Scientifica
RAIDERS of the LOST QUARK

For Key Stage 3 Science

Peter Ellis • Phil Godding • Derek McMonagle
Louise Petheram • Lawrie Ryan
David Sang • Jane Taylor

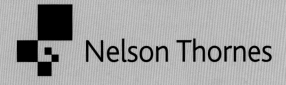

Nelson Thornes

Published in 2005 by:
Nelson Thornes Ltd
Delta Place
27 Bath Road
CHELTENHAM
GL53 7TH
United Kingdom

11 12 13 / 10 9 8

A catalogue record for this book is available from the British Library

ISBN 978 0 7487 7988 8

Illustrations by Mark Draisey, Bede Illustration
Cover illustration by Andy Parker
Page make-up by Wearset Ltd

Printed in China by 1010 Printing International Ltd

Scientifica Course Structure

0 7487 7988 4
Levels 4–7
Student Book

0 7487 7992 2
Complete teacher
guidance
for Levels 4–7

0 7487 8026 2
Teacher Resource
Pack for total
learning support and
extension

0 7487 8027 0
ICT Power
Pack for
Supercharged
lessons!

0 7487 7989 2
Levels 3–6
Student Book

0 7487 7995 7
Complete teacher
guidance
for Levels 3–6

0 7487 8030 0
Formative and
summative
progression tracking

0 7487 9485 9
CD-ROM
and Online
Test and
Assessment

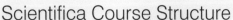

year 8

0 7487 9202 3
Ultimate SEN
support

0 7487 9014 4
Fantastic science
reading

0 7487 9185 X
Low cost.
take-home
personalise

CONTENTS

See which lesson you are studying

This shows what you should hope to learn in this lesson. If you don't understand these things at the end, read through the pages again, and don't be afraid to ask teacher!

LEARN ABOUT
How Scientifica works

LINK UP TO

You can use the things you learn in Science in other subjects too. These panels will help you watch out for things that will help you in other lessons like Maths, Geography and Citizenship. Sometimes they will contain handy hints about other sections of the book.

ICT CHALLENGE

It's really important to develop good computer skills at school. These ICT Challenges will provide lots of interesting activities that help you practice.

Welcome to Scientifica

Why should Science textbooks be boring? We think Science is amazing, and that's why we've packed this book full of great ideas. You'll find tons of amazing facts, gruesome details, clever activities and funny cartoons. There's lots of brilliant Science too!

Here are some of the main features in Scientifica. There are lots more to discover if you look…

Get stuck in

Whenever you see a blue-coloured panel, it means it's time to start doing some science activities. This blue panel provides a set of simple instructions you can follow. Your teacher may also have a sheet to help you and for you to write on.

Meet the Scientifica crew!

Mike Roscope · Pip Ette · Molly Kewell · Pete Ridish · Reese Cycle · Benson Burner

Throughout the book you may see lots of questions, with four possible answers. Only one is correct. The answers **are** in **different colours**. If the teacher gives the class coloured cards to vote with, it will be easy to show your vote.

 Q1 Did you really understand what you just read?

 Q2 Are you sure?

 Q3 Won't these questions help you check?

SUMMARY QUESTIONS

At the end of each lesson, there is a set of questions to see if you understood everything.

☆ See those stars at the beginning of each question?

They tell you whether a question is supposed to be Easy (☆), Medium (☆☆) or Hard (☆☆☆).

 **AMAZING SCIENCE!**

Freaky insects, expanding bridges, boiling hot super stars… These are the most fantastic facts you can find!

Find out how scientists worked out what we know so far. Don't worry! There's plenty for the scientists of the future to find out.

 **IDEAS AND EVIDENCE**

Gruesome science

Lethal clouds of poison gas, dead human skin cells, killer electric eels… Sometimes Science can be just plain nasty! Why not learn about that too?

UNIT REVIEW

There are loads of homework questions at the end of each Unit. There are lots of different types too. If you complete all the SAT-style questions, the teacher may be able to tell you what Level you are working at. Do your best to improve as you go along!

DANGER! AVOID THESE COMMON ERRORS

'Er, the Sun goes out like a light-bulb at night, right?' People make mistakes about science all the time. Before you leave the topic, this will help you make sure you're not one of them!

Phenomenal performance

If you do *brilliantly* in the lesson, your *extraordinary* teacher may ask you to turn towards the back of this *fantastic* book. There are lots of *super* activities for you to try in the *Phenomenal Performance* section.

Key words

amazing
brilliant
phenomenal

Keywords are a handy way of remembering a topic. Some might be scrambled up though!

We think you'll enjoy Scientifica, and hopefully Science too. Best of luck with your studies!

The (other) Scientifica crew – *Lawrie, David and Jane*

8A

Food and digestion

COMING SOON

8A1 Food
8A2 Vitamins and minerals
8A3 Balanced diet
8A4 The digestive system
8A5 Digesting food
8A6 Enzymes

What's it all about?

Do you like chicken and gravy or would you prefer dhal and spinach? How about groundnut stew? One thing's for sure – people all round the world love their food. Food is vital for life. It gives you energy and provides you with the things you need to grow and stay healthy.

In this unit you will find out about nutrients in food, how much of them you need, and how you use them in your body. Your digestive system digests food and absorbs useful substances. You will learn about the organs and how they carry out their functions efficiently.

 # What do you remember?

You already know about:
- the different sorts of foods in a healthy diet.
- why too much fat or sugar is harmful.
- how substances exist as particles that can move around.
- cells, tissues and organs.

1 Which of these foods are good for energy?

   potatoes   **salad**   rice   **fish**

2 Which of these foods are good for growth?

   potatoes   **salad**   rice   **fish**

3 Which of these foods contain a lot of sugar?

   fish   **biscuits**   pasta   **jam**

4 Which of these organs is in the digestive system?

lungs
brain
small intestine
kidney

When you have decided, look at the diagram and choose the letter that shows where the organ is located.

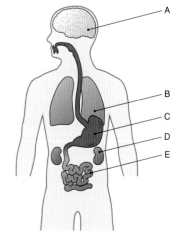

Ideas about food

The Scientifica crew likes the food in their canteen. There's plenty of variety.

QUESTIONS

a) Molly is vegetarian. Benson says that you can't live without meat in your meals. Is he right?

b) Why should you eat five portions of fruit and vegetables every day?

c) Benson and Pete are playing in a match this afternoon. They can't decide whether to have pasta or a chicken wrap for dinner or go without until after the game. What would you choose, and why?

d) Is Mike right? Is that where his stomach is?

LEARN ABOUT
- nutrients

Eating a variety of foods gives us the full range of nutrients

Hair, even modified as a quill, is mainly protein

◉ Eat your greens

Have you ever been told to eat your fish because 'it's good for your brains'? Or that carrots 'help you see in the dark'? These foods actually do help you. They contain substances called **nutrients** that are essential for growth and activity.

◉ Nutrients

Food is a mixture of nutrients. We need large amounts of **carbohydrates**, **proteins**, and **fats** every day. You can see some of the foods that provide them in Table 1.

Starch and **sugars** are two types of carbohydrates in food. They are found in plant foods such as grains, roots and fruits. Plants make them during photosynthesis.

Plant foods also contain **fibre**. We cannot digest fibre and it is not a nutrient, but it is important for our health.

We need **vitamins** and **minerals** each day too, but in very small amounts. There may not be very much of a vitamin or mineral in a food so we may have to eat a lot to get enough. We also need about 1.5 litres of **water** every day.

Q1 Which nutrient in carrots do you think helps you see in the dark?

protein   fat   vitamin   carbohydrate

◉ Protein

We use protein to make new cells, to repair damage and heal wounds, and to grow. Nails, hair, muscle and skin cells are all mainly protein. We also use protein for hormones, antibodies and the enzymes that we use to digest food.

◉ Fats and oils

Fats and oils are not unhealthy – they are important nutrients. The layer of fat under your skin is your energy store. It also conserves heat in your body. We also use fat to make nerve and brain cells, and cell membranes. Two vitamins are found in fats. So when you eat cheese or another food containing fat, you get your vitamins at the same time.

● Carbohydrates

Carbohydrates are our main energy source. It is better for us to eat starchy food than sugary food. Starchy foods also contain other nutrients, particularly vitamins and minerals. Starch takes longer to digest and absorb than sugar so we get a steadier supply of energy.

Table 1 The major nutrients

Nutrient	What we use it for	Good sources
carbohydrate	source of energy for activities and life processes	potatoes, pasta, rice, bread, sugar, cereals
protein	making new cells, growth	meat, fish, nuts, cheese, eggs, beans, peas, lentils, milk
fat	energy source, making cells and hormones, heat insulation	butter, nuts, sunflower oil, red meat, salmon, cheese, margarine, ice cream

Testing foods

- Find out if there is any starch, sugar, protein and fat in the samples of food you have been given.
  You will use these tests again so you will need to be familiar with them.
  Iodine solution turns food that contains starch blue-black.
  Benedict's solution turns from blue to yellow, then orange to red when heated with a food sample containing glucose (a sugar).

- Be a detective! Use your knowledge of food tests, and what is in foods, to decide whether the mixture you have been given is chicken soup or a malted milk drink. Write down your test results and explain your decision.

- Food packets must list how much of each nutrient is in the food, as grams per 100 g of food. Look at food labels to find three foods that are high in   **a)** fat   **b)** protein   **c)** sugar.

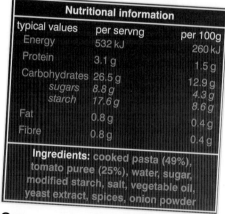

Nutritional information		
typical values	per servng	per 100g
Energy	532 kJ	260 kJ
Protein	3.1 g	1.5 g
Carbohydrates	26.5 g	12.9 g
sugars	8.8 g	4.3 g
starch	17.6 g	8.6 g
Fat	0.8 g	0.4 g
Fibre	0.8 g	0.4 g

Ingredients: cooked pasta (49%), tomato puree (25%), water, sugar, modified starch, salt, vegetable oil, yeast extract, spices, onion powder

Can you guess what food this is?

SUMMARY QUESTIONS

1 ☆ Which nutrients provide energy?

2 ☆ Write out the important nutrients in food.

3 ☆ List three foods that are a good source of   **a)** protein   **b)** starch.

4 ☆ What is protein used for in the body?

Key words

carbohydrate
fat
fibre
nutrient
protein
starch
sugar

Vitamins and minerals

8A2

● Scurvy

Between 1450 and 1800 sailors explored the world for years at a time. These voyages took them far away from land. They ate a poor diet of salted meat and ship's biscuit for months at a time. Many sailors developed an illness called scurvy. They became too ill to work and many died. There was no known cure. Captain Cook even tried feeding his sailors kilos of onions each day, but it did not prevent scurvy.

Sailors did not get scurvy when they had fresh fruit and vegetables. James Lind, a naval surgeon, carefully tested the idea that oranges and lemons kept away scurvy. Even though he was correct he did not know why these fruits were effective. The Royal Navy added preserved lemon or lime juice to its ships' menus and scurvy was brought under control.

Q1 James Lind was testing an idea he had. Was his idea:

an hypothesis?   an evaluation?
a prediction?   a suggestion?

● Vitamins

Citrus fruits contain **vitamin C**. We need vitamin C and other vitamins in minute quantities each day. If we do not have enough we develop **deficiency diseases**, such as scurvy. You can find out about vitamins in Table 1.

The amount of a vitamin that you need each day is your **RDA** – Recommended Daily Amount. You can store some vitamins in your body but not vitamin C. So you must eat fresh fruit and vegetables every day. You will find the chemical names of some vitamins on food packet labels.

● Minerals

We also need small amounts of **minerals** from our food. We use **calcium** to make bones, and **iron** to make red blood cells.

We limey sailors are never scurvy dogs

It could take months to cross the Atlantic

Table 1 Vitamins and Minerals

Nutrient	Use	Deficiency disease	Good food sources
vitamin A	vision, healthy skin	night-blindness	dairy products, oily fish, carrots, dark green vegetables
vitamin B1 (thiamine)	healthy nerves, energy release	beri-beri	wholegrain cereal, yeast, eggs, nuts, liver, peas and beans
vitamin C (ascorbic acid)	used in cell processes, protects cells, absorbing iron	scurvy	oranges, lemons, tomatoes, blackcurrants, kiwi fruit, salad greens
vitamin D	absorbing calcium, depositing calcium in bones	rickets	oily fish, milk, butter, eggs, made in the skin in sunshine
calcium	in bones and teeth, in nerve cells	rickets	cheese, milk, sardines, chocolate, bread, spinach
iron	making red blood cells, releasing energy	anaemia	liver, meat, eggs, cereals, apricots, spinach, cocoa

● Finding out about vitamins

Scientists were interested in what food we needed to live. They discovered that artificial diets made of carbohydrates, fat, protein water and minerals were not enough to keep laboratory animals alive. They knew that if they added milk, their animals stayed healthy. They thought that milk must contain an important factor.

Sir Frederick Gowland Hopkins tested two groups of six female laboratory rats. One set was fed on an artificial diet, the other set was fed on the artificial diet plus 2 cm^3 milk each day. By the 27th day, five of the rats on just the artificial diet had died. You can see the results in the graph.

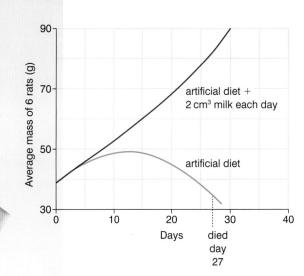

Q2 On which day did these rats stop growing?

In a further experiment, two similar groups of rats were used, but the diets were swapped after 18 days. The group that had received the artificial diet only now had extra milk.

Q3 What do you predict would happen to these rats?

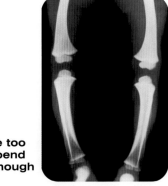

Bones are too soft and bend without enough vitamin D

Research vitamins

● Compare the vitamin C content of two fruit juices. Vitamin C is quickly destroyed in juices. Compare the amount in a juice that has been open for a few days with a fresh juice.

● Research a vitamin such as vitamin A, D or folic acid.

● Make a poster about the early work on deficiency diseases done by Lind with vitamin C, or Eijkman (1905) with vitamin B1, or Mellanby (1919) on rickets.

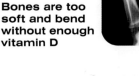
AMAZING SCIENCE!

If you added together the RDA of all the vitamins you need it would be about 0.1 g each day.

SUMMARY QUESTIONS

1 ☆ Why do we need calcium in our diet?

2 ☆ Why does a six-year-old boy need more calcium than his dad?

3 ☆ List three sources of vitamin C. Why do we have to eat vitamin C each day?

4 ☆☆ Look at Table 1. Which two vitamins do you think are fat-soluble?

5 ☆☆ Why do teenage girls need more iron than teenage boys?

Key words

calcium
deficiency disease
iron
mineral
RDA
vitamin

8A3 Balanced diet

So if we eat our greens we should be healthy – right? Not quite. To be healthy we must have the correct balance of nutrients, and enough energy to live and grow.

Energy and food

Food is the fuel that keeps us going. It provides us with **energy**. Carbohydrates are the main energy source in a healthy **diet**.

Q1 What units do we use for energy?

kJ　　Nm　　kg　　km

Carbohydrates release about 17 kJ per gram when burnt. Fats contain more energy per gram. That makes them good for storing energy.

We use energy:

- to maintain our body processes, such as breathing,
- to keep warm,
- to grow,
- for pregnancy,
- to replace or repair damaged tissues,
- to move about.

Different people need different amounts of energy. Year 8 students need lots of energy because they are growing and use plenty of energy in physical activity. You play sports, walk to school, and hang out with your mates out of school.

People whose jobs do not involve much physical activity do not use as much energy. These are **sedentary** jobs. Men have more muscle than women and so need more energy to maintain their bodies. A builder uses more energy than a check-out cashier because the job makes very heavy physical demands. We also use more energy to keep warm when we work outside. Heavy work may use up to 1000 kJ per hour.

The more active you are, the more energy you need

Table 2 Energy needs

	Daily energy need (kJ/day)
baby	4200
child	6800
boy	9600
girl	9200
woman	9500
man	11 500
pregnant woman	10 000

Malnourishment

Malnourished people do not have a balanced diet. They might have too much of one nutrient or not enough of another. They may not have enough food. When people do not have enough to eat they do not grow well.

In some parts of the world a shortage of protein causes a condition called kwashiorkor.

It may surprise you to know that many people in the UK are malnourished. We do not take in enough vitamin C or D, or iron in our food. We also get far too much of our energy from fat. At least 65% of our energy should come from starchy foods and about 25% from fat. Often the proportions are the other way round.

A swollen belly is a symptom of kwashiorkor

● Obesity

When we take in more energy than we need we store the surplus in body fat. Everyone needs some body fat to stay healthy, but if we have too much we become **obese**. This puts a strain on the body, particularly the heart and joints. People who are very overweight in middle-age are more susceptible to diabetes too.

Now that more of us drive to work we need much less energy for walking and keeping warm

How balanced are you?

- Keep a food and energy diary for one ordinary school day.
  Record everything you eat and everything you do.
  Use tables of the energy content of food to find out how much energy you take in.
  Use tables of the energy demand of activities to work out how much energy you use.
  Are you in balance?

- Look at the labels in the picture. If you have a 250 cm³ glass of lemonade and a large dollop (30 g) of ketchup with your meal, how much sugar do you take in? (1 cm³ lemonade weighs 1 g).
  How much fat is there in a 150 g portion of chips?
  Work out how much energy you take in if your lunch is a 500 cm³ bottle of lemonade, 150 g of chips and a 30 g dollop of ketchup.

Kostco Sparkling Lemonade

Nutrition

Typical value	per 100g
Energy	201 kJ
Carbohydrate	12 g
of which sugars	12 g
Fat	less than 0.1 g

McAble Crunchy Oven Chips

Nutritional Information

Typical value	**per 100g**
Energy	1015 kJ
Carbohydrate	41.1 g
Fat	8.4 g

Brandz Tomato Ketchup

Nutrition

Typical Value	per 100g
Energy	456 kJ
Carbohydrate	24.7 g
of which sugars	23.6 g
Fat	0.1 g

AMAZING SCIENCE!

A traditional Christmas dinner contains over 4500 kJ. It's a good job you only eat it once a year.

ICT **CHALLENGE**

Use a spreadsheet to calculate your energy input and output.

LINK UP TO PHYSICS

You found out how to measure the energy content in food in Unit 7I.

SUMMARY QUESTIONS

1 ☆ Why does a 13-year-old girl need more energy than her bank cashier mother?

2 ☆ Why might adult twin brothers need different amounts of energy each day?

3 ☆ Why is eating too many chips and drinking lots of soft drinks bad for you?

4 ☆ Give two reasons why a male footballer needs more energy than a female writer.

Key words

diet
energy
malnutrition
obesity
sedentary

The digestive system

Why do we digest food?

You cannot absorb some of the nutrients in food. Starch, fat and protein molecules are too large to pass through your intestine wall into your blood. They have to be broken down into smaller fragments that can be absorbed.

Mmmm, lovely nutrients...

The digestive system

Your digestive system is in sections. Each section carries out part of the physical and chemical breakdown of food until it is small enough to be absorbed.

You start breaking down food when you chew it. You grind it into much smaller particles. At the same time you mix it with **saliva**. Saliva helps you to swallow your food and it starts to break down starch.

Your food passes to your stomach through your oesophagus. This muscular tube contracts to push a small mass of food along as you swallow. Your food is pushed in this way, by **peristalsis**, all the way through.

Food stays in your **stomach** for hours. Muscles in your stomach wall pound food into a fine paste. Gastric juices start to digest proteins in your food. You also make **hydrochloric acid** that kills bacteria in your food as well as helping in digestion. A thick layer of mucus protects your stomach wall from these digestive juices.

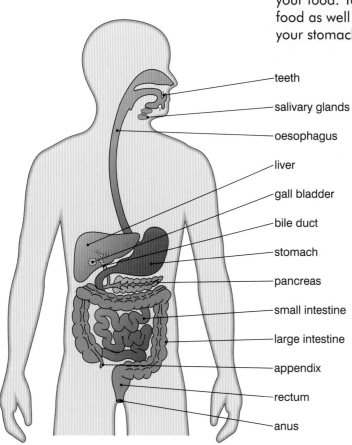

teeth

salivary glands

oesophagus

liver

gall bladder

bile duct

stomach

pancreas

small intestine

large intestine

appendix

rectum

anus

The digestive system

Q1 Is chewing your food and churning it around in your stomach a physical or a chemical change?

Your food is partly digested when it leaves your stomach and enters your **small intestine**. A digestive juice from your **pancreas** is mixed into it. This finishes digesting starch, protein and fats.

Your liver makes bile, which passes into the intestine along the bile duct. Bile helps you digest fats.

Absorbing food

Your small intestine has millions of minute finger-like structures, called **villi**, along its length. These give the intestine lining a much larger surface. It can absorb digested food materials more efficiently. Digested food molecules pass into villi through

Villi

tiny blood vessels inside the villi. They are circulated to your liver and then on to the rest of your body.

● Wastes

You cannot digest everything in your food. You cannot digest fibre, which is mainly cellulose from plant cell walls. Fibre and other undigested foods pass into your **large intestine**, or colon.

Water is reabsorbed from the undigested material in your large intestine. Indigestible material and bacteria living inside your large intestine make up faeces. Faeces are stored in your rectum until they are pushed out.

Although you cannot digest fibre, it helps food move through your intestine. Without it you would become constipated, and may eventually develop bowel cancer.

Modelling intestines

- Visking tubing is an artificial membrane tube that is porous. Use Visking tubing as a model intestine. Fill a length of tubing with a mixture of large starch molecules and small glucose molecules dissolved in water. Put your tubing in a large test tube of warm water and keep it in a water bath. After 20 minutes find out if starch or glucose molecules have been able to pass from inside the tubing into the water.
  What do you predict will happen?
  How will you detect starch or glucose?
  The tubing is a model intestine. The starch and sugar is model food. What is the warm water round the tube a model of?

- Make a 'lift the flap' model of your digestive system.

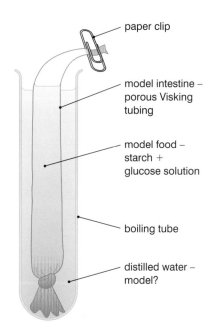

paper clip

model intestine – porous Visking tubing

model food – starch + glucose solution

boiling tube

distilled water – model?

LINK UP TO CHEMISTRY

Unit 8E explains about molecules.

SUMMARY QUESTIONS

1 ☆ Match each part of the gut with its function

stomach	absorbs water
small intestine	makes bile
liver	churns food to a paste
large intestine	absorbs digested food

2 ☆ Name two parts of the body where food is digested.

3 ☆ Why do we need to mix our food with saliva?

4 ☆ How can not eating enough fibre affect our health?

5 ☆☆ Some people get indigestion because they make too much stomach acid. Remedies for indigestion often contain substances such as sodium hydrogencarbonate. Can you explain why this might relieve indigestion?

 AMAZING SCIENCE!

An adult's gut is about 9 metres long from mouth to anus.

Key words

hydrochloric acid
intestine
pancreas
peristalsis
saliva
stomach
villus

8A5 Digesting food

LEARN ABOUT
- how food is digested
- products of digestion

Large molecules

When you digest food you break up large molecules that you cannot absorb into smaller molecules that you can absorb. Proteins and starch are very large molecules. They are made of many smaller molecules linked together in long chains. When they are digested the chain is broken up and the smaller molecules released.

Starch molecules are long chains of **glucose** units. When starch is digested glucose is released.

Proteins

Protein molecules are long chains of **amino acid** units. When protein is digested amino acids are released. There are 20 different amino acids.

There are different combinations of amino acids in different proteins. You have to eat a variety of foods to get all the amino acids you need to make your proteins. You can make some amino acids yourselves but you have to get a few types from the food you eat. These are known as essential amino acids.

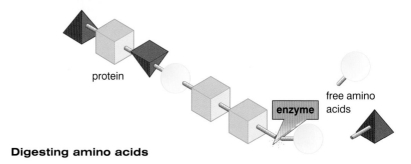

Digesting amino acids

Digesting with enzymes

You use **enzymes** as biological catalysts to speed up the process. Your digestive juices contain enzymes that digest particular nutrients.

Saliva contains an **amylase** enzyme. It begins to break down starch to glucose in your mouth. Amylase is a sort of carbohydrase – an enzyme that breaks down carbohydrates. In your stomach, gastric juice contains a **protease** that digests protein.

In your small intestine a mixture of enzymes includes **lipase** which digests fats. There are also proteases and carbohydrases to finish digesting your food. The molecules made during digestion are called products of digestion.

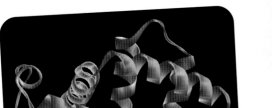

A 3-D model of a muscle protein

Q1 Is breaking a protein into amino acids a physical change or a chemical change?

Gruesome science

Bile carries red and green substances that come from breaking down proteins from old red blood cells. They colour the contents of your intestines.

Food	Product of digestion
protein	amino acids
starch	glucose
fat	fatty acid + glycerol

● What happens next?

Small molecules pass through the intestine wall into blood vessels inside the villi. They are carried in your blood to the liver before being circulated round your body.

You store some useful nutrients such as iron and vitamin B in your liver. You also store some glucose. Glucose is converted to glycogen in your liver and muscles. This acts as your 'front-line' energy store, which you draw on to ensure that your cells have enough glucose for their energy needs.

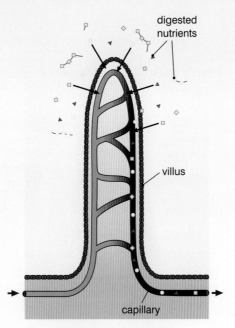

digested nutrients

villus

capillary

Absorbing nutrients

Digesting starch

Investigate how amylase breaks down starch to glucose.

● Warm a solution of starch and a solution of amylase enzyme separately to 37°C.

● Add a small quantity of enzyme to the starch solution.

● Test the mixture with iodine solution regularly to see if the starch has been completely broken down.

● When the starch has been broken down, test the mixture to see if there is any glucose present.

LINK UP TO CHEMISTRY

You learned in Unit 7E that we cannot make essential amino acids, so we have to have them in our food.

SUMMARY QUESTIONS

1 ☆ What are the smaller molecules made when protein, carbohydrate and fats are digested?

2 ☆ What is an enzyme?

3 ☆ How, and where, do we store glucose?

4 ☆☆ Match the food with the type of enzyme digesting it:

butter   protease
beef   amylase
cornflakes   lipase

Key words

amino acid
amylase
enzyme
fatty acid
glucose
lipase
protease

People go to the hairdresser to change their hair's appearance. People with curly hair have it chemically straightened, people with straight hair go to have it permanently curled. Hairdressers can do this because hair is made of protein, and chemicals or heat can alter protein.

An enzyme molecule can work on over 1000 molecules each minute.

Hair strands take on a different form when their proteins are altered by hairdressing solutions

● Denaturing enzymes

The **enzymes** we use to break down food molecules are made of protein. At cool temperatures they work slowly. Human digestive enzymes work best at 37°C.

Enzymes are changed permanently when they are heated to a high **temperature**. Egg white is made of protein – just think of how it changes as you fry an egg. If digestive enzymes are heated above normal body temperature they become **denatured**. Denatured enzymes cannot catalyse chemical reactions and so digestion stops.

Oh no I'm denaturing!

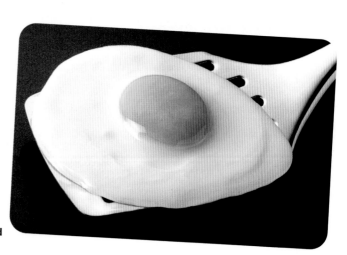

Egg white is a protein called albumen. It changes from clear and runny to white and hard as it denatures.

● Acids, alkalis and enzymes

Enzymes are also affected by the **pH** of their environment. Each of our digestive enzymes works best at a particular pH. Our digestive system is arranged to give them the correct pH for their action.

Q1 Which of these pH values would you expect for
a) a strong acid?   **b)** a weak alkali?

pH 3   pH 6   pH 8   pH 11

Saliva contains a weak alkali. It makes your food slightly alkaline. This is the best pH for salivary amylase. You mix amylase with your food when you chew. It starts working on starch on the surface of food particles. The more you chew the more surface the enzyme can work on.

In your stomach the protease enzyme needs acid conditions. Hydrochloric acid in your stomach produces a pH of 2–3. This is too acid for the salivary amylase and it stops working soon after food reaches your stomach.

When food reaches the small intestine it passes into an alkaline environment again. Here enzymes work on finishing digestion.

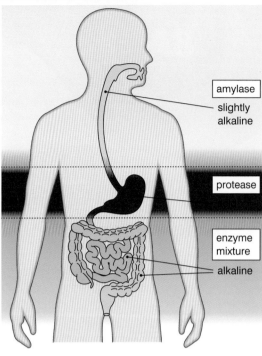

amylase
slightly alkaline

protease

enzyme mixture

alkaline

Different regions of the digestive system have a different pH

How temperature affects enzymes

● Plan and carry out an investigation to find out how quickly amylase breaks down starch at different temperatures.
What procedure can you use to show that amylase breaks down starch?
You will need to think about how you will know when starch has been broken down.
What variables could affect how quickly the reaction will happen?
What quantities of material and equipment will you need? Think about what you have learned from previous experiments with amylase.
Get your teacher to check your plan before you start.

LINK UP TO
CHEMISTRY

You learnt that pH is a measure of acidity and alkalinity in Unit 7E.

SUMMARY QUESTIONS

1 ☆ Why do we have an acid in our stomach?

2 ☆ How does high temperature affect enzymes?

3 ☆☆ In experiments with digestive enzymes we usually keep the food and enzyme mixture at 37°C. Explain why.

Key words

denatured
enzyme
pH
temperature

IDEAS AND EVIDENCE

Using enzymes

After a meal there are always the chores to do – clearing the table and washing up. The plates and saucepans are covered in dried food remains, some of them very crispy and burnt on. Swoosh – you fill the sink with hot water and a good squirt of washing up liquid. Hot water loosens food particles so they can be washed away. **Detergents** in the washing up liquid disperse oily food traces into smaller globules. You just need a bit of 'elbow grease' with a scourer to get sparkling clean washing up.

For some of you washing up is a thing of the past. Your chore is to load and unload the dishwasher. Dishwasher tablets or powders contain **enzymes** that digest food traces sticking to the pots and pans. Large dried on molecules are soaked and broken down to smaller soluble molecules that can be lifted off by the detergent. A dishwasher uses a spray jet of water hotter than your hands could cope with to wash these food traces off the crockery.

Dishwashing enzymes are not human digestive enzymes. Our enzymes would rapidly be denatured at washing temperatures of 50°C or 60°C. These enzymes are from bacteria that are adapted to live in hot springs in volcanic areas.

 SCIENTIFIC PEOPLE

Dieticians have a specialised knowledge of food, how it is digested, and how to adjust someone's diet to cope with a specific medical need.

People are referred by their doctors to a dietician for advice. Pregnant women can have advice on healthy eating to keep their iron and vitamin levels high enough for the baby's needs. Overweight people may need advice to help them lose weight and stay thinner.

A large part of the dietician's work is connected to specific health problems. People suffering with **diabetes** struggle to control the amount of glucose in their blood and may not have glycogen stores for their needs. They need advice on how to regulate their carbohydrate input.

Other people react badly to substances in food such as gluten, a protein found in wheat products such as bread, or lactose the sugar found in milk. A dietician can help them construct a balanced diet that avoids the foods they cannot eat.

Gluten in bread makes some people sick

 CHALLENGE

Use the Internet to find out about lactose and gluten intolerance.

A BALANCED DIET CONTAINS FATS, PROTEINS, CARBOHYDRATES, VITAMINS, MINERALS, WATER, AND FIBRE IN THE CORRECT PROPORTIONS

Proteins are used for growth & repair

FATS ARE USED FOR ENERGY STORES

Food substances are broken down in the gut by enzymes

Carbohydrates are used for energy

Large insoluble molecules are converted to small soluble molecules

Nutrient molecules are transported by blood to the tissues

As long as I have the right nutrients, it's okay to be vegetarian.

Pasta's good for energy... It's got plenty of carbohydrate.

Fruit and veg give me vitamins, minerals and fibre.

Oh, my stomach is up here is it?

DANGER! AVOID THESE COMMON ERRORS

- You use carbohydrates and fats to give you energy. You would only use protein for energy if you were starving.
- **Fibre** is not a nutrient. You cannot digest and absorb it. It is vital in your diet because it helps to keep food moving through your gut.
- Physical activity takes more energy because it involves more physical effort, not because the person is working harder. When the Scientifica crew are doing their homework they may not be making much physical effort but they are working hard.
- Enzymes are not alive – they cannot be killed. They are denatured.

Key words

detergent
diabetes
enzyme
fibre

REVIEW QUESTIONS

1 Copy and complete the following sentences:
   a ... are the food components we need to be healthy.
   b We need carbohydrates, proteins and ... in large amounts.
   c We also need smaller amounts of ... and minerals.
   d Food is digested in the digestive system using ...
   e Digestion is the process of breaking down large molecules to smaller molecules that can be ...
   f Starches are broken down into ..., whereas proteins are broken down into ... ...
   g Digested food is absorbed through ..., which are small finger-like structures in the small intestine.

2 Give one reason why we need each of these in our diet:

   protein   fat   vitamin C   fibre   iron

3 Which one of the following do you need for strong bones and teeth?

   iodine   copper   calcium   iron

4 Link the unbalanced diet factor to the problem it causes:

   too much sugar   bowel cancer
   too much fat   tooth decay
   not enough fibre   obesity
   not enough iron   anaemia

5 Explain why a professional footballer needs a higher energy diet than a receptionist.

6 How do digested nutrients get from inside the small intestine to the cells of the body?

7 Name two nutrients that are absorbed without being digested.

Making more of maths

8 Calculate how much orange juice you need to drink to get your RDA of vitamin C.
   There is 30 mg vitamin C per 100 cm^3 orange juice, your RDA is 75 mg.

Thinking skills

9 Which word is the odd one out? Explain your choice.
   a starch, fat, vitamin
   b protein, fibre, iron
   c glucose, amino acid, cellulose.

SAT-STYLE QUESTIONS

1 Here are some items on the menu in the dining room at Scientifica High.

burger   fries   jacket potato

beans   pasta   salad

doughnut   orange   banana

milkshake   mineral water   fizzy drink

   a Mike chose a 'meal deal' of burger, chips and a fizzy drink for his lunch. Reese thought it wasn't a healthy choice. Give one reason why Mike's could be unhealthy.   (1)
   b Change one item for another that would make his meal healthier.
      Explain why it makes it healthier.   (1)
   c Reese chose pasta and an orange. Give one nutrient in Reese's meal that is not present in Mike's.   (1)

d Choose one food from the foods shown that is rich in
i) protein ii) vitamin C iii) fibre. (3)

2 The diagram shows a villus. Villi line the small intestine, covering the surface. They are covered in a thin layer of cells. You can see two of the cells has been enlarged.

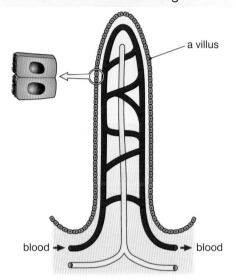

a villus

blood → ← blood

a Give two ways that villi allow us to absorb digested foods efficiently. (2)
b Name one digestive juice that is added to food in the small intestine. (1)
c Name one substance that is not digested in the small intestine. (1)
d Give one function of the large intestine. (1)

3 Pete and Ben were investigating amylase. Pete predicted that amylase was necessary to obtain glucose from starch.

They placed starch solution, distilled water and amylase solution separately in the water bath at 37°C to warm up while they got their equipment ready.
a What is amylase? (1)

They put $15 \, cm^3$ of starch solution inside each of two lengths of Visking tubing. Then they rinsed the outside of the tubing.

Pete added $0.5 \, cm^3$ of amylase to one of the starch solutions as Ben started the stopwatch.

Pete closed the tubing, mixed the contents, and put them into boiling tubes of distilled water. You can see their experiment in the diagram.
b What is the purpose of the tube with just starch? (1)

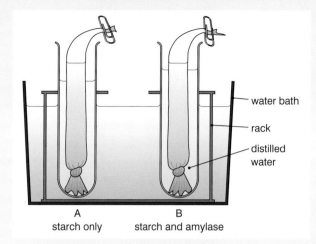

water bath
rack
distilled water

A
starch only

B
starch and amylase

Pete and Ben timed for 20 minutes. They took samples from the distilled water and the contents of the Visking tubing in each boiling tube. They carried out tests for starch and glucose on each of the samples.
c What could Pete and Ben use to detect
i) starch? ii) glucose? (2)

Their results are in the table.

	Starch test		Glucose test	
	colour	present	colour	present
inside tubing with starch only	black	yes	blue	no
inside tubing with starch and amylase	yellow-brown	no	orange	yes
water round starch only	yellow-brown	no	blue	no
water round starch and amylase mix	yellow-brown	no	orange	yes

d Do the results support Pete's prediction? (1)

Pete and Ben wanted reliable results.
e i) Why were they careful to warm everything to 37°C? What would have happened if they had left their experiment on the bench? (2)
ii) Give one other thing they did to make their investigation fair. (1)
f Explain why there was glucose in tube B? How did it get into the water outside the tubing? (2)

Key words

Unscramble these:
harry dabcote
o sing tide
ties boy
miccaul
ise in tent

8B Respiration

I haven't the energy for this! PANT PANT

What's it all about?

You've probably seen adverts for high-energy food and drinks. These give you that extra burst of energy when you are running out of steam. But how does energy in foods end up as energy that keeps your legs moving? In this unit you will find out more about how we release energy from food. This process is **respiration** and it happens in every cell in your body.

Your heart and circulation take digested food, and the energy it contains, to the parts of the body that need it. You might be surprised to learn that your lungs are involved in releasing energy from food too. To find out more, read on.

 ## What do you remember?

You already know about:
- humans needing oxygen from the air to live.
- how gas molecules diffuse.
- how your heart pumps blood through arteries and veins.
- glucose being released from food during digestion.

1 Which of these gases would you expect to find in air?

   oxygen   **carbon dioxide**   nitrogen   **argon**

2 Write a definition of 'diffusion'.

3 Three of these are part of the circulatory system, one isn't. Which?

   heart   **artery**   **capillary**   **pancreas**

4 Three of these are produced from digested food, one isn't. Which?

   fatty acids   **amino acids**   cellulose   **glucose**

5 Make a list of as many ways as you can think of in which we use our energy.

Ideas about energy

It's sports day at Scientifica High. Year 8 has been training hard for their races. Mike and Molly had a good meal of pasta yesterday to prepare for the day's energy demands.

a) Where does the energy for running the race come from?

b) How would a plate of pasta the night before help Mike or Molly?

c) How is Reese's heart rate and breathing rate different from usual after a race?

Why do you think they are different?

Respiration

8B1

● Cells and energy

What have you, your hamster and a geranium got in common? You are all alive. Every living cell needs **energy** to carry out life processes. Our cells use **glucose** as their energy source. Glucose comes from the food we have digested.

Q1 Which type of nutrient releases glucose?

protein   **starch**   fats   **vitamins**

● Respiration

Cells use **respiration** to release energy from glucose. It is a chemical reaction that takes place inside cells. Respiration in our cells also uses oxygen. Glucose and oxygen are brought to cells by blood circulating round your body.

Our cells break down glucose using oxygen to release energy. Carbon dioxide and water are made. During this process energy is released.

We can write the process of respiration as a word equation:

glucose + oxygen → carbon dioxide + water + energy

Respiration that uses oxygen to release energy from nutrients is called **aerobic** respiration.

Water polo uses energy to contract muscles

● What do we use the energy for?

We use this energy for many different things. You can see the main uses in the table.

Use	How we use energy
growth	to make new cells, grow babies, produce biomass
synthesis of new material	to make chemicals that cells need, e.g. protein, cellulose, enzymes
energy stores	animals store energy as fat plants store starch and oils
maintain a constant body temperature	warm-blooded animals use energy for body heat – we keep our body at 37°C
movement	We use energy to move muscles. Even when we are asleep our heart beats and we breathe. Vigorous physical activity uses more energy than quiet activities.
transport	cells use energy to take in some important substances, and to export other chemicals they have made

When we take in more energy than we need, we use the surplus to make fat. We store some fat under our skin. This insulates us so that we conserve body heat. When we are particularly active we can draw on the energy stores we have made.

Detecting respiration

- How can we tell if respiration is taking place? We can look for what respiration produces – carbon dioxide or energy release. Look for carbon dioxide production in the following.
  Mix yeast with sugar solution. Use a delivery tube to pass any gas produced through lime water. What does this tell you about the gas produced? Devise a suitable control experiment.

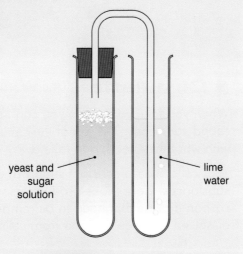

yeast and sugar solution

lime water

- Sodium hydrogencarbonate indicator solution is normally dark red. But even small quantities of carbon dioxide turn it yellow. Place a washed 10 cm length of water weed in sodium hydrogencarbonate indicator solution in a test tube. Place black paper round the tube to block out the light. Put it under a lamp to keep it warm for 30 minutes before you examine it. Has the plant produced carbon dioxide?

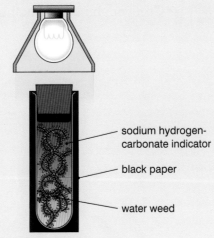

sodium hydrogen-carbonate indicator

black paper

water weed

- Use what you learned about burning fuels to find out which of these foods releases the most energy.

  a plain crisp   a bread crouton
  a rice cracker   a piece of breakfast cereal

AMAZING SCIENCE!

We use almost 80% of our energy intake just to keep warm.

ICT   CHALLENGE

Set up a vacuum flask with germinating peas. Use a data logger to monitor heat production over the next three days.

LINK UP TO
PHYSICS

In Unit 7I you learned that burning fuels for energy releases carbon dioxide.

SUMMARY QUESTIONS

1 ☆ List two things used up in respiration and two products released.

2 ☆ Write out the word equation for respiration.

3 ☆☆ Space probes to Mars have looked for carbon dioxide production in Martian soil samples. Why could this be a sign of life?

4 ☆☆ What do you think happens to the water produced by respiration?

Key words

aerobic
carbon dioxide
energy
glucose
oxygen
respiration

Circulation

When you take your pulse you can feel your blood being pumped round your body. The job of the circulatory system is to supply cells with what they need, and take away what they produce.

Your cells need a constant supply of glucose and oxygen and other substances. Cells make products as well as waste materials such as carbon dioxide that need to be removed. Your blood transports dissolved chemicals to and from cells.

Q1 Can you think of something useful made by your cells?

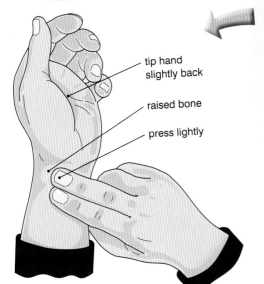

tip hand slightly back

raised bone

press lightly

We can take a pulse wherever an artery passes close to the skin

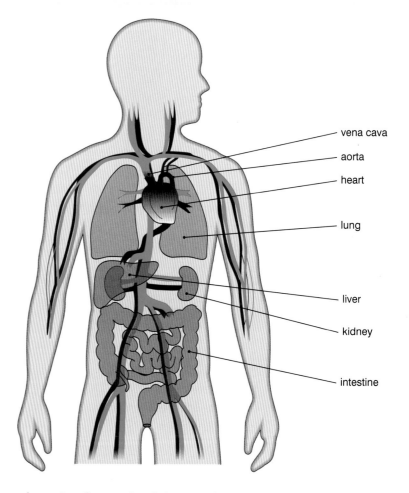

vena cava

aorta

heart

lung

liver

kidney

intestine

The main parts of your circulatory system

Heart

Your **heart** pumps your blood round your body. It is a muscle that contracts, or beats, regularly. Each beat pumps blood into the main blood vessels.

The right side of your heart receives blood from your body. It pumps blood through an artery to your lungs. In your lungs, blood picks up oxygen and loses carbon dioxide. After passing though your lungs, blood returns through a vein to the left-hand side of your heart. The left side of your heart pumps blood to the organs of your body.

Blood vessels

Blood leaving your heart passes through **arteries** to reach your organs. Arteries branch into smaller and smaller blood vessels inside your organs, taking blood to every part. The smallest blood vessels are **capillaries,** which supply cells. Once blood has passed through an organ it passes through **veins** back to your heart.

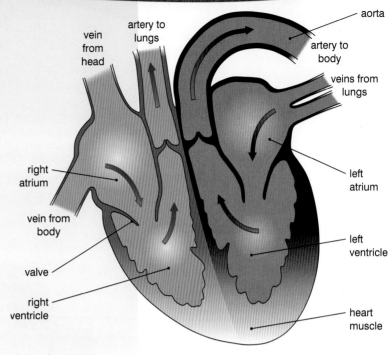

The heart

Q2 Blood travels to and from your heart through the pulmonary artery and vein. Which carries blood towards the lungs – the pulmonary artery or the pulmonary vein?

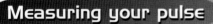

Measuring your pulse

- Measure your pulse. First sit quietly for a few minutes then take your pulse. This is your resting pulse rate. Does everyone have the same resting pulse rate? Collect data from your class and display it in a suitable graph or chart.
  If it is safe to do so, exercise on the spot for one minute. Re-take your pulse. How has it changed? Do other people's pulses change in the same way?

- Draw arrows on an outline drawing of the heart to show the path blood follows as it passes through the heart.

Your heart beats at least 40 million times each year.

Watch a simulation of how the heart pumps blood.

SUMMARY QUESTIONS

1 ☆ What is the function of an artery, a vein, and a capillary?

2 ☆ What is the pulse?

3 ☆☆ When you are more active you need more energy and your pulse increases. How can increasing your pulse rate help you release more energy?

Key words

artery
capillary
heart
vein
ventricle

Supplying cells

● Capillaries

Cells rely on their blood supply to bring them what they need and remove wastes. Capillaries have very thin walls so that oxygen, glucose and other nutrients can pass through easily. The capillary network ensures that every cell is close to a supply line.

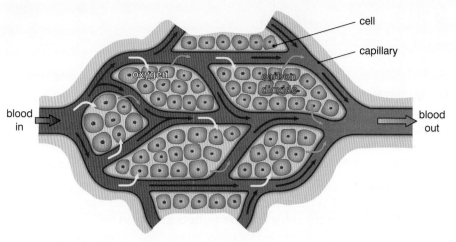

cell

capillary

blood in

blood out

oxygen

carbon dioxide

Cells have several capillaries passing close by. Even if one capillary is damaged another can supply nearby cells.

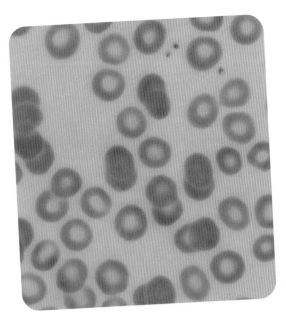

Red blood cells are adapted for transporting oxygen

Substances **diffuse** to cells from blood, and return in the same way. Glucose and other nutrient molecules diffuse through the capillary wall to the cells. **Carbon dioxide** made by the cells during respiration diffuses in the opposite direction, from cells into blood.

Oxygen is transported by **red blood cells**. Red blood cells contain **haemoglobin**. Oxygen bonds to haemoglobin in your lungs to make **oxyhaemoglobin**. When red blood cells pass through tissues, oxyhaemoglobin releases oxygen. **Oxygen** diffuses from the rich supply in your blood to the cells that are using it up.

Q1 Red cells are adapted for transporting oxygen. Can you explain why their shape also makes them efficient at this job?

LINK UP TO **CHEMISTRY**

In Unit 7H you learned that particles move about without you having to mix them.

Anaerobic respiration

A championship 100-metre sprinter runs that distance in around 10 seconds but takes very few breaths. How can sprinters generate enough energy to run at high speed without taking in enormous quantities of oxygen?

Sprinters can do this because we can use anaerobic respiration in our muscles for a short time. Our cells partly break down glucose without using oxygen. They make **lactic acid** and release a much smaller amount of energy. This will keep us going for a short time.

Lactic acid affects muscle cells when it builds up. We develop cramps or 'stitch'. Once the exercise is over we take in oxygen to get rid of lactic acid.

Micro-organisms such as yeast can also use anaerobic respiration. They break down glucose to ethanol, not lactic acid. This is how they ferment sugary fruit juices to wine.

Energy without oxygen

- Use the apparatus in the diagram to show that yeast can **respire** without oxygen.

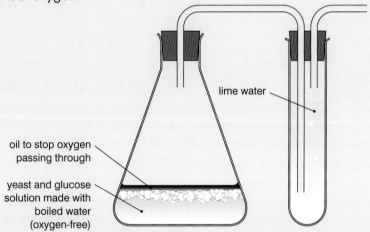

lime water

oil to stop oxygen passing through

yeast and glucose solution made with boiled water (oxygen-free)

- Make a flow chart of the route oxygen takes from the lungs to reach a leg muscle cell. Make another to show the route carbon dioxide takes from a leg muscle cell to the lungs.

Oxygen, someone bring me oxygen.

SUMMARY QUESTIONS

1 ☆ Red blood cells carry oxygen. What substance do they contain that combines with oxygen from the lungs?

2 ☆ How do materials move from blood to cells and cells to blood?

3 ☆ Name one substance that passes *into* the blood from the tissues, and one substance that passes *from* the blood into the tissues.

4 ☆☆ Name two other substances that are transported in blood.

5 ☆☆ What is the difference between aerobic and anaerobic respiration?

Key words

carbon dioxide
diffusion
haemoglobin
lactic acid
oxygen
red blood cell
respire

Breathing

● Breathing

Put your hands on your chest and breathe in and out slowly a couple of times. What do you feel? Your hands move up and out slightly as you breathe. Breathing in is **inhaling**. Your hands drop down again as you breathe out, or **exhale**. When you breathe you move air in and out of your lungs. This is **ventilation**.

● Ventilation

You use muscles to move your chest. You contract muscles that run over your **ribcage** to lift it up and outwards. At the same time your **diaphragm** contracts. Your diaphragm is a dome-shaped sheet of muscle across the bottom of your ribcage. When it contracts it becomes flatter. These actions increase the volume inside your chest, and air enters.

To exhale you relax your muscles and your ribcage drops. The volume inside your chest decreases and air is pushed out. It takes more effort to breathe in than out because you are using your muscles to move your ribcage.

You have a set of muscles that you can contract to exhale. You use these when you cough, sneeze or blow out the candles on your birthday cake.

How we breathe

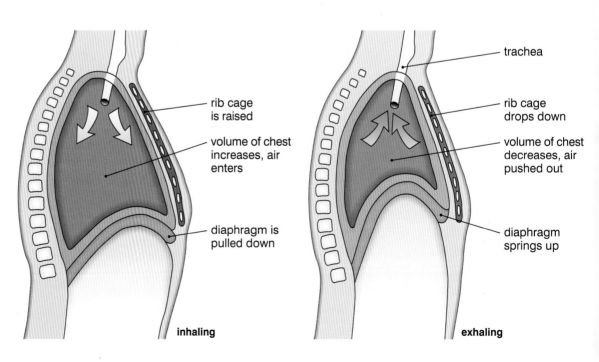

rib cage is raised

volume of chest increases, air enters

diaphragm is pulled down

inhaling

trachea

rib cage drops down

volume of chest decreases, air pushed out

diaphragm springs up

exhaling

Lung capacity

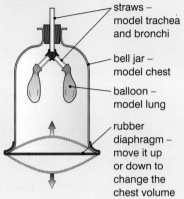

A model chest

straws – model trachea and bronchi

bell jar – model chest

balloon – model lung

rubber diaphragm – move it up or down to change the chest volume

- Use a model chest to see how ventilation works.
- Examine a set of animal lungs. Locate the trachea, rings of cartilage, larynx, left and right lungs, bronchi. Use tubing to partially inflate a lung.
- Measure your lung volume. Plan an investigation to find out whether brass instrument players have a larger than average lung volume.

 **CHALLENGE**

Use a graphing facility to display the range of lung volumes in your class.

● Lungs

Your **lungs** are inside your ribcage. A tube, the **trachea**, connects the back of your throat to your lungs. At the top, air passes through your larynx, which houses your vocal cords. At the lower end, it branches into two **bronchi** that direct air into your right and left lungs. These air passages are held open by rings of cartilage. The bronchi branch again and again. Each bronchiole ends in a cluster of several alveoli.

Q1 How much air is changed when you breathe normally?

$50\,cm^3$ $250\,cm^3$ $500\,cm^3$ $1000\,cm^3$

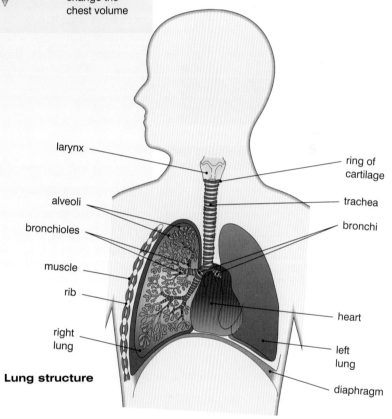

larynx, alveoli, bronchioles, muscle, rib, right lung, ring of cartilage, trachea, bronchi, heart, left lung, diaphragm

Lung structure

SUMMARY QUESTIONS

1. ☆ Identify the structures A–E on the diagram.
2. ☆ Give one function of the rings of cartilage.
3. ☆☆ Explain in your own words how we breathe. Use these words in your answer:

ventilate   **trachea**
exhaled   **inhaled**

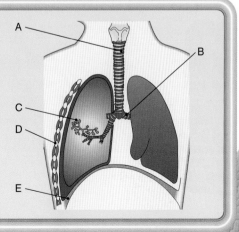

Key words

bronchus
diaphragm
inhale
lung
ribcage
trachea
ventilation

What happens in your lungs?

8B5

LEARN ABOUT
- what happens to air in your lungs?
- alveoli

Air

Do you remember writing your name in the condensation on bus windows or the classroom windows in the winter? The moisture comes from people inside. They breathe out water vapour in their breath. This vapour condenses on the cold window glass. On a frosty morning you can see water vapour in your breath condensing as you breathe out.

As we breathe we take in **oxygen** from the air. We also release **carbon dioxide** into the air. Huge quantities of carbon dioxide enter the atmosphere from the respiration of living things each year. The amount of carbon dioxide we release equals the volume of oxygen we take in. In the table you can see how we change the composition of the air we breathe.

Gas	% of inhaled air	% of exhaled air
oxygen	21	17
carbon dioxide	0.04	4
nitrogen	78	78
noble gases	1	1
water vapour	varies	saturated

What happens in the alveoli?

The working units in our lungs are the **alveoli** clustered around the ends of tiny airways called bronchioles. There are huge numbers of these microscopically small structures in our lungs.

Alveoli are specialised for **gas exchange**, that is taking in oxygen and releasing carbon dioxide. They have very thin walls and a large surface area for exchanging gases. This delicate surface is kept moist and is very easily damaged. A network of capillaries surrounds them.

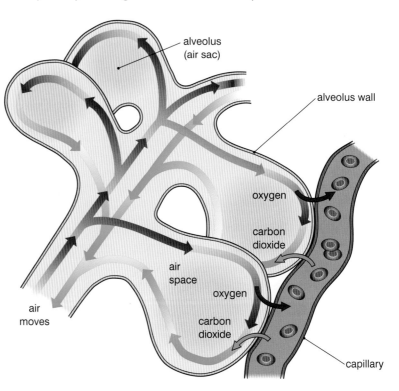

alveolus (air sac)

alveolus wall

oxygen

carbon dioxide

air space

oxygen

air moves

carbon dioxide

capillary

Moisture in the whale's breath condenses in the cold air

Inside each **alveolus**, oxygen **diffuses** into blood which is in the surrounding capillaries. It combines with haemoglobin in red blood cells and is rapidly circulated by the heart to the body.

 What is the name of the compound made when oxygen binds to haemoglobin?

Carbon dioxide arrives in the lungs in blood. It diffuses into the air in the alveolus. Too much carbon dioxide in our blood would make it acidic so it is important to remove it as quickly as possible.

Your breathing rate is controlled by how much carbon dioxide you have in your blood. This is an example of **excretion** because we are removing a harmful material made in our cells.

Our lungs have about 300 million alveoli. These have a surface area about as big as the area of a tennis court.

How do you change air when you breathe?

- Collect samples of inhaled and exhaled air. Compare the amount of carbon dioxide and oxygen in each sample.
- Breathe on to a cold mirror. Test the condensation on the mirror with cobalt chloride paper. What is the liquid?
- Investigate whether other living things release carbon dioxide using the apparatus in the diagram.
  How would you use this experiment to compare the amount of carbon dioxide produced by maggots and germinating peas? Write a plan for your investigation.

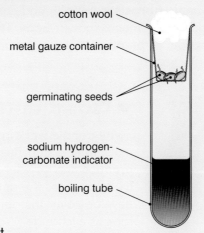

cotton wool
metal gauze container
germinating seeds
sodium hydrogen-carbonate indicator
boiling tube

LINK UP TO CHEMISTRY

Air is a mixture of gases. Carbon dioxide in air makes rain acidic and contributes to global warming.

SUMMARY QUESTIONS

1 ☆ Gases are exchanged in the alveoli. Which gas passes from the air to the blood? Which gas passes from the blood into the alveoli?

2 ☆ How would you detect the presence of carbon dioxide in a sample of air?

3 ☆ Alveoli have very thin walls. How does this help the body exchange gases more efficiently?

4 ☆ Give three differences between the composition of the air Pip breathed in and the air she breathed out. Copy and complete this sentence:

Compared to the air she breathed in, the air she breathed out contains . . .

Key words

alveolus
carbon dioxide
diffusion
excretion
gas exchange
oxygen

8B6 More about breathing

LEARN ABOUT
- factors that affect your breathing
- gas exchange in other animals

The first thing a baby does when it is born is take a breath, usually followed by a yell. Most of us have healthy lungs. Not everyone is so fortunate. Some people have problems breathing.

● Breathing problems

More and more children suffer with **asthma**. No-one is completely sure what causes asthma or why people develop it. In an asthma attack the airways become narrower, sometimes inflamed. This makes it difficult to breathe. Inhalers contain drugs that can reduce obstructions and make it easier to breathe.

Cystic fibrosis is an inherited condition. People make particularly thick and sticky mucus in their body. This can clog their lungs and makes it harder to breathe. It also traps bacteria, which makes it easier to catch infections.

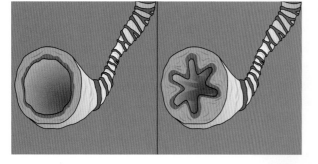

normal   asthmatic attack

● Dust and your lungs

Some people work in dusty environments such as flour mills, mines, quarries and timber yards. All these industries produce fine powdery dusts that can cause **lung damage**. Dusts abrades the delicate alveoli. Thick scar tissue develops over the damaged parts. This reduces the area for gas exchange. Workers should wear face masks to protect their lungs by filtering the air they breathe.

Tiny stone particles in quarry dust abrade the delicate surface of alveoli, scarring them. This is a form of emphysema.

Looking at breathing

● Look at the photograph of alveoli damaged by dust and compare it to the photograph of healthy lung tissue.
Describe any differences you can see in the alveoli. How will this affect the absorbing surface? How could this affect a person with lungs damaged in this way?

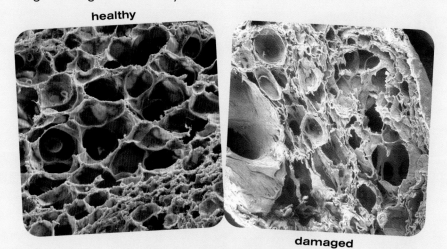

healthy

damaged

● Look at the residue collected in a smoking machine. Cigarette smoke contains hot gases, ash and tar. Explain why a coating of tar and hot gases could affect alveoli.

● How do other animals breathe?

All animals have a gas exchange surface. Mammals, reptiles and birds have lungs like us. Amphibia have lungs as we do but can exchange gases through their skin as well. Fish use **gills**.

Have you ever watched a goldfish as it swims? It slowly opens and closes its mouth as it swims along. It gulps a mouthful of water and pushes it backwards over its gills and out through gill slits. Oxygen dissolved in the water diffuses into blood passing through the fine gill filaments. Carbon dioxide diffuses from the blood into water passing over the gills.

Gruesome science

Dirt trapped in your lungs stays for years, turning them grey.

Water containing oxygen goes in through the mouth and out over its gills

SUMMARY QUESTIONS

1   ☆   Why do people working in flour mills and quarries wear masks?

2   ☆   How does asthma affect someone's breathing?

3   ☆☆   Find out how a frog carries out gas exchange while it is a tadpole.

Key words

asthma
cystic fibrosis
gills
lung damage

IDEAS AND EVIDENCE

William Harvey and solving the circulation problem

It seems obvious that blood flows round the body – but it took centuries of observations and deductions to work out how.

Ancient Greeks had described heart valves by 400 BC but didn't realise how important they were. During the next hundred years people noticed that arteries were different from veins. Arteries were thought to be full of air. This was because they were always empty in dissected corpses. When people cut an artery and bled it was thought that the blood came from veins, somehow, to replace escaping air. Mistaken ideas like this sent people on the wrong track even though they knew all the facts needed to understand blood circulation.

In Roman times, Galen developed a theory of blood **circulation**. He suggested that blood was constantly forming in the body. It passed through the heart then was reabsorbed with each pulse. He showed that arteries held blood and thought it was enriched with 'vital spirit' in the lungs. There were other ideas, for example, Ibn al Naphis argued that blood must pass through the lungs to get from the right to the left side of the heart, not through tiny holes in the heart.

However Galen's ideas lasted until Shakespeare's time. At the University of Padua in Italy, Vesalius found mistakes in Galen's work and people looked at circulation again. They still didn't get it right. For example, Fabricius got the blood flow through valves wrong, suggesting they slowed the blood so it could enter small blood vessels. Leonardo Da Vinci recognised the heart was muscle – but not that it pumped blood.

William Harvey

William Harvey (1578–1657) studied at Padua. He put together the known facts with his own observations to **deduce** how blood circulates. He correctly worked out what heart muscle, arteries and veins did, the blood's route through the heart, and what causes the pulse. He thought blood circulated round the body but didn't know how it passed from arteries to veins. He **inferred** that tiny blood vessels must exist to link them. Finally Professor Malpighi used the newly discovered microscope to confirm that capillaries existed.

- Why hadn't anyone spotted capillaries before?
- Why were the arteries in dissected corpses empty?
- What do you think 'vital spirit' might be?

- All living things, including plants and bacteria, respire.
- Respiration takes place in cells.
- Respiration releases energy from glucose.
- Glucose + oxygen → carbon dioxide + water, energy is released.
- We obtain oxygen and excrete carbon dioxide using lungs.
- Oxygen passes from the air in alveoli into the blood. Carbon dioxide passes in the opposition direction.
- Oxygen is carried round the body by red blood cells.
- Blood releases oxygen in the tissues and carbon dioxide passes into blood.

DANGER! AVOID THESE COMMON ERRORS

The function of cartilage in the trachea is to hold it open, not to protect it.

When people take in *more* energy than they use they *store* the extra as glycogen in muscles, or as fat. They do not become hotter or more active. However if they are more active they will use more energy, and become hotter.

Cells in the trachea protect us from infection. Some cells make sticky mucus that traps dust particles, bacteria and viruses. Cilia on neighbouring cells move mucus, and its load of trapped debris, up into the throat. Cilia cannot make mucus, nor can they go fishing for bacteria.

Excretion is the process of removing harmful materials made by the body. Pushing faeces out of the body is elimination.

Key words

circulation
deduce
infer
William Harvey

SAT-STYLE QUESTIONS

1 Blood contains five million red blood cells in every mm^3. You can see red blood cells in the diagram.

a Give two ways in which they are adapted for carrying oxygen. (2)

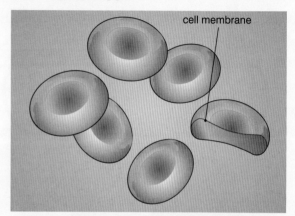

cell membrane

b Some athletes train at high altitude to increase the number of red blood cells in their blood. They do this before running at low altitude. How can this improve their performance in the race? (2)

2 Pip filled a test tube with glucose solution. She added some yeast and mixed it together. She fastened a balloon over the test tube and put it in a water bath at 30°C. Small bubbles of gas formed in the solution and rose to the top. One hour later the balloon had inflated.

a Name the gas given off. (1)

b What is the process that produced the gas? (1)

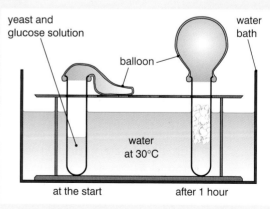

yeast and glucose solution

water bath

balloon

water at 30°C

at the start   after 1 hour

c Write a word equation for this process. (2)

REVIEW QUESTIONS

1 Copy and complete the following sentences:

a Respiration is a chemical reaction that takes place in ... In respiration ... and oxygen produce ... ... and water.

b The heart pumps ... round the body. We can feel its action by the ... at the wrist. The left side of the heart supplies the ... while the right side sends blood to the ... In capillaries oxygen and nutrients ... to nearby cells.

c When we breathe we use muscles that move the ribcage ... The diaphragm ... and becomes flatter. These actions ... the volume inside your chest, and air enters. Oxygen and carbon dioxide are exchanged in small structures in the lungs called ...

2 Write out the word equation for respiration.

3 Describe what happens in alveoli. How can smoking or working in a dusty environment affect what happens in the alveoli?

4 Copy and complete the table:

Gas	Air breathed in (%)	Air breathed out (%)
nitrogen	78	78
oxygen		17
carbon dioxide	0.04	

5 People who do not have enough red cells are anaemic. They do not have much energy. Why do they not have much energy?

6 Make a flow chart of how carbon dioxide produced by a cell is eventually breathed out. Include on your chart places where diffusion is important.

7 Make a concept map that includes the terms

respiration   alveolus   capillary

gas exchange   energy

Pip repeated her work at two different temperatures.

d   Draw the apparatus as you would expect to see it after 1 hour if
  i)   it had been kept at 15°C.   (1)
  ii) it had been kept at 70°C.   (1)

e   Explain your drawings.   (2)

3   A fish exchanges gases through its gills. You can see fish gills in the diagram.

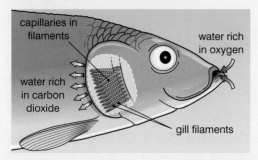

capillaries in filaments
water rich in oxygen
water rich in carbon dioxide
gill filaments

a   What gas does a fish get from water?   (1)
b   How does this gas pass into the gills?   (1)
c   Give two ways in which fish gills are adapted for their function of gas exchange.   (2)

Oxygen from the air dissolves in water. If the water temperature increases, less oxygen can dissolve in it. During very hot spells dead fish can be seen floating in rivers.

d   Explain why the fish have died.   (1)

4   Benson and Mike wanted to investigate respiration. Mike soaked some peas and let them germinate. Then he boiled half of the peas and left them to go cold.

Benson put 40 g of each of the two sets of peas separately in two vacuum flasks. They used a data logger to monitor the temperature for the next five days. The table shows their readings:

		Flask A (°C)	Flask B (°C)
Day 1	11 am	18	18
	11 pm	18	15
Day 2	11 am	18	17
	11 pm	18.5	15
Day 3	11 am	18.5	15
	11 pm	19	14
Day 4	11 am	19	14
	11 pm	19.5	14
Day 5	11 am	19.5	17
	11 pm	20	15

a   Why should they use the same mass of peas in each vacuum flask?   (1)
b   i)   Draw a graph of their results. Label each axis, including the correct units.   (3)
  ii) Describe what happened to the temperature in each flask.   (2)

Mike predicted that the temperature wouldn't change in flask B because the peas had been boiled.

c   i)   Does the data support Mike's prediction?   (1)
  ii) Why would boiled peas be different to the peas in flask A?   (1)

Benson washed both sets of peas with antiseptic solution before he put them in the flasks. This was to kill bacteria or fungi on the peas.

d   Why would microbes in the flask affect his results?   (1)
e   Explain the temperature changes in flask A.   (2)

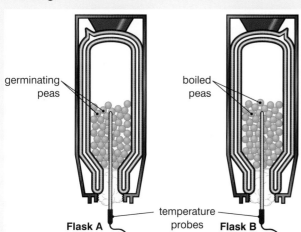

germinating peas
boiled peas
temperature probes
Flask A   Flask B

Key words

Unscramble these:
shrub con
socugle
perrise
biorace
lotte in vain

8C

Microbes and disease

COMING SOON

8C1 Micro-organisms

8C2 Growing micro-organisms

8C3 Microbe factories

8C4 Harmful micro-organisms

8C5 Defending your body

8C6 Immunisation

8C7 Preventing infections

What's it all about?

Atishoo – oh no, not another cold! Last Monday Molly Kewel sneezed all day, and has not been back since. Benson was off yesterday and Pip is off today. This cold is going right round the class.

In this unit we look at micro-organisms, and how infectious micro-organisms pass between people. You will find out about how the body defends itself against infections.

Micro-organisms aren't all bad news though. You will also find out how we can use micro-organisms to make food and other useful things.

What do you remember?

You already know about:

- micro-organisms called bacteria, viruses and fungi.
- how they feed, grow and reproduce.
- how they can cause disease, and make things rot.
- how they are used to make some foods.
- living things using glucose for energy.

1 What sort of living thing is this?

bacterium
virus
fungus
flowering plant

2 What caused Molly Kewel's cold?

getting wet
not enough sleep
not enough vitamins
a virus

3 What is respiration? Is it . . .

making food using light
treating people who have nearly drowned
releasing energy from glucose
breathing in air

Ideas about microbes

Look at the cartoon and then with your partner decide if these are true or false.

a) The nursery rhyme 'Ring a ring o' roses' is about the Black Death, the time that many people in the country died of the plague. True or false?

b) Micro-organisms are used to make cheese. True or false?

c) You can catch diseases by eating dirty food. True or false?

d) Bacteria are always harmful. True or false?

What is the tiniest living thing you can think of? Probably a bacterium. Bacteria are a kind of micro-organism. We need a microscope to see most micro-organisms. The main groups are **bacteria**, **viruses**, **protozoa** and **fungi**. Some micro-organisms have common names – like the 'flu virus, or mould – but we use scientific names for most of them.

⬤ Fungi

Fungi are the biggest micro-organisms. Both mushrooms and tiny yeast cells are fungi. Fungi usually live as fine white threads running through substances. They cause decay of dead animal and plant debris. This is part of recycling materials in the environment. Fungi use useful nutrients from the decayed material to grow. They reproduce by making spores. Some fungi make their spores in structures we call mushrooms and toadstools.

⬤ Protozoa

Protozoa are single-celled animals. They are almost large enough to see. They live in ponds and damp places. They feed on bacteria and particles of debris even smaller than themselves. They are important members of pond and soil food chains.

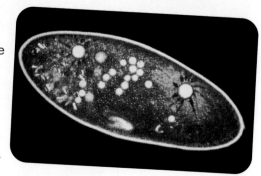

⬤ Bacteria

Bacteria have just one round or capsule shaped cell. They are found everywhere, in soil, in water, and even inside animals. Bacteria in the soil feed on dead leaves and animal matter, causing decay. They reproduce by binary fission.

LINK UP TO BIOLOGY

Binary fission is a form of cell division (see Unit 7A).

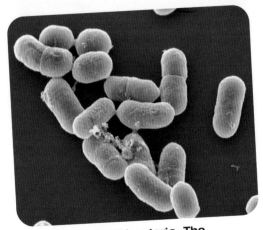

Capsule-shaped bacteria. The 'waistline' shows where a bacterium is dividing into two.

● Virus

Viruses are different from other micro-organisms. They are the smallest and cannot grow and reproduce on their own. They must infect other living cells to reproduce. They do not have cells but have a coat enclosing a few genes. There are viruses that can grow inside every species of living thing – even bacteria have viruses.

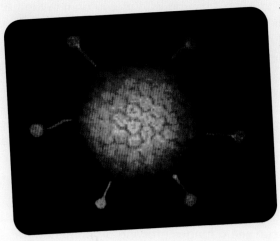

The spikes help this virus attach itself to cells

Q1 Can you recall what a gene is? Is it involved in

inheritance   **respiration**   **classification**   **digestion**

Make a presentation about micro-organisms.

The largest living thing is a fungus growing over one kilometre in area.

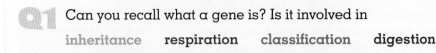
Finding out about micro-organisms

● Look carefully at the samples of micro-organisms that you have been given.
Look at their activity. Describe what you can see and what it tells you about each micro-organism. You should include things such as how big they are and why they are important.

SUMMARY QUESTIONS

1 ☆ Arrange in order of size:

bacteria   **fungi**   **virus**   **protozoa**

2 ☆ Which micro-organisms decay dead material in the environment?

3 ☆☆ How are viruses different from other micro-organisms?

4 ☆☆ Pete was interested in decay. He buried some leaf discs in a mesh bag in the soil. When he dug them up again the leaf discs were much smaller and broken up. Which two groups of micro-organism could have caused the breakdown?

Key words

bacterium
fungus
protozoa
virus

Growing micro-organisms

8C2

Have you ever found a satsuma with mould on it in the fruit bowl? If you leave food out long enough it will grow a fine collection of bacteria and fungi. Scientists grow micro-organisms more carefully – especially if they are infectious.

● Growing bacteria

Scientists can grow bacteria in a laboratory or factory using specialised equipment. Everything they use is **sterilised** before it is used to kill any stray micro-organisms. While they are working, they take care not to let unwanted bacteria in, or to let any of the bacteria they are growing escape.

Bacteria feed on a mixture of nutrients that is made into a liquid broth, or a jelly. You can see a fungus growing on nutrient agar jelly in the picture. To make commercial products, bacteria are grown in large tanks holding thousands of litres of broth.

In a laboratory, scientists often grow bacteria on a layer of **nutrient agar** jelly in a **petri dish**. A sample of bacteria is spread, or **inoculated**, on to the surface of the jelly. The dish is kept in an incubator for a few days at the best temperature for that bacterium to grow. The bacteria form clusters, or **colonies**, as they grow and reproduce.

A fungus growing on nutrient agar jelly. The 'fur' is spores ready to spread through the air.

Q1 What might happen if 'wild' bacteria got into a container of bacteria making fruit yoghurt?

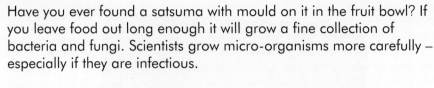

Bacteria grown in these units make protein for medicine

Colonies of bacteria growing on nutrient agar jelly

● Using science

Scientists regularly sample and count the number of bacteria in our drinking water and food supplies to check the cleanliness. If there are too many bacteria, or the wrong sort, there could be trouble.

Hmm, I think something's escaped from the Biology lab!

Growing microbes

It is important that you follow *all* your safety instructions when working with micro-organisms.

● Inoculate bacteria on to two prepared petri dishes of nutrient agar jelly.

● Put one in the warm incubator to grow. Put the other one in a cool place. Don't forget to measure the temperature.

● After a few days compare the colonies on each dish.

● How has the temperature affected how bacteria grow?

AMAZING SCIENCE!

There are more than a hundred million bacteria in a gram of soil.

SUMMARY QUESTIONS

1 ☆ What do bacteria feed on when we grow them in a laboratory?

2 ☆ Name one container we can grow bacteria in.

3 ☆☆ Write definitions of sterile, colony, inoculate.

4 ☆☆ Why is it important to use sterile equipment and materials for growing bacteria?

Key words

colony
inoculate
nutrient agar
petri dish
sterile

Microbe factories

LEARN ABOUT
- making products with micro-organisms

Do you like cheese sandwiches or soy sauce on your food? Micro-organisms help make bread, cheese and soy sauce. They make more than just food. Just as farmers have learnt to keep cows for milk, we have learned how to grow micro-organisms to make products. It would be hard to go for a whole day without using something made with microbes.

What do micro-organisms make?

Micro-organisms make enzymes to digest their food. Washing powder and dishwasher powder contain **enzymes** made by micro-organisms. We use their enzymes to break down food remains and biological stains. Other microbial enzymes are used to turn waste carbohydrate into a sugary syrup for making soft drinks. They are also used to make leather, and finish cotton cloth.

Micro-organisms make medicines such as insulin for treating diabetes. **Antibiotics**, such as penicillin are also made by micro-organisms.

Q1 Can you explain how enzymes might be useful when washing a dirty tablecloth?

Yeast

Yeast is a fungus. It uses sugar for **respiration** and releases carbon dioxide. When we mix yeast with flour and water to make bread it breaks down sugar in the flour. Carbon dioxide collects into bubbles. This makes bread dough rise. At the same time ethanol, a kind of alcohol, is made. When bread is baked the ethanol evaporates so you will not get drunk on your sandwiches.

Brewers use yeast to make drinks such as beer or wine. Yeast is mixed with sugary fruit juice or mashed barley grains. This time carbon dioxide escapes and ethanol stays in the mixture. This sort of process is called **fermentation**. When the process is finished we can extract B vitamins from the yeast.

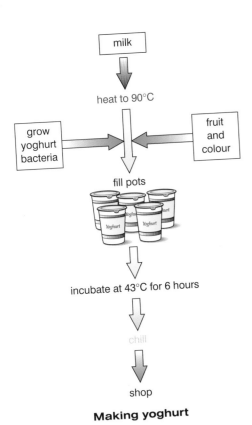

milk
↓
heat to 90°C

grow yoghurt bacteria → ← fruit and colour

fill pots
↓
incubate at 43°C for 6 hours
↓
chill
↓
shop

Making yoghurt

Penicillin is the most commonly prescribed medicine in the world.

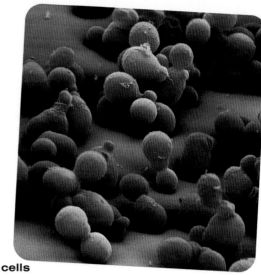

Yeast cells

Making dough

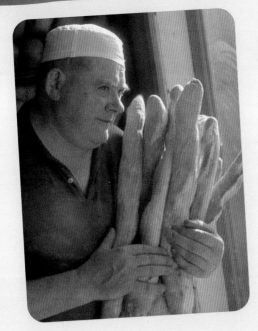

 CHALLENGE

Use a data logger to monitor pH changes in milk as yoghurt bacteria grow.

Bread is first made into dough. Then dough is left to 'prove', or rise, in a warm place. Find out how temperature affects bread dough.

● Mix together yeast, sugar, flour and warm water to make a sloppy dough.
Pour $30\,cm^3$ of the dough into each of three measuring cylinders.
Put one measuring cylinder in a water bath at 50°C, one at 30°C, and leave one at room temperature.
After 30 minutes, measure how far the bread dough has risen.
Draw a graph of the increase in volume at each temperature.
Your 'dough' has risen because yeast releases carbon dioxide when respiring sugar. How could you show that your mixture is releasing carbon dioxide?

● Plan an investigation to find out how changing the amount of sugar affects your dough.

● Find out about growing bacteria or fungi to make a product such as yoghurt, antibiotics, cheese.

LINK UP TO **BIOLOGY**

Respiration is the process of releasing energy from glucose (see Unit 8B).

SUMMARY QUESTIONS

1 ☆ What sort of micro-organism is yeast?

2 ☆ Name one important product made by fungi and one use for microbial enzymes.

3 ☆☆ Benson tried making bread at home. He made dough with flour, water and yeast, then left it on the table to rise. When he came back 30 minutes later it had hardly increased in size at all. Give *two* possible reasons why Benson's dough had not risen.

Key words

antibiotic
enzyme
fermentation
respiration
yeast

LEARN ABOUT
- how disease-causing micro-organisms are passed on

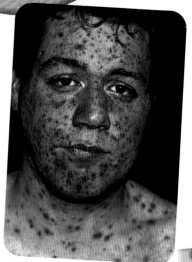

Chickenpox virus multiplies in skin cells and is easily passed on

You wash your cuts to stop an infection. But what's going to infect your cut? In fact you are trying to stop bacteria getting into the wound.

Q1 Why do you think doctors and nurses wear gloves and masks in the operating theatre?

Infectious diseases

Some micro-organisms can grow in your body and cause an infection. In Table 1 you can see some of the illnesses they cause.

Table 1

Micro-organisms	Diseases caused
bacteria	food-poisoning, TB, tetanus, bacterial meningitis
virus	measles, chickenpox, rotavirus, common cold, viral meningitis
fungus	ringworm, athlete's foot
protozoa	food-poisoning, malaria

There are many different ways in which micro-organisms can spread. Table 2 shows you the most common ways that micro-organisms are **transmitted** from one person to another.

Table 2 How micro-organisms are transmitted from person to person

Method of transmission		Examples
droplet	the air we breathe in carries tiny moisture droplets exhaled by other people with infections	common cold, 'flu, TB
oral	you eat food contaminated by micro-organisms or containing faecal traces	salmonella and other food poisonings, listeriosis
water	you drink water contaminated by sewage. Micro-organisms that infect the gut pass in faeces and get into water with untreated sewage	cholera, dysentery typhoid
touch	you touch something the micro-organism is on, or a part of an infected person's body	impetigo, ringworm, conjunctivitis
insect bites	insects carry micro-organisms that enter your body when they bite you	malaria, sleeping sickness, yellow fever
wounds and blood	micro-organisms enter cuts and wounds with dirt or bites or blood	tetanus, rabies, HIV, hepatitis

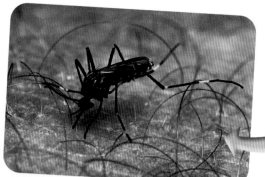

Malaria microbes are injected into your blood when an infected mosquito feeds

● Stopping the spread

- We add **chlorine** to drinking water to kill micro-organisms.
- Sewage is treated to kill harmful micro-organisms.
- People preparing food for supermarkets and restaurants follow regulations designed to stop bacteria getting into food.
- We keep fresh and prepared food in a refrigerator because bacteria multiply more slowly in cold environments.

Q2 Can you think of any other ways in which we try to stop infections spreading?

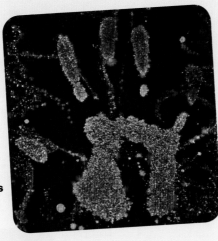

The bacteria on someone's unwashed hands

CHALLENGE

Use the Internet to find out about Dr John Snow. He found how cholera spread in London in the 19th century.

Stopping the spread

- Some people have their holidays spoilt when they catch an **infection** that causes vomiting and diarrhoea. Find out about salmonella and other types of **food-poisoning**. Produce a leaflet that advises holidaymakers on how to avoid such an infection.
- Find out about first aid for cuts and grazes.
- People in the food industry study for a certificate in basic food handling hygiene. Find out about some of the rules for handling meat in a butcher's shop or handling prepared foods in a delicatessen.

LINK UP TO CHEMISTRY

Chlorine is an element you meet in Unit 8E.

Gruesome science

Virus-laden sneeze particles travel at over 45 metres per second from your nose. They can spread for up to 4 metres around you.

SUMMARY QUESTIONS

1 ☆ Explain how colds pass from person to person in a class.

2 ☆ Name one type of organism that can infect a cut.

3 ☆☆ Pip made sandwiches with some left-over cooked chicken. She left her lunch in her desk in the warm classroom but couldn't eat it until very late. Explain why she was at risk of food-poisoning. Suggest one way she could reduce the risk.

4 ☆☆ Why do you think that raw meat is stored separately from cooked meat, such as corned beef in a butcher's shop?

Key words

chlorine
food-poisoning
infection
transmission

8C5 Defending your body

LEARN ABOUT

- how skin protects us
- white blood cells and antibodies

If you are surrounded by millions of micro-organisms in soil, water and air, why aren't you ill more often? You catch so few infections because your body is very well defended.

Keeping microbes out

Skin is good at keeping bacteria out. The outer layer of your skin is hard, dry and constantly flaking off. Bacteria or fungi growing here fall off with dead skin cells. Natural openings in your body are much more promising. Your eyes, nose, throat, sweat glands, and other entrances are warm, moist and have plenty of nutrients – ideal for micro-organisms. Unfortunately for bacteria there are also chemicals that kill them or stop them growing in the moisture.

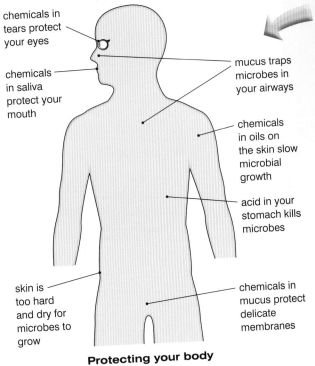

chemicals in tears protect your eyes

chemicals in saliva protect your mouth

mucus traps microbes in your airways

chemicals in oils on the skin slow microbial growth

acid in your stomach kills microbes

skin is too hard and dry for microbes to grow

chemicals in mucus protect delicate membranes

Protecting your body

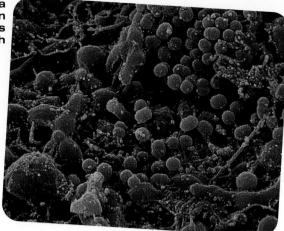

Bacteria growing on food traces around teeth

Internal defences

Your **immune system** protects you from micro-organisms getting into your body, through a wound for example. Most of the work is done by **white blood cells**.

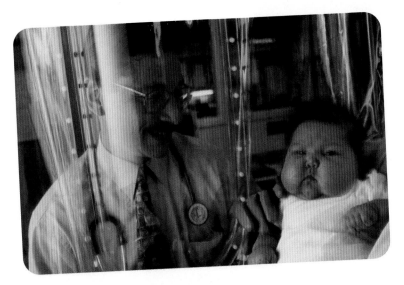

This baby cannot make white blood cells and must live in sterile surroundings

What do white blood cells do?

Micro-organisms are different from human cells. Your white blood cells recognise your own cells and what they are made of, but not 'foreign' substances on microbial cells. White blood cells engulf and destroy any cells with foreign substances, or **antigens**.

Antibodies

Captured micro-organisms are also taken to glands called lymph nodes. Lymph nodes then begin to make new white blood cells called lymphocytes. These cells make **antibodies**. Antibodies stick to the antigens on infecting micro-organisms. This helps other white cells recognise them, sticks them together and stops them infecting our tissues. Antibodies can pass to babies in breast milk and protect new-born babies from infections.

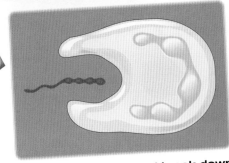

White cells take in and break down bacteria

Q1 Can you think how our immune system stops us accepting a transplanted kidney from an unsuitable donor?

Remembering infections

We remember antigens. If micro-organisms we have met before get into the body again the antigens are recognised. Fresh antibody-making cells are produced rapidly.

Different micro-organisms have different antigens so we have to make a new antibody for every new micro-organism we meet.

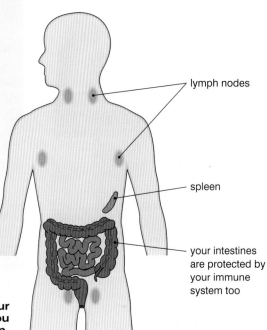

lymph nodes

spleen

your intestines are protected by your immune system too

Lymph nodes. The ones in your neck sometimes swell when you have an infection.

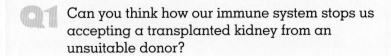

Defending the body

- Use an outline of the human body. Label the places where micro-organisms can enter the body. Beside each, write one defence mechanism.

Gruesome science

The black buboes found on bubonic plague victims were swollen lymph nodes.

SUMMARY QUESTIONS

1 ☆ Give *two* ways in which white blood cells destroy bacteria.

2 ☆ Why is it difficult for bacteria to colonise your skin?

3 ☆☆ Write a short passage about how white blood cells defend against disease.

Key words

antibodies
antigen
immune system
skin
white blood cell

8C6

● Being immune

Once you have had chickenpox you do not usually catch it again. You are **immune**. Being immune means that you are **resistant** to that disease. The chickenpox virus cannot infect you again.

● Immunisation

We use the body's ability to remember antigens to protect people against infections. When you are **immunised** you are given a **vaccination**.

Vaccines contain microbial antigens to provoke your body into making antibodies. It also makes a memory of the antigens. The vaccine doesn't cause a real infection. Should you ever meet the real micro-organism you will be ready for it.

Q1 What is an antigen?

a substance in a microbial cell
something made by a white blood cell

Vaccines are made from killed micro-organisms, or fragments of their cells. They cannot start an infection but they bring your white cells into action. The polio vaccine is different because it contains a weakened form of the virus that provokes immunity to the normal virus.

We have vaccines against many common micro-organisms, such as those causing tetanus and diphtheria. A hundred years ago diseases like these killed tens of thousands of children every year. Now they are very rare. This is because children are vaccinated when they are very young.

Two diseases, smallpox and polio, have been almost eliminated through vaccination. Measles is next on the 'hit' list.

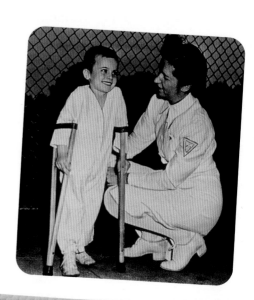

Polio damages the nervous system and leaves people paralysed. Dr Sabin developed the oral polio vaccine.

How do we protect our children?

- Children are offered immunisations from two months old.
  a) Find out which immunisations children are given in their first two years.
  b) Which did you have before you started school?

- From the data in the table, draw a graph of the number of cases of measles between 1989 and 2002. Round the numbers before plotting them.

Year	Number of cases
1989	26 222
1990	13 302
1991	9680
1992	10 268
1993	9612
1994	16 375
1995	7447
1996	5614
1997	3962
1998	3728
1999	2438
2000	2378
2001	2250
2002	3187

The MMR vaccine protects children from dangerous measles infections. On your graph mark
c) when you think the MMR vaccine was introduced.
d) when parents read a health scare about the vaccine.

Scientists can detect every infection you've ever had from the antibodies in your blood.

Visit the World Health Organisation website and find out how the campaign to eradicate polio is progressing.

SUMMARY QUESTIONS

1 ☆ What does immune mean?

2 ☆ How do white blood cells protect you from infection?

3 ☆ What do white blood cells make when you are vaccinated?

4 ☆☆ What is antibody and antigen? How are they linked?

Key words

immune
immunisation
resistant
vaccination
vaccine

8◁7 Preventing infections

LEARN ABOUT
- antibiotics
- disinfectants
- antiseptics

● Antibiotics

Despite your protection you sometimes catch an infection. Your doctor may give you a medicine to help you recover. If it is a bacterial infection, for example an ear and throat infection, you might get an **antibiotic** such as one of the penicillin-based medicines.

Antibiotics stop bacteria growing and reproducing. You have to take them for several days to stop the infection. If you stop too soon the bacteria left alive will quickly reproduce and restart the infection. Antibiotics do not affect viruses at all because viruses grow and reproduce in a different way. So if you have a cold, caused by a virus, you will just have to get better on your own.

Q1 **Penicillin** is an antibiotic. Can you think of the name of another antibiotic?

Penicillium **fungus makes penicillin. Its effects were first noticed by Sir Alexander Fleming.**

● Disinfectants and antiseptics

Disinfectants are very powerful chemicals that damage the cells of micro-organisms so that they die. We use disinfectants on surfaces; in the bathroom, kitchen, hospitals, baby's bottles, and anywhere where there are harmful pathogens. Bleach is a disinfectant that releases **chlorine**. There are many different disinfectant chemicals.

Disinfectants will also harm human cells. We have to use less powerful **antiseptics** to deal with micro-organisms in skin spots, in cuts and grazes, and in the mouth. Antiseptics slow down microbial growth.

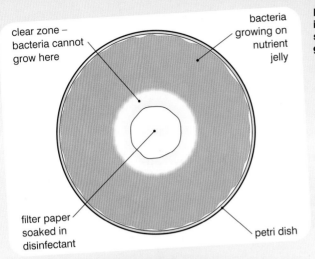

clear zone – bacteria cannot grow here

bacteria growing on nutrient jelly

Disinfectant diffuses into the jelly and stops bacteria growing

filter paper soaked in disinfectant

petri dish

How effective is your disinfectant?

Always follow *all* safety rules when working with microbes.

- Soak numbered discs of filter paper in household anti-microbial chemicals. You could try surface disinfectant, toothpaste, deodorant, antiseptic solution, sterilising solution, mouthwash. You could try cutting a small square of an anti-microbial wipe.
  a) Using forceps, place your discs on nutrient agar jelly that has been seeded with bacteria. Incubate it.
  b) After a few days look to see where bacteria have grown. If the anti-microbial substance has stopped bacteria growing there will be a clear area round its disc.
  c) Which substance seemed to be the most effective against the bacteria you were growing?
  d) Why can't you be sure it's the best?

- Look around your house for the products you use to keep clean. Read the labels and make a list of the disinfectant or antiseptic chemicals.

 CHALLENGE

Penicillin was first observed by Alexander Fleming and developed by Florey and Chain. Write a magazine page about the story of penicillin.

SUMMARY QUESTIONS

1 ☆ Why do antibiotics make people with bacterial infections better?

2 ☆ Match the chemical with the job it is used for:

clean up in the kitchen	antiseptic
clean a graze	antibiotic
treat an eye infection	disinfectant

3 ☆☆ Why doesn't the doctor give you antibiotics when you have a cold or chickenpox?

4 ☆☆ Swimming pool water contains chlorine to keep it clean. Explain why adding chlorine keeps the water safer for swimmers.

Key words

antibiotic
antiseptic
chlorine
disinfectant
penicillin

IDEAS AND EVIDENCE

Louis Pasteur

Louis Pasteur (1822–1895) was one of the first scientists to investigate bacteria. He began as a university chemist looking at crystal structures. He had become a chemistry teacher by the time he was asked by an alcohol manufacturer to look at a problem.

Everyone agreed that **fermenting** sugar into alcohol was linked to brewer's yeast, but no-one knew how. Some of the manufacturer's fermentations had made lactic acid instead of alcohol. The problem, and the new insights it led to, kept Pasteur busy for years.

He examined the fermenting mixes with a microscope. He **observed** that normal fermentations contained minute rounded bodies, but those that would make lactic acid had long bodies. This allowed him to **predict** which batches would be useless.

Pasteur returned to university to work on fermentations. He thought that there must be two different processes going on, not one. He extracted a substance like yeast from the

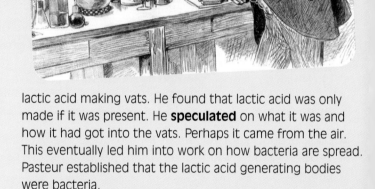

lactic acid making vats. He found that lactic acid was only made if it was present. He **speculated** on what it was and how it had got into the vats. Perhaps it came from the air. This eventually led him into work on how bacteria are spread. Pasteur established that the lactic acid generating bodies were bacteria.

He also showed that brewer's **yeast** was a living organism and watched it reproduce. Others thought that fermentation was the result of brewer's yeast decomposing. By using carefully controlled experiments Pasteur showed that live yeast cells were needed for fermentation. During his investigations into various fermentations he discovered bacteria that did not need oxygen – the first such organism ever found.

Pasteur developed a method of treating wine so that vinegar-producing bacteria did not make it sour. He heated it briefly to about 60°C, which was hot enough to kill the bacteria that make vinegar. This process became known as **pasteurisation**. We use it today to treat milk, beer and fruit juices so they keep better.

Pasteur went on to make vitally important discoveries – what can you find out about him?

Milk leaves the milking cluster and goes straight to a pasteuriser

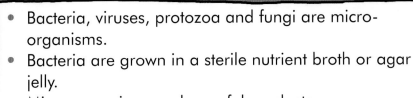

- Bacteria, viruses, protozoa and fungi are micro-organisms.
- Bacteria are grown in a sterile nutrient broth or agar jelly.
- Micro-organisms make useful products.
- Some micro-organisms cause disease.
- Infectious micro-organisms can spread from one person to another.
- Your body has defences against infections.
- White blood cells of the immune system capture micro-organisms and make antibodies. Vaccination mimics this process.
- Antibiotics, disinfectants and antiseptics kill micro-organisms or stop them growing.

You have to handle food hygenically... Not drop it in the muck.

Some people think the ring o roses is the spots and 'atishoo' for how it passed.

So milk bacteria digest milk sugar, and turn milk into cheese.

Only a few sorts of bacteria are harmful, most of them don't affect us at all.

DANGER! AVOID THESE COMMON ERRORS

A *disinfectant* is a very powerful substance that kills micro-organisms. It is used on surfaces such as worktops and sinks.

An *antiseptic* is much more dilute than a disinfectant, so it can be used on delicate human tissue. It will kill some micro-organisms and stop others growing without harming the skin.

Antibiotics are medicines prescribed by a doctor to kill bacteria. They do not kill viruses so we do not take them to cure a cold.

Key words

fermenting
observe
pasteurisation
predict
speculate
yeast

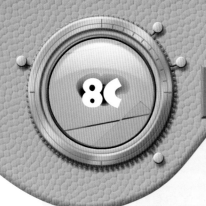

UNIT REVIEW

REVIEW QUESTIONS
Understanding and applying concepts

1 Copy the sentences and fill in the missing words.

   a The four types of micro-organisms are . . . . and . . .

   b Micro-organisms are important for breaking down the remains of dead animals and plants. Two types of micro-organisms do this. They are protozoa and . . .

   c . . . is used to make bread and beer.

   d We are protected from harmful micro-organisms by . . . . . . in our blood. Some of them . . . micro-organisms, others make . . . that stop infections.

2 a What is the name of the substance that is used to grow bacteria?

   b Why should equipment used to grow bacteria be sterile before we use it and after it has been used?

3 In the past many children and young people died of diseases such as diphtheria.

   Why do fewer children catch these diseases today?

4 Write definitions of the following words:

   vaccinate   **sterile**   **ferment**   **incubate**

5 Copy and complete the following table.

Micro-organism	Infection	How it is transmitted
bacterium	food-poisoning	
bacterium		droplets from lungs
	common cold	
virus		
protozoan	malaria	
fungus		contact

Thinking skills

6 Draw a spider diagram of micro-organisms. Include the following words:

   pathogen   **yoghurt**   **white blood cell**
   decay   **immunity**   **virus**   **antiseptic**
   insect

SAT-STYLE QUESTIONS

1 Hib vaccination protects against infections by a bacterium, *Haemophilus influenzae*. This bacterium causes a form of meningitis. Some people have the bacterium but do not show signs of infection.

   The graph shows the number of infections reported in the UK between 1990 and 2001.

   a After which date did the number of infections fall the most? (1)

   b Describe the pattern of infection between 1990 and 1993. (1)

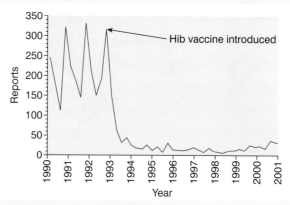

Reports of *Haemophilus influenzae* type B infection

   The arrow shows when the vaccination programme began.

   c Explain the changes in the graph between 1992 and 1996. (2)

   d Predict what will happen if parents do not continue to have their children vaccinated. (1)

   The bacterium is passed in coughs and sneezes.

   e What type of transmission is this? (1)

2 Look at the diagram of a white blood cell.

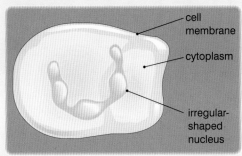

cell membrane
cytoplasm
irregular-shaped nucleus

Blood also contains red blood cells. The structure of white blood cells is different to the structure of red blood cells.

a i) Give one way in which the structure of a white blood cell is different to the structure of a red blood cell. (1)

ii) Give one function of a white blood cell. (1)

b Name one type of micro-organism that can infect through a cut. (1)

Some viruses, such as 'flu, change the composition of their outer layer from time to time. This results in a new strain of 'flu.

c Explain why a vaccine to an older type of 'flu will not be very effective against a new strain. (1)

3 Pip decided to make some bread. She put 250 cm^3 warm water in a jug and stirred in 5 g sugar and 15 g dried yeast. She rested the jug on the radiator. After 15 minutes the mixture was bubbling and there was a froth on the top of the yeast mixture.

a What sort of micro-organism is yeast? (1)

b Why did she add sugar to the yeast mixture? (1)

c Why was the mixture frothy? (2)

She mixed the liquid with 500 g plain flour in a mixing bowl. She kneaded the dough then left it over the radiator to 'prove'. Two hours later the ball of dough was twice as big.

d What is the name of the process that has caused the dough to rise? (1)

e What would have happened if she had left the dough in a cooler place? (1)

Pip kneaded the dough again and put it in a tin. As well as smelling of yeast it smelt slightly alcoholic. After proving again for 30 minutes she baked her bread at 220°C.

f Why wasn't there any alcohol in her bread? (1)

4 Reese and Pete investigated how some household chemicals affected bacterial growth.

Reese predicted that anti-bacterial spray would be most effective at preventing bacterial growth.

They cut circles from filter paper. Reese used sterile forceps to dip them in one of the solutions. They placed them on a petri dish in which bacteria were growing. The dishes of bacteria were incubated.

Reese and Pete knew they had to work carefully.

a i) Why did Reese use sterile forceps to handle the discs of filter paper? (1)

ii) Suggest two other safety precautions they should take working with micro-organisms. (2)

After three days incubation the petri dishes looked like this:

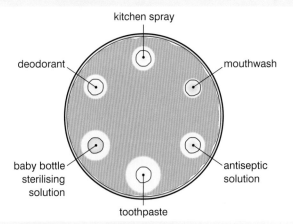

kitchen spray
deodorant
mouthwash
baby bottle sterilising solution
antiseptic solution
toothpaste

b What should Reese and Pete measure to find out about the effect of the anti-microbial substances? (1)

c Do the results support Reese's prediction? (1)

Pete thought that it wasn't a fair comparison because they did not know how much anti-bacterial substance there was in each of their solutions.

d Give one other variable that Pete and Reese could have controlled. (1)

Key words

Unscramble these:

actionule
catabire
tripe hids
eritles

8D Ecological relationships

COMING SOON

8D1 Identifying animals and plants

8D2 Sampling animals

8D3 Sampling plants

8D4 Food webs

8D5 Interactions

8D6 Pyramids and energy flow

What's it all about?

Animals and plants live in complex communities. They are linked to each other. A feeding relationship links organisms with what they eat. Providing something that another species needs is another kind of link. For example, grass benefits from a dollop of cow dung occasionally. In this unit you will explore the relationships within communities of plants and animals.

Energy enters habitats as sunlight. It flows through a community as one species eats another. You will find out about energy flow through a community and how it limits the length of a food chain.

 ## What do you remember?

You already know about:
- classifying plants and animals into groups.
- food chains and food webs.
- how physical factors affect animals and plants in a habitat.
- how animals and plants are adapted to their environment.

1. Three of these are important physical factors in the environment of animals and plants. Which one is not?

    amount of light   rainfall
    highest and lowest temperature each day
    atmospheric pressure

2. Give an example of a predator, a primary consumer, and a producer.

3. Match the animal to the group it belongs to

    snail   **frog**   **ladybird**   **woodlouse**

    crustacean
    amphibian
    mollusc
    insect

A ladybird

Ideas about investigating habitats

The Scientifica crew is sampling the animals and plants in two different areas of the school grounds. They are comparing the wild area by the sports pitch with the rose garden area. They want to know if the communities of animals and plants in the two areas differ.

a) What sorts of animals and plants would you expect to find in the area by the sports pitch?

b) What items of equipment would help Pip identify the bird?

c) What advice would you give the crew for working safely outside?

Identifying animals and plants

LEARN ABOUT
- classifying animals and plants
- arthropods

Imagine it's warm and sunny and you're off for a trip to the coast. What animals and plants do you expect to see? You might see several species of seabirds. Also mussels and limpets and top shells attached to rocks. Maybe you'll see crabs and seaweed, but no jellyfish if you are lucky.

At first glance there probably don't seem to be very many animals and plants in your school grounds. But the first glance is deceptive – it's teeming with life.

There may not be any large animals but there are thousands of small ones living in the zone closest to the ground, among the plants and leaf litter. There will be at least a dozen different flowering plants growing between the grasses on the lawn.

Q1 Where would be a good place to look for animals and plants round the school? What species are you likely to find?

You may not recognise what these small animals are. You need to use your knowledge of the **classification** groups to identify them. You can see how we classify some of the species you may find, opposite.

Most of the animals living in grassy places, among dead leaves and under shrubs are **invertebrates**. Most of these are **arthropods** but there are also plenty of **molluscs** and **segmented worms**.

Arthropods have a body made of distinct segments with a hard outer skeleton – an exoskeleton. They move about using jointed legs. They pass through stages as they grow, and young arthropods, for example caterpillars, may look quite different from the adults. The number of body segments and legs helps us decide what sort of arthropods we are looking at.

You are likely to find herbivores, debris feeders, small predators and **decomposers**. Decomposers decay dead, or dying, plant and animal materials. They break up larger items such as dead leaves into smaller fragments. They recycle nutrients in the community.

You are likely to find flowering plants, both grassy and broad-leaved, and mosses. Don't forget to look up – trees are plants too!

Peacock butterflies look very different from their young

Invertebrates

Segmented worms
- body in many similar segments
- no distinct head
- some bristles
e.g. earthworm

Arthropods
- exoskeleton
- moults to allow growth
- jointed limbs

Molluscs
- muscular foot
- no segments
- usually a shell
e.g. slugs, snails

earthworm

snail

Insects
- body in 3 parts
- 3 pairs of legs
- 1 or 2 pairs of wings
e.g. fungus gnat, beetle, aphid

Myriapods
- head and many body segments with legs
- no wings
e.g. centipede, millipede

Arachnids
- body in 2 parts
- 4 pairs of legs
- no antennae
e.g. spider, harvestman, mite

Crustaceans
- body in 2 parts
- many pairs of walking legs
- gills
- 2 pairs of antennae
e.g. woodlouse

adult beetle   larval beetle

centipede

mite

woodlouse

Classify

● Identify the group the organisms below belong to. Do you know what they are?

(a)

(b)

(c)

(d)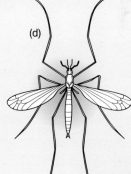

(e)

(f)

(g)

SUMMARY QUESTIONS

1 ☆ What are the general features of an arthropod?

2 ☆ How would you distinguish an insect from a spider?

3 ☆ What is a decomposer?

Key words

arthropod
classification
decomposer
invertebrate
mollusc

How would you find out how many elephants there are in a game reserve? Drive round in a jeep and count? Fly over in a helicopter? We need to be ingenious to find and count animals because they don't stick around to be identified.

Finding animals

We can **observe** large animals, using binoculars in a hide if necessary. A video camera, overlooking a suitable spot can record shy species.

Caught on camera – a badger looking for food at night

Scientists catch animals such as squirrels and mice in humane traps. They are identified, weighed and measured before being released at the spot they were caught.

You can catch small creatures living in vegetation in a **pitfall trap**. **Tree-beating** will uncover the animals feeding or resting in bushes.

Q1 How could you investigate how many blackbirds there are in your school grounds?

Sampling animals

If you want **quantitative** data – that is if you want to know how many individuals there are in a community – you must take samples from a measured area. For example, to estimate the number of animals living in leaf litter you should mark out a square, 30 cm by 30 cm on the surface and use a trowel to dig up the top 10 cm of leaf and soil debris to take back to the lab for careful examination.

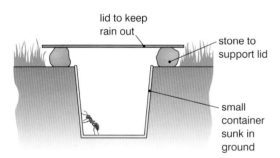

lid to keep rain out

stone to support lid

small container sunk in ground

A pitfall trap

AMAZING SCIENCE!

There are 400 000 soil mites in each m^2 of leaf litter layer in a forest.

Finding animals

- Use a pitfall trap to investigate small ground-dwelling invertebrates.
- Investigate insects and other invertebrates living in shrubs and bushes by tree-beating.
- Investigate a sample of leaf litter to find and identify small invertebrates. Try to estimate how many there are.

Identifying

In the lab use a key and a hand lens and binocular microscope to help you identify the smallest organisms.

As many of these small animals are very fragile pick them up with a paintbrush. They don't stand still so a **pooter** is very useful for catching them as they try to hide.

Investigating different areas

Choose two different areas to investigate.

- Find, identify and record as many species of animals as possible in your two sites.
  Research the species you have identified. Include what it eats and its major predators. Pool your information with other groups to construct a database of information.

 CHALLENGE

Use the Internet to find out about how bird populations are monitored. Construct a database of information about the species you have identified.

SUMMARY QUESTIONS

1. ☆ How would you assess how many a) ground beetles b) woodlice there are in a community?

2. ☆ Give an example of quantitative data that you have collected in science activities.

3. ☆☆ Why do you think it is important to replace animals in the same spot you found them in?

Key words

observe
pitfall trap
pooter
quantitative
tree-beating

Sampling plants

When we go for a walk we remember the colourful flowers of dandelions and gorse. We don't notice small plain plants. Ecologists collect data about plants scientifically to make sure they do not overlook species.

Our eyes are drawn to vivid flowers and we ignore the rest

Sampling

Ideally we should identify and count every plant in an area. This is too difficult and time consuming in a forest, or across a county. Instead we take **samples**. We investigate small areas thoroughly within a larger area.

It is important to take random samples that represent all parts of the area. We assume that the rest is like the samples, and that our results are typical.

Q1 Try to think why these actions could give us biased data:

avoiding the soggy part of a field

sampling near to but not in the clump of bushes

A **transect** is a long line running across an area. We sample plants at regular intervals along the line. Transects are useful to find out how the plant population changes with different physical conditions.

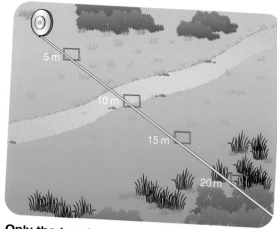

Only the toughest plants can survive being trampled on the path

Quadrats

Each sample should be the same size. A **quadrat** defines the area, and as they are 0.5 m square we can use them to **estimate** numbers per m². Quadrat sampling can tell us whether a plant is present or not, how many there are per m², and what percentage of the ground is covered by a particular species. **Percentage cover** is useful when we cannot see individual plants, for example, clover and daisies.

A quadrat. Daisies occur in 5 squares therefore the percentage cover is 20%.

Using quadrats

- Identify the plants growing in two different areas. Use quadrats to estimate the percentage cover for each species.
- Measure the light intensity, soil and air temperatures in the two areas you are comparing. Are there any other factors it would be useful to measure?
- Construct a database of the species you identified.

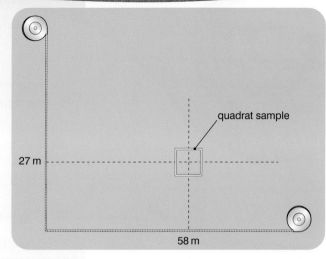

27 m

58 m

quadrat sample

Mike's phone number ends in 5827. The group has used it to select a random sample site.

SUMMARY QUESTIONS

1 The Scientifica crew were investigating plants in the school grounds. They could not decide how many quadrat samples to take. They looked at a graph constructed by Nina in Year 13 as part of her ecology coursework. It showed the number of plant species discovered when various numbers of samples were taken.

They used Nina's graph to decide how many samples to take.

a) Describe the pattern shown by Nina's graph.

b) How many samples should they take? Explain why you reached that decision.

(Graph: vertical axis "Total number of species found" from 0 to 40; horizontal axis "Number of quadrats sampled" from 0 to 40)

Nina's graph

2 Reese and Pip used a 0.5 m x 0.5 m quadrat to investigate the distribution of ribwort plantain plants. You can see where they sampled in the diagram. Their results are shown in the table.

Ribwort plantain

Square	1	2	3	4	5
Number of ribwort plantain	3	5	6	3	7

a) Using Reese and Pip's data, estimate how many ribwort plantain plants there are in the whole area.

b) Reese and Pip's results may not be reliable – why not?

c) How could Reese and Pip make their investigation more reliable?

Key words
estimate
percentage cover
quadrat
sampling
transect

Food webs

8D4

Life would be very boring if we only ate bread. We eat a variety of foods and so do most animals.

The foods that animals eat change. Summer fruit eaters may switch to seeds in the autumn. A tiny frog tadpole eats microscopic algae. As it grows it eats small water organisms, but it eats flies and worms as an adult frog. Food choices are shown in a **food web**.

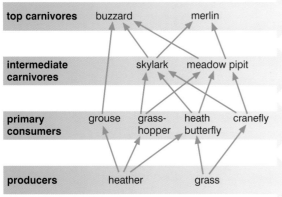

● Food webs

A food web shows the feeding relationships in a community. **Producers**, the plants, convert light energy into chemical energy. The substances they make provide energy for the rest of the food web. Animals that get their energy from plants or other animals are **consumers**.

Organisms on the same level in a food chain **compete** for food. This limits how many animals can co-exist on one level.

The size of an animal population depends on

- how much food is available,
- how much competition there is from other species for that food,
- how many predators feed on them.

For example, the number of red squirrels is linked to how many tree seeds there are in a year. They rear fewer young in years when there is less seed available, and their numbers decline.

top carnivores	buzzard	merlin
intermediate carnivores	skylark	meadow pipit
primary consumers	grouse	grass-hopper	heath butterfly	cranefly
producers	heather	grass

decomposition
fungi
bacteria
also
earthworms
springtails
mites

A moorland food web. The cranefly eats grass roots when it is a larva.

Q1 Can you think of any factors that might result in trees making less seed than usual?

Dead plants and animals are food for **decomposers**. Decomposers decay remains from all levels of a food web. Decomposers are primary consumers because they consume plant material.

Q2 Pick out two animals in the food web that are in competition for a food source.

Q3 Pick out a food chain with a grasshopper in it from the moorland food web.

Red squirrels thrive best in mixed woodlands with plenty of tree seed

Changes in the web

Anything that changes the numbers of one species in a food web also affects other species, directly or indirectly.

The small tortoiseshell butterfly larva (caterpillar) feeds on nettles. Adults feed on nectar from many flowers. If we clear nettles from an area there are no food plants for the adult to lay eggs on. There will be no caterpillars, and in time no adults.

We lose nectar-producing plants when we flail hedges instead of cutting, mow grassy areas more often, and cultivate fields right to the edges. Fewer flowers results in fewer nectar feeding insects and fewer fruits. In turn there will be fewer of the animals that feed on them.

Alien invaders

Alien species are plants and animals that arrive as a result of international trade. Some plants have spread from gardens. For example, rhododendrons now grow in woods and Himalayan balsam has spread along hundreds of miles of rivers in a few decades.

Grey squirrels, muntjac deer and mink arrived as exotic pets or farmed animals that later escaped or were released. Marine animals are carried as very small larval stages in ballast water in ships. They are deposited in foreign waters when ships discharge it.

Alien species compete with native species in food webs. They may be better at getting food and have no predators. Alien plants may not be as good a food source as native species. For example, Sitka spruce is not as good a food source for red squirrels as native conifers. Bark beetles in timber carried a fungus that killed most English elm trees.

ICT CHALLENGE

Find out about an alien species such as grey squirrels, muntjac deer, mink, Himalayan balsam or sycamore. Make a presentation about it and how it arrived.

Grey squirrels were introduced in 1876. By 1937 they had become such a nuisance in woodlands that laws were passed about releasing them.

Making a web

- Use the database you made in 8D3 to construct food chains for your areas.
  Try to link the food chains into a food web.

- Make a poster to display a food web in your environment.

SUMMARY QUESTIONS

1 ☆ Look at the moorland food web (opposite). Write out a food chain from the web. Identify a herbivore, a predator and a prey item.

2 ☆ Give three factors that can affect the size of the population of a particular animal species.

3 ☆☆ Red squirrels live and find food in the treetops but grey squirrels forage more on the ground. Explain how this could help grey squirrels compete for food.

Key words

alien species
compete
consumer
decomposer
food web
producer

8D5

Plants compete with each other. They compete for space, for water, for **minerals** from the soil, and for **light**. Each species has adaptations that help it compete more effectively.

Plants may grow differently in different light intensities. Ivy clinging to a tree grows larger leaves on the shady side so that they can collect enough light for making food. Other plants grow taller when shaded. They get their leaves above those of their competitors.

Q1 Moss can make food using less light than grass. How would you expect this to affect the amounts of grass and moss in a lawn, and in a wood?

(a) growing in a shaded area

(b) growing in full sun

The periwinkle plant growing in the shaded area needs larger leaves to collect as much light energy as stems from the same plant growing in the sun

Q2 Estimate the leaf area in the sun and in the shade.

Marsh plants can tolerate little oxygen around their roots and acid soil, which allows them to grow where other plants cannot. Conversely stinging nettles thrive where there is a high nitrate content in the soil. Nitrate is one of the minerals plants need in order to grow.

● Predators and prey

In some years there are so many ladybirds that they get everywhere. This **population boom** happens after there have been lots of aphids (greenfly) on plants. Adult and larval ladybirds are predators that eat aphids. When there are plenty of aphids most of the ladybird larvae survive to become adults, and the population booms. The aphids become very scarce.

Populations of **predators** and their **prey** are very closely linked. Predators depend on catching enough prey to stay alive, and to reproduce successfully. If there isn't enough food then the predators cannot survive and breed so well, and their numbers go down.

Stinging nettles are often a sign of an old farm muck heap or the place where the privy was emptied before modern sanitation. They cope with high nitrate content in the soil.

The number of prey animals, such as rabbits, is affected by the size of the predator population. When there are large numbers of predators, the rabbit population goes down. If there aren't many predators more rabbits survive to maturity and breed, so the rabbit population increases.

Over many years we can see the populations changing together, the boom in predator numbers always follows a boom in prey numbers.

Number per leaf — — number of red spider mites (prey) / — number of predator mites

June July Aug. Sept.

Month

Changing populations of apple red spider mite and its predator

Reporting findings

- Use the information you have gathered about the two areas you have investigated and the animals and plants living there to write a report comparing the two communities.

- Include in your report any factors you have identified that may affect the size of the populations.

ICT CHALLENGE

Prepare a PowerPoint or similar presentation comparing the two sites you have investigated.

SUMMARY QUESTIONS

1 In the diagram you can see dandelion plants from two different areas, one by a sports pitch, the other from a region of unmown grass.

The difference in growth can be explained by a difference in an important physical factor.
- ☆ **a)** Which physical factor could have caused this? How does this factor differ in the two areas?
- ☆☆ **b)** Explain how human activity could also have resulted in this difference.

2 ☆ Look at the graph above showing the population of red spider mites. Explain what would happen to the numbers of red spider mites if there were fewer predatory mites.

3 ☆☆ Ladybirds survive the winter by hibernating in a sheltered spot. Aphids die in the winter but replacements migrate north from warmer parts of Europe in early summer. Many ladybirds do not survive long cold winters. How would the population of aphids be affected the following year if there had been a very mild winter?

Key words

light
minerals
population boom
predator
prey

Pyramids and energy flow

- pyramids of numbers
- how energy is lost from a food chain

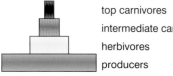

Hay stacks catch fire because so much heat is produced by microbial respiration in dried grass.

Pyramids

A food chain tells us what eats what – Molly Kewel eats tomatoes for example. Ecologists also use **quantitative data**, such as how many organisms are involved in a particular food chain.

We can show how many animals and plants are involved in a food chain with a **pyramid of numbers**. Each step in the pyramid shows how many organisms there are at that level.

The base is usually the broadest. It shows the number of plants. The more there are, the wider the step. The next step shows the number of herbivores. It is usually much narrower than the first step because each herbivore needs a lot of plants to supply its needs.

The third step is the intermediate carnivore, the animal that eats the herbivore. The last step is the top carnivore.

Q1 Choose the term from the list that best describes
a) the herbivore and **b)** the intermediate carnivore.

producer **primary consumer**
secondary consumer **decomposer**

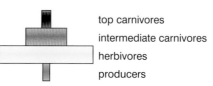

an inverted pyramid

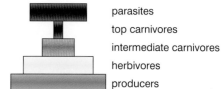

including parasites

Pyramids of numbers

Energy transfer

Energy flows along a food chain. When an animal or plant is eaten the energy it contains passes to the animal that has eaten it.

Food chains are short because at each transfer only a small proportion of the energy taken in ends up stored in tissues. The rest is lost in various ways. Very little of the light energy that entered the chain is left by the third or fourth step of the chain.

We can look at the transfers more closely. A plant uses some of the food it makes in **respiration**. Only a small proportion of the light energy falling on a plant ends up as stored energy in its tissues.

Stored energy in plants is transferred when herbivores eat them. Herbivores digest vegetation and absorb energy-containing nutrients. The nutrients are stored or used to make new tissues. Energy in undigested materials is lost in faeces.

Herbivores also respire and use energy to move about for example. Most energy is lost as heat. Energy also passes out of the body in waste materials such as urea in urine. Overall less than 10% of the energy in plants ends up as stored energy in herbivores.

Energy is transferred from a herbivore to a carnivore when it is eaten. Carnivores lose energy in the same ways as herbivores.

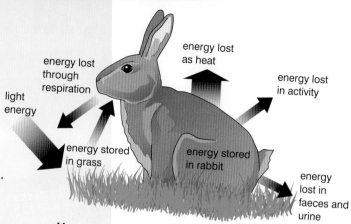

How energy is lost from a food chain

 What do you think happens to the energy in dead animals and plants?

Construct a pyramid

- The leaves from a small apple tree fall on to the earth below. In a 10 cm by 10 cm section of apple leaf litter beneath the tree there were the following animals:
  - 8 small centipedes,
  - 200 springtails,
  - 1 harvestman spider,
  - 4 parasitic mites on the spider.

  Harvestmen eat small centipedes.
  Springtails eat fallen apple leaves.
  Centipedes eat springtails.
  Use this information to construct a pyramid of numbers.

LINK UP TO BIOLOGY

Living things use energy from respiration to maintain tissues, for activities, and for growth and reproduction (see Unit 8B).

SUMMARY QUESTIONS

1 ☆ Match the food chains below to the appropriate pyramid of numbers.
   a) Grass → crane fly (larvae) → swallow.
   b) Rose bush → aphid → blue tit.

2 ☆ Draw a flow chart showing the flow of energy through a food chain.

3 ☆ Give two ways in which energy is lost from a food chain.

4 ☆ Explain why there are usually only four or five steps in a food chain.

Key words

energy
pyramid of numbers
quantitative data
respiration

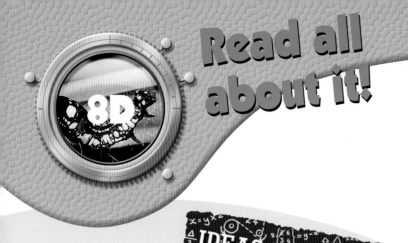

Read all about it!

8D

  ## SCIENTIFIC PEOPLE

IDEAS AND EVIDENCE

The case of the disappearing codfish

How many portions of cod are left in the North Sea? We have been fishing for cod for hundreds of years – but it looks as though a fish and chip supper might become a thing of the past.

There are fewer cod in the North Sea because we have been **over-fishing**. We have taken more cod from the ecosystem than are being added through reproduction. The fish caught now are smaller because they are younger. In the past, fish would have reproduced several times before they were caught. Now there is more chance of a fish being caught by modern well-equipped fishing boats before it has reproduced, so there are fewer replacements coming into the population.

We could reduce the number of cod we catch, or ban cod fishing. A whaling ban helped to slow down the decline in whale populations. However banning cod fishing would throw thousands of people out of work. Many coastal communities depend on fishing.

Currently there is a **quota** system, in which fishermen have a licence to catch a certain number of cod. This has not halted the decline. Cod swim in mixed shoals with haddock, whiting, herrings and sprats. It is hard not to catch them while fishing for other fish. Any that are caught accidentally above the quota have to be dumped.

What can you do to help the situation?

Cod

Marine ecologists and **fishery scientists** investigate the ecology of the North Sea and other important fishing areas. Estuaries, the **littoral zone,** which is shallow water near the shore, and deep water are just three of the habitats in a sea.

Marine life is difficult to observe and we have much to learn. We can monitor fish movement by marking fish, or using radio-tracking tags on young fish, and regularly sampling at particular sites to see how the community changes. We can investigate some basic fish biology in a laboratory with captive fish – rather like a giant aquarium.

One important job is to monitor the numbers of different fish species from year to year to find out what is happening to fish populations. If they stay steady we are happy, but if the numbers go down then scientists have to try and find out why. The decline could be due to adverse physical conditions during the breeding season, causing a temporary fall in the population. Or it could be due to an epidemic disease or a change in the population of something else in the complex North Sea food web.

If it is due to over-fishing by humans then advice must be given to try to conserve fish stocks.

A biologist tagging Atlantic sturgeon. They are an endangered species.

- Animals and plants compete for what they need.
- Plants are affected by their physical environment.
- Animals and plants are linked together in food webs.
- Anything that changes the numbers of one species in a food web will affect other species too.
- The number of predators depends on how many prey are available.
- A pyramid of numbers shows the numbers of plants and animals in a food chain.
- Energy is lost from a food chain because of respiration, undigested material and wastes.

We found dandelions in 20% of the squares, daisies in 60% and plantain in 30%.

The plants all had flattened leaves in a circle. They would survive here where plants get trampled a lot.

Can I have the binoculars? If the bird has speckles it's a thrush.

You are responsible for the equipment. After you have taken it back, wash your hands carefully.

DANGER! AVOID THESE COMMON ERRORS

When the bottom step of a pyramid of numbers is very narrow it is because the food chain involves a large plant such as a tree.

Plants lose energy through respiration at the same time as they gain energy through photosynthesis. Plants do not lose as much energy through respiration as animals because they do not move about.

Key words

fishery scientist
littoral zone
over-fishing
quota

REVIEW QUESTIONS

1　Copy and complete the following sentences.
　a　Food . . . in a community interlink forming a food web.
　b　Decomposers are organisms that use . . . as a food source.
　c　Plants compete for resources such as . . ., minerals and water.
　d　When predator numbers increase, prey numbers . . .
　e　Animals lose energy in food through . . ., by egesting indigestible materials and in excreting wastes.
　f　The numbers of individuals in a food chain are represented by a . . . of numbers.

2　Write definitions of each of the following.

producer　　consumer　　decomposer
predator　　prey　　sampling

3　What would you use each of the following for?

quadrat　　pooter　　pitfall trap
transect

4　You are surveying the distribution of bluebells in a wood. Give one technique you could use to avoid bias in your data.

5　Which of these pyramids of number pictured below best represents this food chain.

Grass → cow (dung) → dung beetle → badger

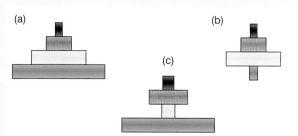

Thinking skills

6　Which is the odd one out in each of these groups? Explain your reasons.
　a　Food chain, food web, predator–prey relationship.
　b　Peacock butterfly, grasshopper, centipede.
　c　Fox, bear, lion, badger.
　d　Light, water, minerals, shade.
　e　Arthropod, mollusc, earthworm.

Ways with numbers

7　Draw a pyramid of numbers for the following food chain:

10 cabbages
95 large white butterfly caterpillars
1 robin

SAT-STYLE QUESTIONS

1　The food web below shows the feeding relationships between some of the inhabitants of a heath land.

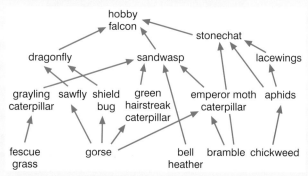

A heath land food web

　a　Identify one food chain from the food web. (1)
　b　Select one producer and one consumer from the food web. (2)
　c　Select one predator and its prey from the web. (2)

Fires are common on heath land. Plants such as heather, bracken and gorse can shoot again from underground parts that are protected from the fire's heat, or from seed. Ants too can survive in the deepest underground parts of their nests.

　d　Which animals in the food web are most likely to be affected by a fire? (1)

2 Whiteflies are small insects that feed on plants. They grow and breed very rapidly. They can become a very serious pest in greenhouses.

Some gardeners do not like to spray insecticides over their plants. Instead they use biological control of the whitefly. A small wasp, *Encarsia*, parasitises whiteflies and kills them. Gardeners can buy cultures of the wasp to put in their greenhouses.

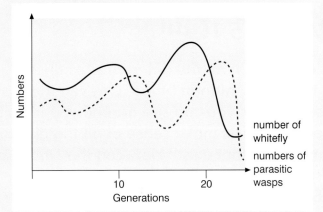

The graph shows what happens when whiteflies and wasps are kept together.

a Describe what happens to the whiteflies after 10 generations. (1)

b Why does the population of whiteflies rise between 12 and 18 generations? (1)

c Why do you think the population of wasps falls to such low numbers after 20 generations? (1)

3 Beech trees are grown in woodlands to provide wood for furniture. They are deciduous. In April new leaves grow in an arrangement that is very efficient for using sunlight.

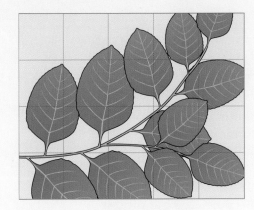

a What does deciduous mean? (1)

b Explain why this leaf arrangement is very efficient for using sunlight. (2)

In spring the ground in a beech wood is covered with bluebells. Bluebells grow from bulbs that put out leaves in March and flower in April. Their leaves die off by May. In summer there are no plants growing under the beech trees.

c Explain why bluebells can grow and flower in the beech woods in the spring but no other plants can grow and flower in the summer. (1)

d Old beech trees sometimes fall in a storm. The following summer the clear area round a fallen beech tree is full of plants. Why is this? (1)

4 Benson and Pete spent one afternoon carrying out an ecological survey on a field next to their school that is used for hay. A sample of their results can be seen in the table.

Quadrat	ox-eye daisy		corn cockle		meadow buttercup		cocks-foot grass		meadow grass	
	squares	% cover	squares	% cover	squares	% cover	squares	% cover	squares	% cover
1	3	12	5	20	0	–	0	–	16	64
2	0	–	3	12	0	–	0	–	12	48
3	5	20	1	4	3	12	14	56	3	12
4	2	8	0	–	0	–	0	–	2	8
5	4	16	1	4	3	12	0	–	20	80
6	0	0	3	12	2	8	0	–	16	64
7	12	48	0	–			8	32		

a How do you think they found out the percentage cover of corn cockle? (1)

b Why would it be better for Benson and Pete to measure environmental factors on more than one occasion? (1)

c Benson and Pete could see the white flowers of ox-eye daisies all over the field. They thought that ox-eye daisies must be evenly distributed. Do their results support this first impression? (1)

d For many years the farmer has been letting the grass grow long then cutting it for hay. What differences might Benson and Pete see in the plants growing in the field if the farmer decided to graze cows instead? (1)

Key words

Unscramble these:
etpoor
andy roif berpmum
ming laps
pooedcrems
scantter

8E

Elements and atoms

COMING SOON

8E1 Different substances

8E2 Atoms

8E3 Looking at elements

8E4 Making molecules

8E5 Reacting elements

Do I look like a model?

Yes... A very hot particle.

What's it all about?

Just think of all the different substances that make up a human being. Or even the many substances you can see around you now. How can scientists make sense of all the different materials that exist? How can they make new substances that have never been made before?

To find the answers to these questions we can look at the basic particles that make up substances. You have met particles before in unit 7G and other units, but here we will develop our particle model. We will then be able to explain more about materials and the way they behave.

How can scientists explain all the different substances that go together to make a new person?

What do you remember?

You already know about:
- the differences between solids, liquids and gases.
- changes of state.
- how we can use models to explain our observations.

1. Which state(s) of matter can we compress easily?

   solid   liquid
   gas   solid and liquid

2. What do we call the process in which a gas turns into a liquid?

   melting   evaporation
   condensation   boiling

3. In the particle model, why does a solid expand when we heat it?

   the particles get bigger
   air inside the particles expands
   the particles need heat to grow
   the particles vibrate more vigorously

Ideas about elements and atoms

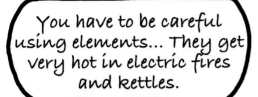

"You have to be careful using elements... They get very hot in electric fires and kettles."

"Let's see if we can see the atoms in this plant cell."

"There must be millions of different types of atoms if there are millions of different substances on Earth."

"Can we say that gases and liquids are materials... surely all materials are solids?"

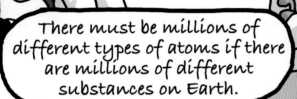

QUESTIONS

Look at the cartoons above and discuss these questions with your partner.

a) The word element has more than one meaning. Find out some definitions of 'element'.

b) Do you think Mike will be able to see an atom through a microscope? What small things have you seen using a microscope?

c) How many different types of atoms do you think there might be (roughly)? Why did you choose that number?

d) Why is Benson wrong to think that liquids and gases are not materials? Why is he confused?

Different substances

LEARN ABOUT

- the huge variety of materials
- the relatively small number of elements from which all other materials are made

Loads of substances

It's difficult for us to imagine all the different **substances** there are on Earth. There are many millions known to scientists, and new ones are being made all the time. So nobody knows the exact number. Scientists try to make sense of all these substances by classifying them in different ways.

You looked at solids, liquids and gases in unit 7G – this is one way of **classifying** substances. This grouping is based on the arrangement of particles in a substance at 20°C.

Look at the substances below:

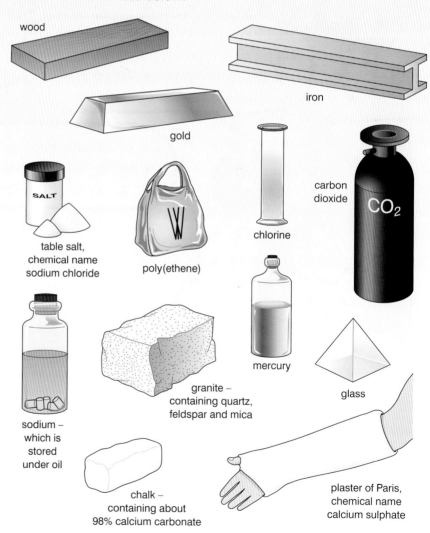

wood

iron

gold

table salt, chemical name sodium chloride

poly(ethene)

chlorine

carbon dioxide CO₂

mercury

sodium – which is stored under oil

granite – containing quartz, feldspar and mica

glass

chalk – containing about 98% calcium carbonate

plaster of Paris, chemical name calcium sulphate

People sometimes refer to substances as materials. However, the everyday use of the word 'material', meaning a piece of cloth, can be confusing. Stick with 'substance'!

Classifying substances

- Sort the substances in the picture into different groups according to your own criteria. (Don't tell anyone else how you have done it.)

- Ask a partner to guess how you have classified the substances.
  a) Did the people in your group use different criteria? Discuss which criteria would be most useful to a scientist trying to make sense of the great variety of substances on Earth.
  b) How can you decide by experiment which substances are metals?
  c) Make a list of the metals shown.

AMAZING SCIENCE!

Over 5000 new substances are registered by scientists every day.

Nature's building blocks

Look at the substances on the previous page. There are some substances that we call **chemical elements** (or just **elements**). Substances like chlorine, iron, sodium, gold and mercury. Altogether, there are only 92 elements that occur naturally on Earth. About another 20 elements have been made artificially by scientists.

All the other substances that exist (we can think of them as 'non-elements' for now) are made up from just these one hundred or so elements. The chemical elements are like nature's building blocks.

The chemical elements are the building blocks of all substances.

We can use models to help us to understand this.

I think you could register this as a new substance, Mike!

Model 1

Imagine the chemical elements as the letters of the alphabet. For example,

C + A + T

These letters represent three substances that are elements.
In this model, all the words in a dictionary represent the different substances ('non-elements') that exist. For example,

CAT

This word represents a substance that is one of the millions of 'non-elements'.

Model 2

Imagine that the chemical elements are the building bricks in a Lego set. The other substances ('non-elements') are all the different structures you can make by joining bricks together.

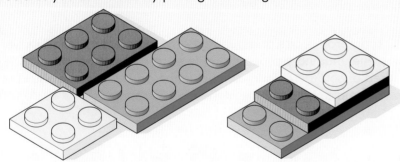

These bricks represent three substances that are elements

This structure represents a substance that is one of the millions of 'non-elements'

AMAZING SCIENCE!

The human body is made up of just 26 different elements.

SUMMARY QUESTIONS

1 ☆ Copy this sentence. Complete it by filling in the gaps.

There are only about 100 different . . . but these can combine in many different ways to make the . . . of different . . . that exist.

2 ☆☆☆ Think up another model that you could use to explain the different numbers of substances that are elements and those that are 'non-elements'.

Key words

chemical element
classifying
substance

Atoms

LEARN ABOUT
- the difference between elements and other substances
- using models to show things we can't see

What are atoms?

You've probably heard of 'atoms' before. The word 'atom' comes from a Greek word describing something that can't be divided up. We know that atoms are something to do with the **particles** that make up solids, liquids and gases. But what exactly are they?

Imagine that you had a magic knife and started chopping up a piece of a chemical element, such as iron. You keep cutting and cutting until the bits of iron are really tiny – smaller than the smallest thing we can see through a normal microscope.

Eventually the smallest particle you would get to, that could still be called iron, would be an **atom**. It would be an individual atom of iron.

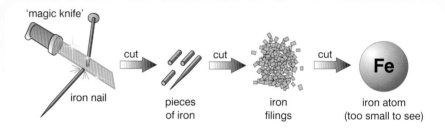

'magic knife'

iron nail → cut → pieces of iron → cut → iron filings → cut → **Fe** iron atom (too small to see)

As you know, iron is one of a hundred or so different elements. If we do the same imaginary chopping up to each element, we will arrive at a hundred or so different atoms. Each atom differs from the others by its size and mass, but we think of them all as spheres.

an atom of hydrogen an atom of oxygen an atom of sulphur

Atom	Symbol	Atom	Symbol
hydrogen	H	zinc	Zn
carbon	C	iron	Fe
nitrogen	N	sodium	Na
sulphur	S	potassium	K
oxygen	O	copper	Cu
chlorine	Cl	helium	He

Chemical symbols

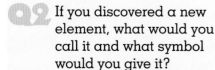

Q1 Find the names of all the elements whose symbols start with the letter 'H'.

Q2 If you discovered a new element, what would you call it and what symbol would you give it?

Notice the letter on each atom. This is called the chemical **symbol** of the atom (or of the element). To a chemist, the symbol H represents one atom of the element hydrogen. Look at the symbols of some common elements in the table.

You can see that the symbol for some atoms is a single capital letter. Others have two letters – a capital followed by a lower case letter. Notice that the symbol for some atoms comes from their Latin name. For example, iron's symbol is Fe, which comes from its Latin name, ferrum.

● Making models

We also have *model kits* to show how atoms join (or bond) to each other. One of these kits has coloured plastic balls with holes in them. Each ball has a set number of holes. In the kit you also get plastic sticks that fit into the holes and join one ball to another.

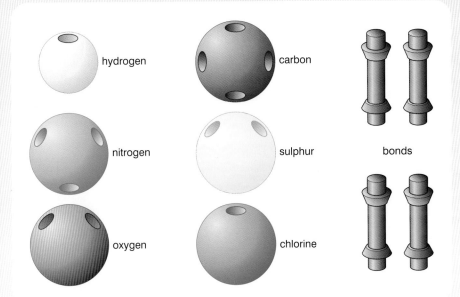

hydrogen

carbon

nitrogen

sulphur

bonds

oxygen

chlorine

Make your own model

● Use a kit to design your own model.
There are a couple of rules you have to follow.
1 No plastic ball should have any holes without sticks in them.
2 All sticks must have plastic balls at either end of them.

● Compare your model with others in your group. Were any two models the same?
You can see how a few 'building blocks' can make lots and lots of different substances. Were the models that you made elements or not? (See below.)

Look at these models on the right:

These show how the atoms are joined together in three of the chemical elements. Notice how each model contains only one type of plastic ball.

An element is a substance made of only one type of atom.

Look at the models on the right:

When you take these apart, you are left with two or more different types of atom, unlike the elements. So we can also define an element like this:

An element is a substance that can't be broken down into simpler substances.

elements

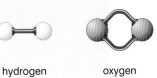

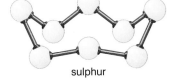

hydrogen   oxygen

sulphur

'non-elements'

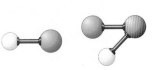

SUMMARY QUESTIONS

1 ☆ Copy these sentences. Complete them by filling in the gaps.

An ... is a substance made up of only one type of ...

They cannot be ... down into any ... substances.

2 ☆☆ Why don't we use C as the symbol for chlorine? What is the rule about capital and lower case letters in chemical symbols?

Find five more atoms (elements) whose symbols start with the letter 'C'.

Key words

atom
element
particle
symbol

Looking at elements

LEARN ABOUT
- how elements vary in their appearance and state
- researching some of the elements

The chemical elements

Trying to make sense of the many millions of different substances on Earth sounds a very difficult job. Fortunately, not many of these substances are elements. We only have around 100 different elements to find out about. But even this number is daunting. However, many of the elements have things in common, so studying them is made a lot easier!

Researching elements

Your teacher will give each group about five elements to find out about.

You will need to use books, videos, CD ROMs or the Internet.

- Find out for each of your elements:
  a) its symbol
  b) its state at 20°C
  c) whether it is described as a **metal**, a **non-metal** or a **metalloid** (semi-metal)
  d) whether it is magnetic or not
  e) its appearance
  f) any other interesting information about it.

You will be looking for patterns in the information the whole class gathers.

To help us find patterns, record the information on the sides of a cube made from card.

- Record each piece of information on a different side of the cube for each element.

- Write the word metal in blue, non-metal in red and metalloid in green.

- Use a large capital S for solids, an L for liquids and a G for gases.

This information will be used in the next activity.

There must be some way to make sense of all these different substances.

Gruesome science

Atoms of new elements were discovered in the aftermath of the first nuclear bomb. It was dropped on Hiroshima, Japan in 1945.

AMAZING SCIENCE!

The element helium was discovered on the Sun before it was found on Earth.

Sorting out the elements

In 1869, a Russian chemist called Dmitri Mendeleev arranged the elements in order of atomic mass. He started with the lightest atoms, getting heavier. He formed new rows so that similar elements lined up in vertical columns. The columns are called **groups**. He called the arrangement the **Periodic Table**. Periodic means 'repeated at regular intervals'.

Here is a modern version of his table:

The Periodic Table of elements

H Hydrogen																	He Helium
Li Lithium	Be Beryllium											B Boron	C Carbon	N Nitrogen	O Oxygen	F Fluorine	Ne Neon
Na Sodium	Mg Magnesium											Al Aluminium	Si Silicon	P Phosphorus	S Sulphur	Cl Chlorine	Ar Argon
K Potassium	Ca Calcium	Sc Scandium	Ti Titanium	V Vanadium	Cr Chromium	Mn Manganese	Fe Iron	Co Cobalt	Ni Nickel	Cu Copper	Zn Zinc	Ga Gallium	Ge Germanium	As Arsenic	Se Selenium	Br Bromine	Kr Krypton
Rb Rubidium	Sr Strontium	Y Yttrium	Zr Zirconium	Nb Niobium	Mo Molybdenum	Tc Technetium	Ru Ruthenium	Rh Rhodium	Pd Palladium	Ag Silver	Cd Cadmium	In Indium	Sn Tin	Sb Antimony	Te Tellurium	I Iodine	Xe Xenon
Cs Caesium	Ba Barium	La Lanthanum	Hf Hafnium	Ta Tantalum	W Tungsten	Re Rhenium	Os Osmium	Ir Iridium	Pt Platinum	Au Gold	Hg Mercury	Tl Thallium	Pb Lead	Bi Bismuth	Po Polonium	At Astatine	Rn Radon
Fr Francium	Ra Radium	Ac Actinium															

Ce Cerium	Pr Praseodymium	Nd Neodymium	Pm Promethium	Sm Samarium	Eu Europium	Gd Gadolinium	Tb Terbium	Dy Dysprosium	Ho Holmium	Er Erbium	Tm Thulium	Yb Ytterbium	Lu Lutetium
Th Thorium	Pa Protactinium	U Uranium	Np Neptunium	Pu Plutonium	Am Americium	Cm Curium	Bk Berkelium	Cf Californium	Es Einsteinium	Fm Fermium	Md Mendelevium	No Nobelium	Lr Lawrencium

Q1 Why is the table called the Periodic Table?

Q2 Why are the chemical symbols for elements useful for scientists from different countries?

 ICT CHALLENGE

A database for the elements
Set up a database to store your information about the elements in the Periodic Table. Include the number which shows their position in the Periodic Table (called the **atomic number**). Also record melting points and boiling points.

Looking for patterns in the elements

Clear a space on the floor and place your cubes in the positions they would be in the Periodic Table.

- Turn all the cubes to show metal, non-metal or metalloid.
  a) What do you notice? Are there more metals or non-metals?

  Describe which part of the Periodic Table contains metals and which contains non-metals. Where are the metalloids (or semi-metals) found?

- Now turn the cubes to show the state of the elements at 20°C (solid, liquid or gas).
  b) What can you say about the numbers of solids, liquids and gases?

- Now show which elements are magnetic and which are non-magnetic.
  c) What do you notice?
  d) Note any generalisations you can make about the chemical elements and the Periodic Table.

- Get your own copy of the Periodic Table to stick in your book. Use colour coding and a key to show your findings.

SUMMARY QUESTIONS

1 ☆ Copy these sentences. Complete them by filling in the gaps.
   The elements can be sorted out into . . ., non-metals and a few . . .
   The Periodic . . . shows elements with . . . properties in the same column.
   The columns are called . . .

2 ☆☆ **a)** How many of the chemical elements are liquids at 20°C? Name them.
   b) Work out roughly the percentage of elements that are metals.

3 ☆☆ Name one metalloid. What is special about its properties?

Key words

atomic number
groups
metal
metalloid
non-metal
Periodic Table

LEARN ABOUT

- new substances made when atoms combine
- molecules and compounds
- chemical formulae

● Joining atoms up

You have already seen how we use models to represent atoms.

You have also tried linking the model atoms together. We call the links between atoms 'bonds'. When atoms join together, we say that the atoms **bond** to each other.

Q1 Explain how we can have millions of different substances if only 92 different types of atom exist naturally on Earth.

When atoms bond together, the new particles they make are called **molecules**. Look at the two molecules below:

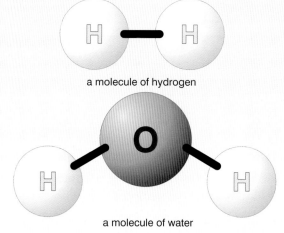

a molecule of hydrogen

a molecule of water

Two or more atoms bonded together are called molecules.

Notice that the atoms in a molecule of hydrogen are both the same. We can say that hydrogen is made up of molecules of an element.

On the other hand, a water molecule contains two types of atom – hydrogen and oxygen. When a substance is made up of two or more different types of atom, we call it a **compound**. So compounds are the substances we have referred to before as 'non-elements'.

A compound is made up of two or more different types of atom.

It's alright for you... my molecule's not going to be very exciting, is it?

Making molecular models

- Using a kit, make your own models of:
  – a molecule of an element, and
  – a molecule of a compound.
- Draw diagrams to represent each molecule.

● Chemical formula

Scientists use their own short-hand way of showing a molecule. Rather than drawing a molecule, they use its **chemical formula**. It shows us how many of each type of atom there are in a molecule. The formula does this by using the **symbols** of atoms, and subscript numbers.

Here's the formula of a larger molecule – insulin.
Its formula is: $C_{254}H_{377}N_{65}O_{75}S_6$!

Q2 You've probably heard people talk about 'H-two-O' and know that it is water. We write this formula as H_2O.

Explain why the formula of water is H_2O.

You can see that if a molecule contains just one atom of a certain element, we don't bother writing a number 1 in its formula.

Look at the examples below:

Name of molecule	Diagram of molecule	Chemical formula
hydrogen sulphide		H_2S
chlorine		Cl_2
methane		CH_4

Q3 Look at the molecule of hydrogen on page 84. Now write the chemical formula of hydrogen gas.

SUMMARY QUESTIONS

1 ☆ Copy these sentences. Complete them by filling in the gaps.
When two or more . . . bond together, we get a . . .
If a substance is made up of two or more different types of . . . it is called a . . .
We can represent molecules by their chemical . . . For example, the formula of water is . . .

2 ☆☆ The chemical formula of carbon dioxide is CO_2.
Explain why carbon dioxide is a compound, and not an element.

Key words

bond
chemical formula
compound
molecule
symbol

Reacting elements

LEARN ABOUT
- atoms combining to form compounds
- new substances made in reactions
- using word equations and models to show reactions

From elements to compounds

You have seen elements reacting together to make compounds. In Year 7 you saw different elements react with oxygen. The compounds made are called **oxides**.

We represented the reaction by word equations. For example,

magnesium + oxygen → magnesium oxide

Remember that the substances we start with before the reaction are called **reactants**.

The substances formed in reactions are called **products**.

Other non-metals, such as sulphur, chlorine and bromine, also react with other elements to form compounds.

Sulphur makes compounds called **sulphides,** for example, magnesium sulphide.

Chlorine makes **chlorides**, and bromine makes **bromides**.

Q1 What do you think we call the compounds made from iodine?

Q2 Write a word equation that shows the reaction between magnesium and sulphur.

Combining two elements

- Watch your teacher demonstrate the following reactions:
  hydrogen + oxygen
  magnesium + oxygen
  sodium + chlorine
  copper + sulphur
  zinc + sulphur

- Record your results in a table that describes the reactants and the products, and also what happens as the elements react.
  a) Write a word equation for each reaction.
  b) How can you tell that chemical reactions took place? What signs of reaction did you see?

In a chemical reaction, the atoms in the reactants re-arrange to form the products. The new substances formed as products are often nothing like the reactants you started with. We can use models to show a reaction taking place.

Look at the model of hydrogen reacting with oxygen below:

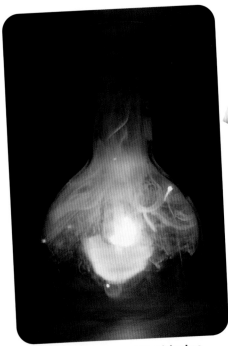

Sodium reacting with chlorine

Modelling reactions

- Use a molecular model kit to show what happens in the reaction between hydrogen and oxygen.

- Now use the kit to model the reaction between a carbon atom and an oxygen molecule.
  Draw a diagram to show what happens to the atoms and bonds.
  Now explain your diagram in your own words.

My dance now.

Now that might cause a reaction if she swaps partners!

Breaking down compounds

We have seen that all the atoms in an element are the same type. So we can't break elements down into simpler substances in a chemical reaction.

However, compounds contain atoms of different types. So we should be able to break down compounds into simpler substances.

We can break down some compounds by heating them up. We say that they **decompose**. Others are broken down by passing electricity through the compound once it is melted or dissolved in water.

Splitting up

- Watch your teacher break down water back into its elements.
  a) Write a word equation to describe this chemical change.

Your teacher will give you a powder to find out if it is an element or a compound.

- Plan a safe test to solve the problem.
  Let your teacher check your plan before you start any practical work.

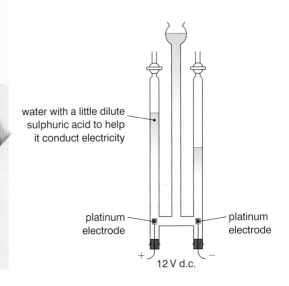

water with a little dilute sulphuric acid to help it conduct electricity

platinum electrode

platinum electrode

+ 12 V d.c. −

SUMMARY QUESTIONS

1 ☆ Copy these sentences. Complete them by filling in the gaps.

Some elements can react together to form c ... For example, oxygen reacts to form ... and chlorine forms ...

We can describe these chemical reactions by ... equations. For example, iron + ... → ... bromide.

2 ☆☆☆ Draw a diagram to show how hydrogen (H_2) reacts with chlorine (Cl_2) and forms hydrogen chloride (HCl).

Key words

bromides
chlorides
decompose
oxides
products
reactants
sulphides

Read all about it!

CHEMICAL GIANTS

John Dalton

By the start of the 1800s science had become more firmly based on evidence from experiments. A Cumbrian scientist called John Dalton, who taught in Manchester, loved experimenting. He liked to work alone and never trusted the results of other scientists. His careful experiments suggested to him that all matter is made up of tiny particles. He thought that these particles could not be broken down into anything smaller.

He called the particles atoms, taken from an ancient Greek word.

John drew up a list of elements – substances that were made of only one type of atom and couldn't be broken down into simpler substances. He visualised atoms as hard, indestructible spheres with each element having atoms of a different mass.

Here is a list of Dalton's elements:

ELEMENTS		
⊙ Hydrogen 7	⊕ Strontian	46
① Azote 5	⊖ Barytes	68
● Carbon 54	① Iron	50
○ Oxygen 7	② Zinc	56
☿ Phosphorus 9	© Copper	56
⊕ Sulphur 13	ⓛ Lead	90
◐ Magnesia 20	⑤ Silver	190
⊖ Lime 24	ⓓ Gold	190
⓪ Soda 28	℗ Platina	190
⓪ Potash 42	✸ Mercury	167

An element was defined as something that couldn't be broken down into any simpler substances. However, this led to some compounds getting on John's list of elements. These compounds were very difficult (impossible at the time) to split up so he thought they must be elements. It's little wonder that scientists at the time had trouble making any sense of the chemical elements. Most had not yet been discovered and others were actually compounds. It was a bit like trying to do a jigsaw puzzle without the picture, with half the pieces missing and with some pieces thrown in from a different jigsaw – not an easy task!

John Dalton was co-founder of the British Association for the Advancement of Science, and over 40 000 people attended his funeral in Manchester in 1844

Dmitri Mendeleev

Dmitri Mendeleev (1834–1907). He was the youngest of 17 children.

Chemistry was changed forever when a Russian chemist discovered how to sort out the chemical elements in his Periodic Table. It was at the end of the 1860s that the real breakthrough was made by Dmitri Mendeleev.

Dmitri was writing a textbook and wanted to organise the elements properly. So he wrote each element onto its own card to help him sort them out. Dmitri enjoyed playing cards, especially patience, and one evening he dosed off while working. He had a dream in which the element cards lined up in rows, just like a game of patience.

When he woke, he realised that he should put the elements in order of atomic mass, but then turn the line so that similar elements lined up under each other. His first table (in 1869) had 17 columns, but he revised it a couple of years later to one with 8 columns. Dmitri called his table the Periodic Table because of the regular repeating pattern of elements.

Chemists still took some persuading that Dmitri had cracked the code that could make sense of chemistry. His Periodic Table had quite a few gaps left in it. He explained these by saying that these spaces would be filled by new elements as they were discovered. But this failed to convince some of his fellow scientists.

However, we can judge a good theory by its power to make predictions that are later proved to be correct. Sure enough, Dmitri had the perfect model to predict the properties of elements that were not yet discovered. When his predictions closely matched the properties of newly discovered elements, it became very difficult to question his Periodic Table.

Now I know that the word 'element' can have different meanings. If the element in this kettle is made of iron then it is a chemical element too!

No, we can't see atoms through our microscopes in school... atoms are much too small for that! Even a tiny plant cell contains millions and millions of atoms.

- **Elements** are substances that cannot be broken down into any simpler substances. Elements are made up of only one type of atom.
- The smallest part of an element, which we can still recognise as the element, is an **atom**.
- When atoms bond together they form **molecules**.
- If the atoms in a molecule are not all the same type, then we have a **compound**.
- There are about 100 elements but millions of compounds. Most of the elements are metals, with less than a quarter being non-metals.
- Each atom has a **symbol** (for example, carbon's is C, chlorine's is Cl).
- We can show the number and type of each atom in a molecule by its chemical formula. For example, the formula of carbon dioxide is CO_2.
- The elements have been sorted out into a useful structure called the **Periodic Table**. This shows us patterns in the properties of elements.

No, the relatively small number of different atoms on Earth can bond to each other in loads of combinations to make millions of different molecules.

We use the word material, or substance, for anything made up from atoms or molecules.

DANGER! AVOID THESE COMMON ERRORS

People often get confused between the words **A**tom, **M**olecule, **E**lement and **C**ompound. Try building up the ideas in the order **AMEC**.

- **A**toms are the smallest particles.
- They join together to make **M**olecules.
- If the atoms in a molecule are all the same, you have an **E**lement.
- If there are different types of atom in a molecule, you have a **C**ompound.

When using a formula remember there is really a '1' after a symbol if no number is written. So in a CO_2 molecule there is 1 carbon atom and 2 oxygen atoms. We can tell when a new atom starts in a formula by its capital letter – so in Cl_2 there are only 2 atoms of chlorine. The symbol Co stands for 1 atom of cobalt, but CO represents a molecule of carbon monoxide (made of 1 carbon atom and 1 oxygen atom bonded together).

atoms

molecules of elements

molecule of a compound

Key words

atom
compound
element
formula
molecule
Periodic Table
symbol

REVIEW QUESTIONS
Understanding and applying concepts

1 **a** Draw diagrams to represent the following molecules:
  i) HBr
  ii) BF_3
  iii) PCl_5
  iv) CH_3Br
  v) S_8
  b Which of the molecules in part **a**
  i) is *not* a compound? Explain your answer.
  ii) is a compound containing atoms of three different elements?
  iii) could be broken down into two elements?
  iv) contain hydrogen atoms?
  c Draw a table showing the number of atoms in each molecule listed in part **a**.

2 The chemical symbol of lead is Pb, taken from its Latin name, *plumbum*.
  a Find five other elements whose atoms have symbols derived from their Latin names. Give their names and symbols.
  b Find out the Latin names of the elements listed in part **a**.
  c Name the atom whose symbol is:
  i) O
  ii) N
  iii) He
  iv) Zn
  v) Mg
  vi) Br

3 Write a word equation to describe the reaction between:
  a zinc and oxygen
  b potassium and chlorine
  c copper and sulphur
  d iron and bromine
  e aluminium and iodine.

4 Look at the molecule below:

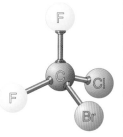

What is the chemical formula of the compound?

5 Draw a concept map using the words:

  atom   molecule   element
  compound   Periodic Table

Ways with words

6 Imagine you are a hydrogen atom.
  Using page 86, describe how you existed within a molecule of hydrogen gas, and the day you reacted with oxygen to form water.

Making more of maths

7 Sort these substances in a Venn diagram like the one shown below:

  iron   gold   carbon   chlorine
  water   oxygen   sulphur   sodium
  copper sulphide   silicon   magnesium
  zinc   iodine   germanium

substances

metallic elements   non-metallic elements

8 **a** Draw a bar chart to display this data:

Group 1 element	Density (g/cm³)
lithium	0.53
sodium	0.97
potassium	0.86
rubidium	1.53
caesium	1.88

b What is the pattern you see as you go down the Group 1 elements?

Thinking skills

9 Magnesium and oxygen always react together in the same proportions.

A student did some research and found that 6 g of magnesium react with 4 g of oxygen.

a How much magnesium will react completely with:
  i) 8 g of oxygen?
  ii) 80 g of oxygen?
  iii) 1 g of oxygen?

b How much oxygen will react completely with:
  i) 60 g of magnesium?
  ii) 3 g of magnesium?
  iii) 24 g of magnesium?

Extension question

10 Carry out some research into the discovery of the Periodic Table.
   Then draw a time-line showing the scientists involved and their contributions.

SAT-STYLE QUESTIONS

1 The chemical formula of ammonium nitrate is NH_4NO_3.
  a Is ammonium nitrate an element or a compound? Explain your answer. (1)
  b What is the total number of atoms represented by the formula NH_4NO_3? (1)
  c Ammonium nitrate decomposes on heating to form nitrogen(I) oxide and water.
    Write a word equation to show this reaction. (1)

2 Read this information:

Sodium, aluminium and zinc are elements that conduct electricity.

Iodine and sulphur are elements which do not conduct electricity.

If zinc and sulphur are heated together, they react vigorously to form a new substance called zinc sulphide.

  a Using the information given above:
    i) Name two metals. (2)
    ii) Name two non-metals. (2)
    iii) Give the name of a compound. (1)
  b i) Write a word equation for the reaction of zinc with sulphur. (1)
    ii) Why would you carry out the reaction between zinc and sulphur in a fume-cupboard? (2)
    iii) Write the name of the compound formed when magnesium reacts with sulphur. (1)

3 Look at this outline of the areas in the Periodic Table:

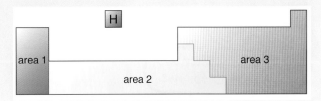

  a What does the symbol H stand for? (1)
  b In which areas of the Periodic Table would you find:
    i) metallic elements? (2)
    ii) non-metals, such as nitrogen and phosphorus? (1)
    iii) very reactive metals, such as sodium and potassium? (1)
    iv) less reactive metals, such as iron and zinc? (1)
  c Why is sodium chloride not found in the Periodic Table? (1)

8F

Compounds and mixtures

COMING SOON

8F1 Making compounds and mixtures

8F2 Reacting compounds

8F3 More about mixtures

8F4 Pure or impure?

There's nothing like a good mixture when you're thirsty.

I prefer a compound... Straight H₂O for me.

Milkshake is a tasty mixture!

What's it all about?

In this unit you will build on the work done in unit 8E. You already know about compounds, but now we will concentrate on differences between compounds and mixtures.

Most of our chemical industry is all about making useful compounds. However, the raw materials are often mixtures, such as air or rocks. We also manufacture many useful mixtures, such as paints and cosmetics.

What do you remember?

You already know about:

- the 100 or so elements each containing only their own atoms.
- compounds being formed when atoms of different elements bond together.
- some chemical reactions.
- making and separating mixtures.

1 Which of the following is an element?

sodium   water
copper sulphate   common salt

2 How would you separate the different dyes from a coloured ink?

filtration   evaporation
chromatography   distillation

3 Which types of atom are contained in a molecule of water?

hydrogen and chlorine
oxygen and helium
helium and hydrogen
hydrogen and oxygen

4 All chemical reactions . . . ?

. . . cause explosions.
. . . form new substances.
. . . are easily reversible.
. . . give out light and sound energy.

Ideas about compounds and mixtures

"You can't have molecules of an element, can you? I thought compounds were made when atoms join together."

Br_2

"This is clearly the formula of a compound... It has one atom of B and two atoms of R in its molecules... So it has 2 types of atom."

"Why has this been marked wrong? I put 'When magnesium burns in air, we get a mixture of magnesium and oxygen.' What's wrong with that?"

"Can you ever have _pure_ water? Even if there is nothing dissolved in it, there's still a mixture of hydrogen and oxygen in the H_2O, isn't there?"

Look at the cartoons above and discuss these questions with your partner.

a) What is wrong with Pip's ideas about compounds?

b) Do you agree that Br_2 is the formula of a compound? Explain your reasoning to Pete.

c) Add a teacher comment to explain the cross on Molly's book.

d) What do you think of Mike's ideas about water? Do you think water from a tap is pure water? Why?

QUESTIONS

Making compounds and mixtures

8F1

LEARN ABOUT

- combining elements to make compounds
- the new properties of the compound made
- differences between a mixture and a compound

● Elements combining

In unit 8E we looked at elements reacting together to form compounds.

Q1 Predict what will be formed when iron reacts with sulphur.

Reacting iron and sulphur

Now you can look at a mixture of elements before they react together.
Then in the next activity you will compare the mixture with the compound formed in the reaction.

- Collect some iron filings on a piece of paper.

- Then collect a spatula of sulphur on another piece of paper.

- Now thoroughly mix the iron and sulphur together.

iron   sulphur

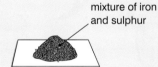

mixture of iron and sulphur

a) Describe each element.

b) Do you think a compound has formed? How can you tell? Think of two ways to separate the iron and sulphur.

- Next heat the **mixture** of elements in an ignition tube with a loose plug of mineral wool in its mouth. (The mineral wool is to reduce the chance of sulphur vapour igniting and forming toxic sulphur dioxide gas. Take care not to inhale any vapours.)

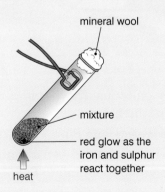

mineral wool

mixture

red glow as the iron and sulphur react together

heat

Focus your heating on the bottom of the tube. When you see the first signs of a reaction, stop heating and see if the reaction continues.

c) How can you tell when the reaction starts?

d) Describe the product formed.

e) Write a word equation for the reaction between iron and sulphur.

SAFETY: Do this in a fume-cupboard or well-ventilated lab.

Symbol equation

The formula of iron sulphide is FeS. So we can write an equation, using symbols and the formula, showing how we made iron sulphide.

$$Fe + S \rightarrow FeS$$

We call this a **symbol equation**. Notice that we have the same number of each type of atom on either side of the equation. We can then say that this is a 'balanced symbol equation'.

Q2 Write a symbol equation for the reaction between zinc and sulphur.

Comparing a mixture and a compound **SAFETY**

- Look at a sample of iron sulphide and compare it with a mixture of iron and sulphur.
  a) What differences do you notice?
- Use a magnet wrapped in plastic film to test the compound and the mixture.
- Add iron sulphide to some water in a beaker and stir. Compare this by doing the same thing with the mixture of iron and sulphur.
  b) What happens in each test?
- Watch your teacher add some dilute hydrochloric acid to the compound and to the mixture in a fume-cupboard.
  c) What differences do you notice between the reactions?

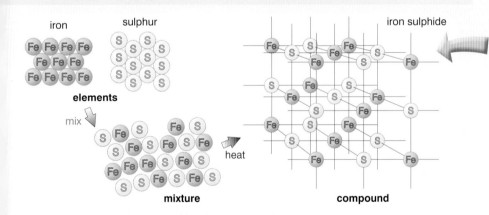

iron   sulphur   iron sulphide
elements
mix
mixture   heat   compound

The ratio of iron and sulphur atoms in any sample of the compound iron sulphide will always be the same. The ratio in this case is 1 : 1 and that's why its formula is FeS. However, the proportions in a mixture can vary. We could mix one part iron with two parts sulphur, or three parts iron with one part sulphur, and so on.

Any **compound** always has **fixed proportions** of its elements (as shown by its chemical formula).

SUMMARY QUESTIONS

1 ☆ Copy the sentences. Complete them by filling in the gaps.
The properties of a compound differ from those of the . . . it is made from. A compound always has . . . proportions of each element (shown by its chemical . . .). However, in a . . . the proportions can . . .

2 ☆☆☆ Do some research to find out the differences between the following compounds and the elements that make them up:
a) potassium iodide **b)** silicon dioxide **c)** silver bromide.

Key words
balanced
compound
fixed proportions
mixture
symbol equation

Reacting compounds

LEARN ABOUT
- making observations and drawing conclusions
- compounds undergoing chemical changes
- differences between mixtures and compounds

● Physical and chemical changes

So far you have looked at elements reacting to make compounds. You have seen that in chemical reactions we get new substances formed. Reactions are also accompanied by temperature changes.

Q1 How can you tell that a reaction takes place when magnesium burns in air?

Chemical changes	Physical changes
new substances are formed	no new substances are formed
often cannot be reversed	usually easy to reverse

We also refer to reactions as 'chemical changes'. These are the opposite of 'physical changes'. Here is a table showing the differences between physical and chemical changes.

Examples of chemical changes that you have come across are neutralisation and combustion (burning). On the other hand, changes of state are not chemical changes. No new substances are formed and the changes are easily reversed. So melting and freezing are examples of physical changes.

Q2 Give two more examples of physical changes.

Sorry! I think my beaker has just undergone a physical change.

Q3 Is dissolving salt a physical or chemical change? Explain your answer.

Can compounds react too?

In the next experiment you will use compounds as reactants in chemical changes.

- Mix the following pairs of substances together in separate test tubes. Use a different pipette for each solution and record your observations.
  1. Sodium carbonate solution and iron(II) chloride solution.
  2. Dilute hydrochloric acid and solid magnesium carbonate.
  3. Ammonia solution and copper sulphate solution.
  4. Lead nitrate solution and sodium iodide solution.
     (Avoid contact with skin and be sure to wash your hands.)
- Write a short paragraph to show your evidence that compounds can be the reactants in reactions.
- Read the evidence produced by another group. Do their ideas agree with yours?

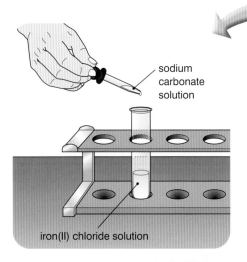

sodium carbonate solution

iron(II) chloride solution

● Compounds and mixtures

You have seen that there are differences between **mixtures** and **compounds**.

Here is a table to summarise these differences:

Compounds	Mixtures
Have a fixed **composition** (will always have the same **proportion** of elements in any particular compound)	Have no fixed **composition** (the **proportions** vary depending on the amount of each substance mixed together)
Need chemical reactions to separate the elements in them	The substances can be separated again quite easily (by physical means using the differences in properties of each substance in the mixture)
Are single substances	Contain two or more substances
Have properties different to those of the elements combined in the compound	Have properties similar to those of the substances in the mixture

● Predicting the formula

When you use molecular model kits the 'atoms' have holes for the 'bonds' to slot into. When you made models of molecules on page 81 we said that there were a couple of rules to follow:

1 No 'atoms' should have any holes without 'bonds' in them.
2 All 'bonds' must have 'atoms' at either end of them.

Following these rules means that the formula of a compound is set and can't be changed. We can think of the number of bonds an atom can form as its '**combining power**'.

Look at a molecular model kit or think back to making the models:

Hydrogen has a combining power of 1 (it can only form one bond).

Oxygen has a combining power of 2 (it can form two bonds).

So 1 oxygen atom can bond to 2 hydrogen atoms. Therefore the formula of hydrogen oxide, water, is H_2O.

Here is a table showing the combining powers of some atoms.

Atoms don't always obey the rules above, but they do work for lots of compounds.

Gruesome science

We all drink water (H_2O), but drinking hydrogen peroxide (H_2O_2) would burn and blister your mouth and insides.

Element	Symbol	'Combining power'
hydrogen	H	1
carbon	C	4
nitrogen	N	3
sulphur	S	2
oxygen	O	2
chlorine	Cl	1

SUMMARY QUESTIONS

1 ☆ Copy these sentences. Complete them by filling in the gaps.

Compounds have a fixed c... but the proportions in a ... can vary.

We can ... the elements from a mixture quite easily, but a chemical ... is needed to break down a compound into its elements.

2 ☆☆☆ Using the 'combining powers' in the table above, work out the formula of a compound formed between:
a) hydrogen and chlorine
b) chlorine and oxygen
c) nitrogen and hydrogen.

Key words

combining power
composition
compound
mixture
proportion

More about mixtures

8F3

LEARN ABOUT
- some useful mixtures
- the mixture of gases in air
- separating these gases and some of their uses

Emulsions – a mixture containing two liquids, such as oil and water

Foams – a mixture containing a gas trapped in a liquid

USEFUL MIXTURES

hair gel   chocolate
hair mousse   butter
deodorant   Salad cream
perfume   mayonnaise
airfreshener   whipped cream

Useful mixtures

We use lots of mixtures in everyday life. We can make all sorts of useful mixtures by mixing substances that don't dissolve well in each other.

When one of the substances is finely spread throughout the other substance, we call the mixture a colloid.

Aerosol sprays are examples of colloids. You have fine droplets of liquid mixed with the gas that spurts out of the can. You can see some other useful colloids in the photos opposite.

There are other types of mixture, such as a sol. In a sol, fine particles of an insoluble solid are spread through a liquid. You can also get solid foams. In these a gas is spread throughout a solid, like in a sponge.

Q1 Think of an example of a solid foam that you can eat.

Raw materials

Here are some useful mixtures that we use as **raw materials**. These are the starting materials used in the chemical industry to make new products:

air **sea water** **crude oil** **rocks** (some are called ores)

In Year 7 you saw how air is not a single substance, but a mixture of different gases.

The table shows the gases we find in air:

Gases in the air	Formula of gas	Approximate proportions (%)
nitrogen	N_2	78
oxygen	O_2	21
carbon dioxide (about 0.04%) water vapour (varies) argon (about 0.9%) and other noble gases various pollutants	CO_2 H_2O Ar He, Ne, Kr, Xe, Ra e.g. SO_2 or NO_2 or CH_4	1

Separating the gases from liquid air

We can separate and collect liquids with different boiling points from a mixture. The process is called **fractional distillation**. But how can we get air cold enough for it to condense into a liquid? It's not easy because the air has to be cooled to a temperature of almost −200°C.

In industry they do this by first of all compressing the air to about 150 times atmospheric pressure. This warms the air up. So then it has to be cooled down to normal temperatures by passing it over pipes of cold water.

But the main cooling takes place when the pressure is released and the air expands rapidly. If this is repeated, the air gets cold enough for the gases to condense (liquefy).

The carbon dioxide and water can be removed easily from the mixture as they are solids at this low temperature.

The table on the right shows the boiling points of the main substances left in the liquid mixture.

The liquid is then allowed to warm up and at −196°C nitrogen boils off first and is collected from the top of a tall column. The remaining mixture contains mainly oxygen.

Uses of gases from air

NITROGEN
- making fertilisers
- freezing specimens in hospitals
- inside food packaging

AIR

OXYGEN
- breathing apparatus
- welding
- steel making

CARBON DIOXIDE
- fire extinguishers
- cold storage
- stage 'smoke'

ARGON
- in light bulbs
- advertising signs

Gruesome science

People working with liquid air have to take special care. Exposure to the extreme cold, even for just a few seconds, results in terrible frostbite and permanent tissue damage.

Substance	Boiling point (°C)
nitrogen	−196
argon	−186
oxygen	−183

Q2 Which of the gases in the table has the lowest boiling point?

ICT CHALLENGE

Working as a group, produce an information booklet for government officials on the importance of air as a raw material for industry.
You can use ICT to find the information you need and to present your findings in a professional way.

SUMMARY QUESTIONS

1 ☆ Copy these sentences. Complete them by filling in the gaps.

We can make many useful materials by . . . substances that do not . . . well in each other. Examples include . . . paint and shaving . . .

Air is a . . . of gases. Most of the air is made up of . . . and oxygen.

We can separate the gases from . . . air using . . . distillation.

2 ☆☆☆ Think of some other mixtures that are emulsions, liquid foams, solid foams or sols. Write a list and say which type of mixture each product is.

Key words
argon
carbon dioxide
fractional distillation
nitrogen
oxygen
raw material

Pure or impure?

LEARN ABOUT
- melting points and boiling points
- pure and impure substances

Pure water?

Look at this label from a bottle of mineral water:

Q1 Would you call mineral water 'pure' water?

Q2 How could you get a sample of pure water from mineral water?

Q3 What would be the best way to describe mineral water?

an element

a compound

a mixture

a mineral

Aquavic water is specially produced to be fresh and light. We use our own formula to blend a unique balance of ingredients to create maximum refreshment.

Composition in mg/litre:

Calcium	78	Bicarbonates	357
Magnesium	24	Sulphates	10
Sodium	5		
Potassium	1	Chlorides	4.5
Silica	13.5	Nitrates	3.8

AQUAVIC

Melting points and boiling points

We have a great range of **melting points** and **boiling points** amongst the chemical elements. Look at the examples below:

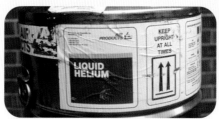

Liquid helium boils at −269°C. That is only 4 degrees above the minimum temperature possible (−273°C, known as absolute zero).

The melting point of gold is 1064°C

We can show the melting point and boiling point of a substance on a temperature line. For example, the data for bromine has been put on this line:

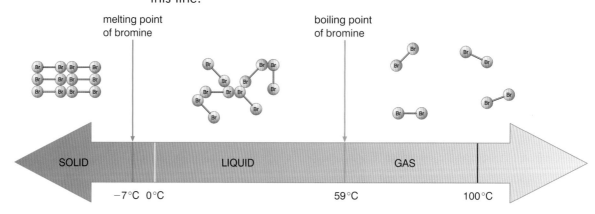

melting point of bromine

boiling point of bromine

SOLID   LIQUID   GAS

−7°C 0°C   59°C   100°C

This shows that the element bromine is a solid below −7°C. It melts at −7°C, turning into liquid bromine. The liquid boils at 59°C, turning into a gas. So at room temperature (taken as 20°C) bromine is a liquid.

Pure substances and mixtures

We can use boiling points and melting points to identify pure substances.

Do you remember a test for water? It turns white anhydrous copper sulphate blue. But that only tells us that water is present. It doesn't tell us if the water is pure or not. The test for **pure** water is that its melting point is exactly 0°C, and its boiling point is exactly 100°C. The melting and boiling points of an element or a compound are called its **fixed points**.

Pure substances can be compounds or elements, but they contain only one substance. An **impure** substance is a mixture of two or more different substances.

We can use melting points or boiling points to identify substances because pure substances have characteristic temperatures at which they melt and boil.

The melting point and boiling point of a mixture will vary depending on the composition of the mixture. A mixture does not have a sharp melting point or boiling point. It changes state over a range of temperatures. Impurities in a substance tend to lower its melting point and raise its boiling point.

I'm glad ice cream is a mixture... Imagine if it had a sharp melting point!

Which is pure?

Your teacher will give you two liquids in boiling tubes. One is pure water and one is salt water (sodium chloride solution). You will also have an ice/salt mixture to cool the tubes down.

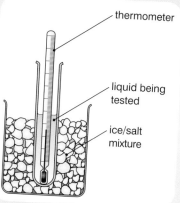

thermometer

liquid being tested

ice/salt mixture

- Your task is to record the temperature of each liquid as it cools down. You might use a temperature sensor and data logger or do the experiment using a thermometer and clock.

- From the lines on your graph deduce which liquid is pure water and which is salt water.

 CHALLENGE

Interrogate your database
In 8E3 you constructed a database for the melting points and boiling points of the chemical elements. Use your database to answer these questions.
a) Which element has the lowest boiling point?
b) Which element has the highest melting point?
c) Is the boiling point of an element always lower than its melting point? Display your evidence on a graph.

SUMMARY QUESTIONS

1 ☆ Copy these sentences. Complete them by filling in the gaps.

A pure element or c... can be identified from its f... points.

However, a... will change s... over a r... of temperatures, depending on its c...

2 ☆☆☆ Bromine is one of only two elements that exist as a liquid at 20°C. Name the other liquid element. Give one use of this element and explain an advantage and a disadvantage of using this particular element.

Key words

boiling point
fixed points
impure
melting point
pure

8F

Read all about it!

IDEAS AND EVIDENCE

Chocoholics – can you resist the mixture we know as chocolate?

Why is chocolate so gorgeous? Why do some of us crave it so much? But why do we feel guilty after indulging our urges to eat that yummiest of all mixtures? Chemical research has revealed some, but not all, of the answers.

It turns out that chocolate is a mixture of around 300 different substances. Some of these are chemicals that can act like drugs and affect the way your brain works. Although these are only present in tiny quantities, they might explain our liking for chocolate.

Chocolate is mainly a mixture of cocoa butter, sugar and dried milk. Like all mixtures, its composition can vary. It is obvious that plain, dark chocolate must contain a different mix to milk chocolate or white chocolate. Chocolate bars are made so that they are solid at normal room temperature and can be snapped into pieces. The trick is to vary the components of the mixture so that the chocolate will also melt at the slightly warmer temperature inside your mouth.

Chocolate gets its taste from chemicals extracted from cocoa beans. But the mixture of chemicals even differs in cocoa from different parts of the world.

Gruesome science

Chocolate can act as a poison to some animals, such as dogs. The animal can experience vomiting and diarrhoea.

The Latin name for the cocoa tree is *Theobroma cacao*. One of the trace chemicals is called theobromine. Its chemical formula is $C_7H_8N_4O_2$. Look at the model of one of its molecules below (notice there is no bromine atom – the compound was named after the tree it is extracted from):

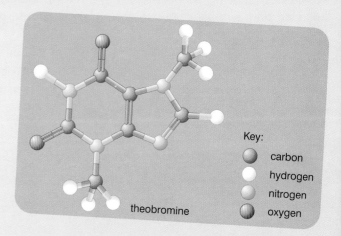

theobromine

Key:
- carbon
- hydrogen
- nitrogen
- oxygen

This compound is only a weak stimulant, although it may account for chocolate making you feel good. The stimulant caffeine, which is found in much larger amounts in coffee, is also present in chocolate. Other 'mood-affecting' compounds include serotonin, a chemical also released in the brain when we feel pleasure. However, lots of other foods also contain traces of these chemicals and people don't get strong urges to eat them. Therefore, we need more research to explain our cravings. It could have nothing to do with the chemicals from cocoa at all. Some think it is more likely to be the fact that chocolate is associated with 'treats' from an early age. So when we feel a bit low, we look to chocolate to spoil ourselves and make us feel better.

There is no doubt that for some people it works, even though warnings of the fat and high sugar content leave many of us feeling guilty for giving in to the pleasures of chocolate!

Other choco-facts

- The chemicals in red wine that protect against heart disease are also found in chocolate. There is the same amount in one square of milk chocolate as there is in a whole glass of red wine.
- The average person in the UK eats about 9 kg of chocolate each year. Only Swiss chocoholics can beat that, with 10 kg per year.

- **Compounds** contain more than one type of atom bonded together.
- The **ratio** (or **proportion**) of each element is fixed for any particular compound. For example, the ratio of calcium : carbon : oxygen in any sample of calcium carbonate is always 1 : 1 : 3 and its formula is $CaCO_3$. The elements in a compound can only be separated in some kind of chemical reaction.
- On the other hand, **mixtures** do not have any fixed **composition**. The amount of each substance in a mixture can vary.
- Because no new substances have been formed, it is usually possible to separate out the different substances in a mixture. (Methods such as filtration, evaporation, distillation and chromatography can be used.)
- We can use melting points and boiling points to identify pure substances from values given in data books or databases. However, the melting point and boiling point of a mixture will vary depending on its composition.

You can have molecules of elements... If all the atoms bonded together are the same type, just like we have in the model.

No, this is the formula of an element... There's a capital B and a little r meaning there are 2 atoms of Br in Br_2... So only one type of atom here!

There is a chemical reaction when magnesium burns in air to make magnesium oxide. There are bonds between magnesium and oxygen in the new compound made... You can't call it a mixture.

Now I see that you can have pure water if the only substance in the beaker is H_2O. If there is anything dissolved in it, you get a mixture.

DANGER! AVOID THESE COMMON ERRORS

Some people confuse 'compounds' and 'mixtures'.

Compounds contain atoms of different elements bonded together. The properties of the new compound made are not related at al to those of its elements.

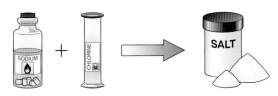

Fortunately, salt is nothing like sodium or chlorine!

All compounds also have their own chemical formula, unlike mixtures.

The properties of a mixture are just a combination of the properties of the substances mixed together.

Because there are no new chemical bonds formed on mixing, the substances can be separated easily from a mixture. However, separating the elements from a compound needs a chemical reaction to take place.

Key words

compound
element
formula
impure
mixture
pure
ratio

REVIEW QUESTIONS
Understanding and applying concepts

1 Explain the difference between a mixture of elements and a compound.
Use diagrams to help your explanation.

2 Look at the boxes below:

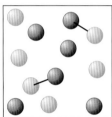

Box A

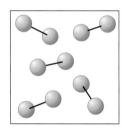

Box B

Box C

Box D

a Which boxes contain mixtures?
b Which boxes contain a pure substance?
c Which box contains a pure element?
d Which box contains a mixture of compounds?
e Which box shows a chemical reaction in progress?
f Which box contains ammonia, NH_3?

3 Look back to page 102 and answer **a** and **b**.
a Which elements make up theobromine?
b How many atoms are there in each theobromine molecule?
c Why does theobromine have a sharp melting point while chocolate melts over a range of temperatures?

4 On page 85 we saw that the chemical formula of insulin is $C_{254}H_{377}N_{65}O_{75}S_6$.
a Name the elements that make up insulin.
b How many atoms are there in an insulin molecule?

5 Explain these statements.
a Rock salt is put on roads when there is a forecast of freezing conditions.
b Boiled potatoes cook slightly more quickly if you add salt to the water in the pan.

6 The gases in air can be separated by fractional distillation of liquid air.
a How are water and carbon dioxide removed from the air before the gases enter the tall fractionating column?

Look at the boiling points of the substances in the liquid mixture:

Substance	Boiling point (^{o}C)
nitrogen	−196
argon	−186
oxygen	−183

b Which gas boils off after nitrogen?
c Why is it difficult to obtain 100% pure oxygen?
d Using the table on page 98, give the formulae of any gases in the air that can be described as:
  i) atoms of elements
  ii) molecules of elements
  iii) molecules of compounds.
e Explain why there is no such thing as the 'chemical formula of air'.

Ways with words

7 **a** Does the word 'pure' mean the same in the food and drink industry as it does to a scientist? If not, what is the difference in meaning?
b What do advertisers imply by the word 'pure' when describing a product?
c Try to think of some products that are advertised as 'pure'.

Making more of maths

8 The ratio of the elements in a compound is always fixed. In a sample of a compound of phosphorus and oxygen, there are 8×10^5 atoms of phosphorus and 2×10^6 atoms of oxygen. Work out the simplest ratio to find the chemical formula of this oxide of phosphorus?

Extension question

9 Look at these natural mixtures that we use as raw materials in the chemical industry:

sea water   crude oil
rocks (sometimes called ores)

Choose one of the mixtures above and find out some of the products that are made from that raw material. Write word equations for any chemical reactions involved.

SAT-STYLE QUESTIONS

1 The diagrams show the different arrangement of atoms in six substances.

Each atom is represented by a circle labelled with its chemical symbol.

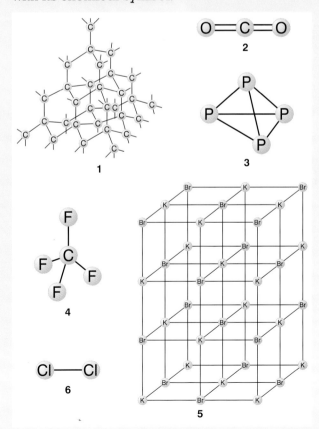

a i) Which of the diagrams represent the structures of chemical elements? Write down the correct numbers. (1)
  ii) Explain how you decided which are elements. (1)
b Give the formula of two of the compounds represented in the diagrams. (2)
c Give the name of the substance labelled 5. (1)
d Which of the diagrams represents a molecule made of 4 atoms? (1)
e How many atoms are in the molecule labelled 2? (1)
f Give the names of the chemical elements whose atoms can be represented by the following symbols:
  i)   C
  ii) Cl
  iii) Cu (3)

2 The table gives the melting points and boiling points of some substances present in air:

Substance	Melting point (°C)	Boiling point (°C)
oxygen	−219	−183
water vapour	i)	ii)
nitrogen	−210	−196
carbon dioxide	−78 (sublimes)	−78 (sublimes)

a What are the missing data in the table? (2)
b What would happen if solid carbon dioxide was warmed from −95°C to −78°C? (1)
c 'Liquid air' is a mixture of nitrogen and oxygen. Use the table to suggest how liquid oxygen could be separated from the mixture. (1)

Key words

Unscramble these:
uprime
meetlen
pocmundo
otari

8G

Rocks and weathering

COMING SOON

8G1 Looking at rocks

8G2 Chemical weathering

8G3 Physical weathering

8G4 Fragments in motion

8G5 Forming layers

8G6 Evidence from layers

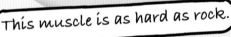
This muscle is as hard as rock.

I've heard some rocks are actually very soft.

What's it all about?

We are never very far away from rocks. We find them beneath the concrete and tarmac of our cities. The soil in fields and gardens contains fragments of rock. In the countryside we can often see the bare rock piercing the surface. But how do the rocks make all those interesting shapes? How do they get into the soil? How can they be broken down in nature?

In this unit we will start looking at the answers to these and other questions about rocks.

How on earth did these form?

 ## What do you remember?

You already know about:

- soils coming from rocks, and rocks being under the surface of the Earth.
- some examples and uses of rocks.
- the particles in solids, liquids and gases.
- the pH scale.
- what happens when solutions evaporate.

1 Which of these rocks can you see in the face of a white cliff?

granite **slate** sandstone **chalk**

2 Which of the following is the best use of slate?

bricks **roof tiles** gutters **fence posts**

3 In which of these states of matter are particles perfectly still (stationary)?

solids **liquids** gases **none of these**

4 If you leave sea water to evaporate in a glass, what are you left with in the glass?

blue liquid **white solid**
pure water **nothing**

Ideas about rocks and weathering

QUESTIONS

Look at the cartoon above and discuss these questions with your partner.

a) What do you think rocks are like? Can you generalise and say 'All rocks are . . .'?

b) How do you think that underground caverns could form in limestone regions?

c) Do you think Pete is right about the strange rock? Try to think of another way that the rock could have got there?

d) Think of some things that you know about the history of the Earth from millions of years ago. What evidence convinces you to believe it?

LEARN ABOUT

- the mixtures of mineral grains in rocks
- the textures of rocks
- using experimental evidence and models to explain different textures

Diamond is a mineral that is an element. It is one form of the element carbon.

Halite is a mineral that is a compound. Its chemical name is sodium chloride (NaCl).

● What are rocks?

There are many different rocks. They are usually made up of different *mixtures of minerals*.

A **mineral** *is a solid compound or element found naturally in the ground.*

For example, diamond is a mineral that is an element. It is an element made up of carbon atoms. On the other hand, halite is a mineral that is a compound. It is made up of sodium chloride. Most minerals are compounds.

Q1 Which elements make up halite?

Q2 Why do minerals have a chemical formula but rocks do not?

Look at the photo of granite rock opposite:

Granite is a rock made from a mixture of minerals. This type is called blue pearl granite.

Comparing rocks

You can now look at different rocks in detail to compare them.

- Use a hand lens to help you observe the rock samples.
  a) Record your descriptions of the different rocks provided.
  b) Sort the rocks into groups using your observations.

Compare your groupings with others in your class.

● Texture

The **texture** of a rock describes the way its grains fit together. There are two main types of texture in rocks:

- **Crystalline texture**. The mineral grains are crystals in the rock. The grains all interlock. There are no gaps between the crystals.
- **Fragmental texture**. The minerals form randomly shaped fragments or grains that do not fit together neatly. Another mineral often 'cements' the grains to each other.

The textures of granite and sandstone

- Use an hand lens to look at the structure of granite and sandstone.
  a) What do you notice about the way that individual 'grains' interlock? Which rock has grains that do not interlock?
  b) Classify the rocks as having a crystalline or fragmental texture.

● Porosity

The **porosity** of a rock tells us how well it soaks up water.

Q3 Predict whether granite or sandstone will be better at soaking up water. In other words, which rock is more porous? Explain your reasoning.

The porosity of granite and sandstone

- Weigh a dry sample of each rock (granite and sandstone).
- Record the masses in a table like the one below:

Rock	Mass when dry (g)	Mass after soaking (g)	Increase in mass (g)	Percentage increase in mass (%)
granite				
sandstone				

- Now place each rock under water in a beaker.
  a) What do you notice?
- Remove them from the water and let the excess drip off. Then weigh the rocks again.
- Record your results in the table. Then fill in the other columns.
  b) What is your conclusion? Was your prediction correct?

The grains in sandstone are non-interlocking

Rocks that have spaces between their grains can soak up water better than rocks with interlocking crystals. The water fills the gaps between grains in rocks like sandstone.

water in the gaps

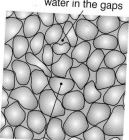

Porous rocks have grains that do not interlock

grains in the rock

SUMMARY QUESTIONS

1 ☆ Copy the sentences. Complete them by filling in the gaps.

Minerals are . . . elements or . . . found naturally. Most rocks are . . . of minerals. There are two main types of rock . . . called crystalline and . . .

When the grains in a rock do not . . . the rock is . . ., meaning it can . . . up water.

2 ☆☆☆ Try to think up a model you could use to help explain the porosity of rocks to a child in Year 6. It should demonstrate the interlocking and non-interlocking grains.

Key words

crystalline
fragmental
granite
mineral
porosity
sandstone
texture

Chemical weathering

8G2

LEARN ABOUT
- the breakdown of rocks in chemical changes
- how to record results over a period of time
- explaining changes that happen to rocks over time

● Breaking down rocks

You might have heard the saying 'As hard as rock', and some rocks, such as granite, are very hard indeed. But even the surface of granite is broken down by the action of rain water. We say that the granite gets **weathered** by the rain water.

Weathering *breaks down rocks*.

Rain water is slightly acidic. It always has been, even before the days of pollution and acid rain. That's because of carbon dioxide gas in the air.

I knew weathering could be slow, but this is ridiculous!

Q1 Why do you think the proportion of carbon dioxide in the air can vary from place to place?

Carbon dioxide gas dissolves slightly in water. It forms a *weakly acidic* solution of carbonic acid. Over time, this acid can chemically attack some of the minerals in rocks.

Acid on carbonate rocks SAFETY

Let's see what happens when we add acid to three types of rock containing carbonates.

We can test limestone, chalk and marble. We will use dilute hydrochloric acid, instead of a solution of carbon dioxide. This will speed up the effect of the acid.

● Carry out the experiment shown here:
  a) What happens to the rocks?
  b) What gas is given off? How could you test for this gas?

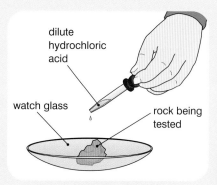

dilute hydrochloric acid

watch glass

rock being tested

Limestone can be weathered over time to form caverns

Limestones (which include chalk) and marble contain the mineral **calcite**.

Its chemical name is calcium carbonate ($CaCO_3$). Other rocks also contain carbonates, such as magnesium carbonate or copper carbonate.

You might recall from unit 7F that acids react with carbonates. They form a salt, plus carbon dioxide and water. The salt formed is often soluble in water. So any carbonate in the rock breaks down in acid and forms a solution. That's how carbonate rock gets weathered by acids in soil or in rain water.

Q2 The soluble salt formed when calcium carbonate reacts with carbonic acid is called calcium hydrogencarbonate. Write a word equation for this reaction.

Chemical weathering of granite

We can also model the effect of rain water on granite rock. The reaction that causes weathering of granite is much slower than the reaction that weathers limestone.

The effect of acid on granite

- Use a mixture of dilute hydrochloric acid and hydrogen peroxide solution to cover a piece of granite in a small beaker. The hydrochloric acid will speed up the action of acids in soil and in rain water. The hydrogen peroxide will speed up the reaction of oxygen over time.
- Cover the top of the beaker. Make sure that it is not disturbed.
- You will have to use time-lapse photography to observe the slow changes. Take your photos from exactly the same place over a couple of weeks.
- Arrange the photos in a sequence to show the effect of weathering on granite.
  a) Describe your observations.
  b) Evaluate time-lapse photography as a way of recording observations.

Stalactites and stalagmites form from solutions of weathered limestone. When the water evaporates, it leaves behind tiny crystals of calcite.

Granite is a mixture of three types of mineral – quartz, feldspar and mica. The acid in rain water attacks the feldspar and mica minerals. Eventually the granite is weathered into small particles of clay. These are carried away by the water, along with any compounds formed in solution.

The breakdown of rock by reactions is called **chemical weathering**.

SUMMARY QUESTIONS

1 ☆ Copy these sentences. Complete them by filling in the gaps.
   When rocks are . . . down in nature, we say that the rocks have been . . .
   This can happen as a result of c. . . reactions with a. . . in rain water or in soil.

2 ☆☆ Carry out a survey of school building materials that have been weathered.

Key words

calcite
chemical weathering
granite
limestones
weathered

8G3 Physical weathering

LEARN ABOUT
- freeze/thaw weathering
- weathering caused by temperature changes

Forces that break down rock

We have seen how rocks can be broken down by chemical changes to their minerals.

They are also broken down in nature by forces caused by physical processes. We call this **physical weathering**.

Freeze/thaw

Most liquids contract slightly when they solidify.

Q1 Why do most liquids contract slightly when they change to a solid?

However, water is the exception to this rule. It expands as it freezes to form ice. Sometimes water collects in rocky places, then repeatedly freezes and thaws. This process can break off pieces of rock.

Ice breaker

- Watch your teacher fill a glass screw-top bottle to the brim with water, then replace the top tightly.

- The bottle is placed in a sealed plastic bag and then left in a freezer until next lesson.
  a) Predict what will happen.
  b) Check the results next lesson. Was your prediction correct?

Look at the diagrams below:

AMAZING SCIENCE!

Rocks can also be broken down physically by plant and tree roots. Even burrowing animals can scrape away at the surface of rocks, breaking bits off. Some people call this biological weathering.

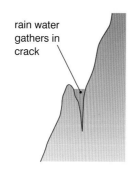

rain water gathers in crack

water freezes and expands

the crack gets bigger

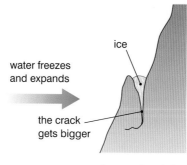

ice

eventually a piece of rock breaks off

temperature falls below 0°C

The effect of freeze/thaw

Water collects in cracks in rocks when it rains. If the temperature drops to 0°C or below, the water freezes. As it turns to ice, it expands and opens the crack a little wider. When this has been repeated many times the crack gets big enough to physically break off a rock fragment.

The fragments of broken rock can collect at the bottom of the rock face. This is called a **scree slope**.

A scree slope in the Lake District

● Changing temperatures

As you know, when solid materials get hot they expand.

When they cool down they contract.

 Q2 Why do solids expand and contract with changes in temperature?

Rocks in a desert will get very hot in the baking sun. However, the temperature quickly drops at night time. This repeated heating and cooling of rocks is another cause of physical weathering.

In the activity opposite we will model the effects of changing temperatures on rocks.

Rocks are mixtures of minerals. During heating and cooling, each of the minerals expands and contracts at different rates. This sets up stress forces within the rock that eventually causes the surface to crack and break away.

On individual pieces of rock we can get an effect called 'onion-skinning'. The rock splits into layers that eventually fall away. It's like peeling off layers of an onion. On large masses of rock this flaking off is called **exfoliation**.

If the climate is right, the cracks can also be subject to the forces of freeze/thaw weathering. Small cracks can be opened up wider, as explained at the top of the page.

It is important to realise that rocks will undergo many types of weathering at the same time, For example, once cracks open up, chemical weathering will also have a greater effect. The cracked rock will have more surface exposed to attack by acidic solutions.

Expanding and contracting rocks
SAFETY

● Your teacher will heat a piece of granite strongly in a Bunsen burner flame.

● Then the rock will be plunged into a trough of cold water. What happens?

SUMMARY QUESTIONS

1 ☆ Copy these sentences. Complete them by filling in the gaps.

   Water that collects in a c... in a rock can ... and expand.

   This splits the rock further until a f... breaks off. Rocks can also be b... by stress forces produced within rocks by changes of ....

2 ☆☆ Give a similarity and a difference between physical weathering and chemical weathering?

Key words

exfoliation
freeze/thaw
physical weathering
scree slope

Fragments in motion

8G4

LEARN ABOUT
- how rock fragments become sediment grains
- how rock fragments and sediments are moved and deposited

⚫ Transporting fragments

We know that weathering breaks down rock. But what happens to the bits that come away from the body of the rock? The **fragments** or minerals in solution, formed by weathering, get moved to another place. They are **transported** by:

- gravity
- wind
- ice (in glaciers – rivers of ice)
- water (in streams, rivers and seas).

Q1 How will minerals in solution, formed as a result of chemical weathering, be carried away?

Modelling transport by water

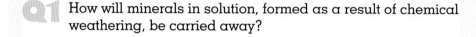

- Use a length of square guttering to channel water into a deep trough.
- Use some ink to investigate the water currents in the guttering and trough.
- Find out where the current is fastest and where it is slowest.
  a) Predict where differently sized particles will be deposited.

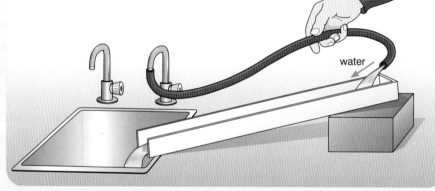

water

- Add some rock fragments of different sizes. For example, try a mixture of gravel, sand and clay soil.
  b) Record your results and decide if the evidence gathered supports your prediction.
  c) How is the size of the rock fragments deposited affected by the speed or volume of the water flow?
- Choose another question to investigate using the equipment already set up. Make a prediction and carry out your investigation.
  CARE! Mop up any spills. Do not let rock fragments block the sink or drains.

It has been estimated that the Mississippi River in the USA deposits almost two million tonnes of material each day at its delta.

⚫ Depositing sediments

Weathered rock is often carried away in streams and in rivers. At first, high in the mountains, fast flowing water races down steep slopes. Here it has enough energy to carry quite large pieces of rock. They bounce along the bottom of the river.

The river starts to slow down as the land levels off. Then the larger bits of rock get **deposited** on the riverbed. They might be moved on again, for example, in times of flood, when the river has more energy for a while.

Deposited pieces of rock are called **sediments**.
The smaller pieces of rock get carried along further before they are also deposited.

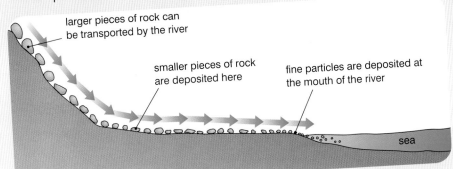

larger pieces of rock can be transported by the river

smaller pieces of rock are deposited here

fine particles are deposited at the mouth of the river

sea

Sediments tend to be sorted by size as the river deposits them along its course to the sea

So the greater the energy of the moving water, the larger the rock fragments it can carry along.

The fine bits of rock, such as clay, can be carried all the way to the river mouth (estuary) where it meets the sea. If it is deposited there, we can get the fine sediments building up to form a **delta**.

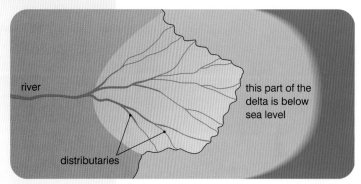

river

this part of the delta is below sea level

distributaries

The fine sediments deposited at the mouth of a river can form a delta

● Erosion

Erosion is the wearing away of rock as surfaces rub against each other.

Weathered fragments will erode the rock that they pass over. For example, rocks in riverbeds will be worn away as fragments scrape and bounce along down the river.

The weathered fragments themselves also get worn down (eroded), losing their sharp edges. They will get smaller and smaller, the longer they get carried along by the river.

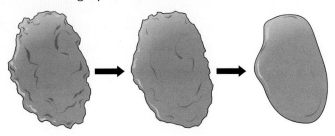

Q2 Is erosion a physical change or a chemical change? Why?

SUMMARY QUESTIONS

1 ☆ Copy the sentences. Complete them by filling in the gaps.

Weathered rock can be . . . by gravity, . . ., ice and . . .

The weathered pieces of rock become . . ., smoother and rounder as they get e. . .

2 ☆☆☆ Describe how the energy of a river at different stages affects the transport, deposition and erosion of rock.

Key words

delta
deposit
erosion
fragments
sediments
transport

Forming layers

LEARN ABOUT
- forming sedimentary layers
- suggesting explanations for observations

Layers of sediment

We have seen how sediments get deposited. Eventually these sediments turn into rock (see 8H1). Different types of sediment form layers of different rocks.

Look at these two rocks taken from different layers in a cliff face:

Q1 What can you say about the sediments that were deposited to form the two rocks in the photos?

Look at the photo showing layers of rock formed from sediments deposited millions of years ago:

Layers of sediment formed these layers of rock

Q2 Why can we see the layers now?

Sandstone rock

Conglomerate rock

The layers of rock are called **beds**. The boundaries between different layers are called **bedding planes**.

The rock layer at the bottom of a sequence of layers is usually the oldest. Its sediment was probably laid down before the others. However, we can't be certain of this from the sequence. That's because sometimes layers are put under great stress by powerful movements in the Earth's crust. They can be snapped, folded and even turned upside down.

You can investigate how sediments are laid down in layers in the next activity.

AMAZING SCIENCE!

A three metre depth of sea water must evaporate to leave a layer of minerals 5 cm thick. The seam of rock salt under Cheshire is up to 2000 metres thick in places.

Looking at layers

mixture of sand, gravel and clay is shaken up

- Shake up a mixture of sand, gravel and clay in a jar three-quarters full of water.
- Allow the sediments to settle in the jar.
  a) Describe the layers in the jar.
    - Are there sharp boundaries between layers or do they blend into each other?
    - Why do layers merge at their boundaries?
  b) Which sediments settle out more quickly – large fragments or small fragments of rock?

When we look at layers of rock we sometimes get a sharp **boundary** at a bedding plane. This gives us evidence that there was a gap in time between the **deposition** of one sediment and the next.

Layers of minerals

We can also get layers of minerals that were once dissolved in water forming layers of rock. These were mainly formed when ancient seas evaporated and left behind the salts dissolved in them.

The salts come out of the sea water as solids in sequence. The least soluble solid **precipitates** out first as the water evaporates off. So the first solid (precipitate) is usually calcium carbonate (see page 129).

This can happen in lagoons that repeatedly evaporate, but fill up before the level of water goes down too much. The calcium carbonate falls to the bottom of the lagoon and can build up in layers.

About 90% of the water has to evaporate from sea water before common salt (sodium chloride) comes out of solution. This is thought to have happened when seas became cut off and surrounded by land. Eventually the water evaporated, leaving the layers of minerals behind. The sea can return and evaporate many times. This builds up thick layers of the rock. We call rocks formed like this **evaporites**.

Q3 What would you see at the boundary between two layers if there was a period when both types of sediment were deposited at the same time?

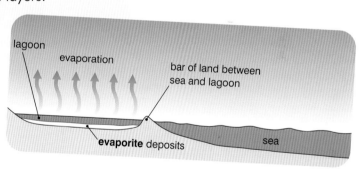

lagoon
evaporation
bar of land between sea and lagoon
evaporite deposits
sea

SUMMARY QUESTIONS

1 ☆ Copy these sentences. Complete them by filling in the gaps.

Older layers (or . . .) of rock are usually found . . . layers made from . . . laid down in more recent times. Other layers of rock can be formed when . . . evaporates from sea water. Rock formed like this is called an . . .

2 ☆☆☆ A layer of evaporite rock was found to contain mainly sodium chloride, but also narrow bands of other minerals. Explain how these bands could have been formed.

Key words

bedding plane
beds
boundary
deposition
evaporite
precipitate

Evidence from layers

LEARN ABOUT

- sediments from once living organisms
- using evidence from rocks to sequence events
- using evidence from fossils

● Evidence in the rock

We have already seen how we can observe the sediments that were deposited millions of years ago in rocks exposed today.

Q1 Why do sediments vary in size?

We can make deductions from the layers of rock we see.

For example, look at the layers below:

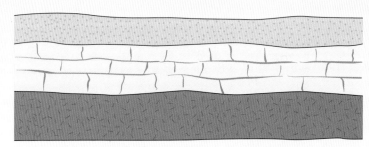

rock salt

shelly limestone

mudstone

From these three layers we can say that a sediment of mud was laid down first, followed by the limestone, then the salt. That's because the oldest rocks usually come at the bottom of a sequence of layers.

We can guess that the mud was deposited at the mouth of an ancient river where it met the sea. Sometime later this part of the shore became covered by the sea. The shells of sea creatures were deposited as sediment to form the layer of limestone.

This part of the sea must then have been cut off from the rest of the ocean. The new in-land sea was surrounded by land. The water evaporated from the sea, leaving behind a layer of rock salt.

It's a bit like being a detective really. You can try to piece together the events from the clues left in the rocks.

● Layers from living things

We have seen how sediment from weathered rock that has been transported can settle in layers.

However, sometimes the layers of sediment found in rock can be formed from the remains of plants or animals. These often lived in the sea. For example, most limestones are formed from the shelly bits of sea creatures. Chalk was made from the 'hard bits' of a tiny sea plant called **coccolith**. The sediments from living things **accumulate** (build up) in layers.

The chalk, laid down in thick layers, is clearly visible in these cliffs in Kent

Coal is another rock made from sediments. It was formed millions of years ago from layers of plant material. The plants lived in tropical swamps. When they died, they were buried in mud at the bottom of the swamp. There was little oxygen down there so they didn't decompose like most plants. The layers built up and were compressed, eventually turning into coal.

● Evidence from fossils

Some rocks formed from sediments contain **fossils**. A fossil can show an imprint made by a living thing in the sediments before they turned to rock. They also form from the hard skeletons of the once living things.

These fossils help us to compare the age of rocks found in different parts of the world. Rocks containing fossils of the same species must have been formed at about the same time.

They can also give us clues about the conditions on Earth at the time. For example, we find tropical fern-like fossils in the coal seams under Britain.

This suggests that our climate was very different millions of years ago. In fact most scientists believe that over time Britain has moved slowly from near the equator to its present position.

The same fossils in different parts of the world have given scientists evidence that continents were once joined together (see page 136).

This is a fern fossil in coal. The fern lived about 300 million years ago.

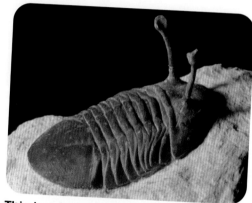

This is a fossil of an extinct species of sea creature called a trilobite

Playing detective!

Draw a diagram of the layers you would expect to find from the evidence below:

Millions of years ago a sediment of sand built up on the bed of an ancient sea. Then the landscape changed and the next layer to build up came from more turbulent conditions. Pebbles and stones were deposited.

This was followed by more changes. A period of calm arrived. Sea levels were high now in this part of the world. The only sediment coming to rest on this part of the seabed were the remains of tiny sea plants called coccoliths.

Although each coccolith only measures a few thousandths of a millimetre across, layers of chalk 1000 metres thick have been formed – now that's a lot of coccolith!

SUMMARY QUESTIONS

1 ☆ Copy these sentences. Complete them by filling in the gaps.

Rocks and f. . . give us clues to events that happened . . . of years ago.

Rocks, such as limestone, . . . and . . . were formed from once living organisms.

2 ☆☆☆ Chalk contains about 98% of the mineral calcite (calcium carbonate). What can you deduce about the conditions when the sediments were laid down?

Key words

accumulate
coccolith
fossil

Read all about it!

IDEAS AND EVIDENCE

Mary Anning – famous fossil hunter (1799–1847)

Mary's great find

Discovering the fossil of a large prehistoric creature intact is a rare event. But a girl called Mary Anning did just that when she was only 11 years old. She discovered the fossil of a complete Ichthyosaurus. Her brother first spotted the position of the fossil. She returned to the spot later. Mary carefully brushed the earth away, and there it was – the remains of a reptile 30 metres long!

The fossil is now kept in the Natural History Museum in London.

Mary carried on collecting and has been described as the greatest fossil collector ever. She was one of the first ever palaeontologists – they are people who study fossils and evidence from prehistoric times.

The life and times of Mary Anning

Mary was born in 1799. The odds were stacked against Mary ever reaching adulthood. She arrived into a poor family. It is thought that her mother had given birth to as many as 10 children, but only Mary and her brother managed to survive.

Mary's father was a furniture maker, but the family struggled to make ends meet. The family lived in Lyme Regis, a seaside town in Dorset. There were lots of fossils in the rocks exposed along the coastline. In fact, her father collected fossils to sell to tourists in their home town. This helped bring in a bit more cash to live on. However, the family still owed money when he died in 1810.

An ammonite fossil found at Lyme Regis

The family had all become really skilful at finding fossils as they scoured the beaches with their father. Mary had even trained her dog to mark the spot where she found a fossil. The dog would sit patiently as she went off to get her digging tools. One day she returned to find her helper was dead. The dog was killed when it was buried in a landslide. A close escape for Mary, but that didn't make her feel any better.

It is thought that Mary Anning gave rise to the tongue-twister 'She sells sea shells on the sea shore'

Mary eventually took over the fossil hunting business. She managed to earn just enough for the family to get by.

Mary's place in science

Mary did not really gain the recognition that her discoveries and great knowledge about fossils deserved.

At the start of the 19th century, men dominated British society. Women were treated as second-class citizens.

Poor people were also looked down upon by those with wealth and power. Schooling was not provided for all children. The rich and the clergy did receive a good education. But even rich women couldn't go to university.

The world of science reflected these attitudes. Many scientists were wealthy men who enjoyed science as a hobby. Little wonder that Mary struggled to get respect from fellow scientists. She was poor, had received little formal education and was a woman!

However, eventually she did win over the scientists of her time. She discovered the first ever fossil of a Plesiosaur. But at first even this was not accepted. A famous French scientist doubted her fossil. He insisted on checking it out himself in person. He was soon convinced though, and had to agree that Mary's new fossil was an important scientific discovery. This helped to get her welcomed by fellow scientists as part of their 'club'.

She discussed scientific theories on equal terms with eminent geologists. She was delighted to be made an honorary member of the Geological Society of London before she died.

- Rocks are broken down by weathering.
  Chemical weathering happens when the rock is attacked by weakly acidic rain water. A reaction results in new substances being made. These are often washed away in solution.
- Rocks are also broken down by **physical weathering**. Changes in temperature and freeze/thaw create stress in the rock. Fragments can be broken off in these processes.
- The weathered rock is then **transported** to another place, often by moving water. On its journey the rock fragment will get smaller, smoother and rounder the further it is carried along. It will also wear away rock that it passes over. This is called **erosion**.
- Eventually, the rock fragment is **deposited** as a **sediment**. These sediments build up in layers. The sediments can be made from the remains of animals and plants as well as bits of rock. Other layers are formed when dissolved compounds come out of solution as solids as the water evaporates. These are called **evaporites**.

Not all rocks are hard, you know. Did you know that talc is a soft rock?

We can't see the chemical weathering as it happens... It's too slow... But it has had millions of years to break down the rock!

Glaciers are rivers of ice. They can carry large boulders along and dump them where they melt.

There are all kinds of clues in rocks if you know what to look for. Look at this fossil and the sediments that make up the rock.

DANGER! AVOID THESE COMMON ERRORS

Many people think that the words 'weathering' and 'erosion' mean the same thing. However, weathering takes place at the site of the original rock. The rock is *broken down* in weathering. When bits of rock are moved along and then collide with other rock, erosion takes place and the rocks get *worn away*.

Some people don't recognise coal as a rock because it is also a fuel. Geologists refer to sand, peat and clay as rocks too!

Key words

deposit
erosion
evaporites
sediment
transport
weathering

REVIEW QUESTIONS
Understanding and applying concepts

1 **a** Why might you need a plumber if you go on holiday in winter and forget to leave some kind of heating on? Explain what happens and why. How does this same process result in the physical weathering of rocks?

b Here is a scree slope:

The rock fragments on the scree slope are increasing in number.
What can you say about the climate?

c A scree slope in Greenland is not getting any new deposits of rock.
What can you say about the climate and how it has changed over time?

d Give another set of conditions in which the formation of scree will not happen.

e How are the rock fragments on a scree slope transported originally?

2 **a** Bits of weathered rock can be transported by several different means before their journey ends. Name these.

b Think up a situation that could involve three different methods of transporting rock fragments.

c If a piece of weathered rock falls into a fast-flowing river, parts of it may eventually end up deposited by the river as fine particles called silt. Explain how this happens. Include diagrams in your answer.

3 **a** In which environment do you think that rocks undergo regular large and rapid changes of temperature?

b Explain how a rock undergoes the process called exfoliation.

c Explain how rock fragments can be sorted by size on a beach.

d Draw a plan view of a meandering river (one that curves from side to side as it crosses the land). Indicate on your drawing where you would expect most bits of rock to be deposited. Explain your choice of sites.

4 Imagine a river with a large lake half way along its course to the sea.

a Predict what sediments you would find at the bottom of the lake.

b How might this river's estuary differ from another identical river without a lake?

5 Look at the sequence of layers found at the face of a cliff:

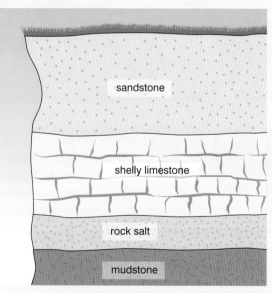

Describe a possible sequence of events that led to the formation of the layers.

6 Draw a concept map linking these terms together. Don't forget to label your links, explaining what the connection is.

> weathering   erosion   rock fragment
> sediment   layer of rock

Ways with words

7 Write definitions for the following terms:

> chemical weathering
> physical weathering
> transport
> erosion
> deposition
> sediment
> evaporite
> coal

8 Write a poem about the processes of weathering, transportation, erosion and deposition.

Making more of maths

9 It has been estimated that it would take about 30 years for a layer of chalk 1 mm thick to build up from the remains of coccoliths.

> Calculate how long it took to build up a layer of chalk that is 1000 m thick. (Remember that the Earth is very old – about 4600 million years old!)

Thinking skills

10 a What climatic conditions will give rise to the fastest rate of chemical weathering?

   b Plan an investigation into one of the factors you identified in part a. You can model the process of chemical weathering using marble chips and dilute hydrochloric acid.

Extension question

11 Carry out research into the formation of fossils. Write a booklet for use with Year 6 children. Explain clearly how fossils can form in different ways.

SAT-STYLE QUESTIONS

1 Weathering breaks down rocks. This can happen when:
 – Water collects in cracks in rocks.
 – The water turns to ice at its freezing point and expands.
 – Pieces of rock get split off.

What other things must happen during this type of weathering? Choose *two* of these options:
 A The temperature does not change.
 B The temperature rises above 0°C.
 C The temperature remains below 0°C.
 D Expansion forces all the water out of the cracks.
 E Expansion causes the cracks to widen.
 F Expansion forces the cracks to close up.
 (2)

2 There are potholes, caves and caverns in limestone regions.

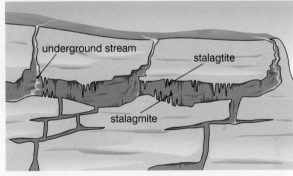

a Explain how chemical weathering can cause caverns to form in the limestone. (2)
b Explain how stalactites form in the caves. (2)
c Limestone can absorb water. It is a porous rock.
Describe how this causes the physical weathering of limestone. (2)

Key Words

Unscramble these:
sotepid
roonies
poisartvee
rotprants

8H

The rock cycle

I don't think that's the rock cycle we'll be studying!

What's it all about?

The Earth's crust is made of lots of different rocks. Have you ever wondered how different types of rock were formed? Why are some rocks really hard, but others crumble in your hands? Why are they different colours and densities? Why are some made of crystals and others of grains?

Understanding the processes that form rocks will help you answer these questions. It will also make you think more deeply about your environment. Who knows, you might even become a geologist?

 ## What do you remember?

You already know about:

- rocks under the surface of the Earth and that soils come from rocks.
- the names of some rocks and their textures.
- weathering processes and how sediments are formed.
- the differences between the way particles are arranged in solids and liquids.

1 What do we call the process in which weathered rock fragments wear away rocks they come into contact with?

deposition   **erosion**
accumulation   **sedimentation**

2 Which of the following describes the texture of sandstone?

intermingling   **non-intermingling**
interlocking   **non-interlocking**

3 Which of these processes is described as chemical weathering?

freeze/thaw   **changes in temperature**
attack by acid   **breakdown by tree roots**

4 The particles are very close together, touching, and slipping and sliding over each other. Which state of matter does this describe?

solids   **liquids**
gases   **none of these**

Ideas about rocks

Every rock on Earth must be millions and millions of years old.

They say 'Diamonds are forever'... But I suppose rocks are too.

This rock can't be made of sediments... It's really hard.

Do you know the chemical formula of granite?

Can you find fossils in any kind of rock? Let's look closely at granite.

That can't be limestone... it looks nothing like the limestone we used at school.

QUESTIONS

Look at the cartoon above and discuss these questions with your partner.

a) The Earth is about 4600 million years old. Are all rocks that age too?

b) Do rocks last forever? What might change them?

c) How do you think you can get hard rocks made from sediments?

d) Why will it be useless trying to find the formula of granite?

e) Which type of rocks do you know that fossils are found in? Under what conditions might fossils be destroyed as a new rock forms?

f) Why do you think that different kinds of limestone can look so different?

LAUNCH

LEARN ABOUT
- how sedimentary rock can form
- the characteristics of sedimentary rocks

● How do sediments turn to rock?

We have seen in unit 8G how weathered rock:

1 is transported by water, wind, gravity, and/or ice,

2 is eroded on its journey, then

3 eventually settles as a sediment (often with other bits of rock of a similar size).

Over time, layers of sediment build up. The individual bits of rock become a layer (or bed) of rock. But how does this happen?

Sand and sandstone

- Squeeze a handful of wet sand.
  a) What do you see happen?

- Now compare your damp sand with a piece of sandstone. You can use a hand lens or microscope to help your observations.
  b) From your observations, how do you think the grains in sandstone are held together?

You can imagine the pressure building up as layer upon layer of sediment is deposited. This squeezes water out from the gaps between the grains of sediment. Under this pressure, the edges of the grains can fuse together. This is called **compaction**.

Sand grains as they are deposited; water fills spaces between grains

As more sediments build up, the pressure increases and pushes grains of sand closer together, squeezing out the water

The edges of the grains can fuse together under this pressure, forming solid rock

Sometimes, for example in rough conditions in the sea, we get mixed sizes of sediment laid down. As layers build up, fine bits of silt or clay fuse together under pressure, binding the larger fragments together into rock.

Another process also helps the sediments to form rock. Water that passes between the gaps in grains can evaporate, leaving behind any solids that were in solution. The solid that comes out of solution acts like cement, sticking the grains of sediment together.

This is called **cementation**.

The mineral that acts as the cement between grains might have been dissolved from the sediment itself. Alternatively, it might have been in solution before the water seeped into the layers of sediment. Rocks formed like this are called **sedimentary rock**.

Sedimentary rocks are formed by the processes of compaction and cementation.

The individual pieces of sediment are compressed and 'cemented' together to form rock.

There are many different sedimentary rocks. Geologists can classify different sedimentary rocks by their **texture**. Their texture partly results from the size of the sediment that formed the rock.

Look at the examples:

Sandstone is made of sand with particles between 0.5 mm and 2 mm in diameter. These are called **medium grained**.

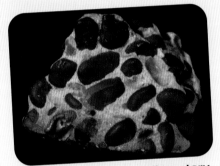
Conglomerate is a sedimentary rock made from a sediment containing pebbles. These are called **coarse grained** sedimentary rock.

Mudstone is classed as **fine grained** sedimentary rock. The particles of clay sediment are less than 0.5 mm in diameter.

From this lesson and your work in unit 8G we can say that sedimentary rocks:

- are **porous** (absorb water)
- usually have **fragmental** textures (grains that don't interlock)
- can contain fossils.

Q1 Sometimes fine particles of sediment (such as clay or silt) settle between pebbles. Under pressure from the layers above, the fine sediment can join together. This helps to bind the pebbles into a rock called conglomerate.

Is this description an example of compaction or cementation?

Q2 What else is likely to happen to form the conglomerate rock (as well as the process described in question 1)?

Observing texture

- Use a hand lens or microscope to examine some samples of sedimentary rock. You could observe rocks such as sandstone, chalk, limestone, shale, or breccia.
  a) Describe the sediment that has made the rock.
  b) Can you see any **mineral** 'cement' between grains in any of the rocks?

SUMMARY QUESTIONS

1 ☆ Copy these sentences. Complete them by filling in the gaps.

Sedimentary rock is formed by the processes of . . . and . . .

The p. . . increases as . . . of sediment and rock build up above.

This causes the edges of g. . . to fuse together, and water is squeezed out.

S. . . left behind act as a c. . . between the grains, forming rock.

2 ☆☆☆ Think of a situation from which a sedimentary rock with
  a) fine grains, and
  b) mixed grains, was formed.

Key words
cementation
compaction
fragmental
mineral
porous
sedimentary
texture

Looking at limestones

LEARN ABOUT

- trialling your ideas to solve a practical problem
- describing and evaluating your method and conclusions
- the composition and formation of limestones

What is limestone?

Limestone paving and tiles have become very popular. These are an attractive light beige colour. But there are lots of different rocks called limestone.

Limestones are sedimentary rocks. The main mineral in all limestones is calcite (**calcium carbonate, CaCO$_3$**). The calcite can precipitate out of water directly to form sediment or an evaporite rock. Stalactites and stalagmites build up as water evaporates from solution, leaving behind calcium carbonate.

Often the calcium carbonate has been concentrated into the 'hard bits' of sea creatures and plants. They use the calcite to make their shells and skeletons. When they die, these accumulate on the seabed. Over long periods of time, they form sedimentary rock.

Limestone is a popular building material

How much calcium carbonate in limestones?

SAFETY

Can you recall the reaction between calcium carbonate and dilute acid? (See page 110.)

You can use this reaction to find out the proportion of calcium carbonate in different types of limestone.

- Plan your investigation. Let your teacher check that the plan is safe.
- Carry out a trial run if necessary. You might need to modify your plan in some way.
- Record your results in a table.
- Put the limestones in order. Place the one containing the highest proportion of calcium carbonate at the top.
- Evaluate your working method and those of other groups. Suggest improvements and comment on the validity of your conclusions. Can you trust the order you arrived at?

Formation of limestones

Different types of limestone were formed under different conditions.

Shelly limestones
These formed from sediments of shells accumulated on ancient seabeds. Sea creatures extract calcium carbonate to form their shells. These are often broken up by water currents before settling as a sediment.

Brown limestone containing minerals of iron

In clear waters, these shells will be the main sediment collecting on the seabed. Then we find a high proportion of calcium carbonate in the limestone. If there are other sediments mixed with the shelly bits, then the proportion of calcium carbonate is reduced. For example, brown limestone has iron minerals mixed in with the calcium carbonate.

Chalks

We have already seen how **chalk** formed slowly over millions of years from the remains of **coccoliths**. The purity of the calcium carbonate (about 98%) in chalk means that there were few other sediments settling on the seabed at the same time.

One theory suggests that sea levels were very high at the time when chalk was laid down. So there was not much land exposed. This meant there was little sediment carried to the sea by rivers. At present, similar deposits of sediment are only found at the bottom of oceans well away from land.

Q1 Which part of Britain is famous for its 'white cliffs'?

● Other types of limestone

Coral reefs are made up of the shells of sea creatures that fasten themselves to the bottom of the sea in warm conditions. These reefs build up over time and form a very hard rock called **reef limestone**.

Q2 Do you think that selling coral to tourists should be banned? Why?

Sometimes calcium carbonate comes out of solution when some sea water evaporates off. If this happens in calm waters, for example in a lagoon, the tiny crystals of calcium carbonate that form will sink to the seabed. They form a fine white mud (called micrite). Under compaction this can form rock. The sediment is often mixed with mud so the rock formed is dark grey with very fine grains, called **lime 'mudstone'**.

The fine white mud of calcium carbonate can also coat other bits of sediment that roll gently across it. In effect you get tiny snowballs with an outer layer of calcium carbonate. These can go on to form another type of limestone (**oolitic limestone**).

In a sample of chalk you can see the remains of the tiny plants (coccoliths) that died millions of years ago, but you need a powerful electron microscope to do it.

The shells of corals form very hard deposits of calcium carbonate

Oolitic limestone

SUMMARY QUESTIONS

1 ☆ Copy these sentences. Complete them by filling in the gaps.

All limestones are s. . . rocks. Their main mineral is . . . carbonate.

Their characterictics depend on how they were f. . .

2 ☆☆☆ a) Read the information above and draw a 'spider diagram' with the word *limestone* in the middle. Your diagram should explain how each type of limestone mentioned is formed.

b) Link the way that a limestone is formed to its proportion of calcium carbonate.

Key words

calcium carbonate
chalk
coccoliths
coral
limestones
oolitic

LEARN ABOUT

■ how metamorphic rocks are formed
■ some examples of metamorphic rocks

● Slate – a metamorphic rock

Do you have many houses with slate roofs where you live? Have you ever seen slate being split to make tiles? Slate can be split into very thin sheets along one direction. Look at the photo:

Slate was made from mudstone or shale, both examples of sedimentary rock. In mudstone the clay minerals are mainly jumbled up. In shale some minerals are lined up as the rock formed under the moderate pressure of layers above.

Sometimes sedimentary rocks are subjected to very high temperatures and/or pressures. When this happens, chemical reactions take place in the solid rock. New minerals form and recrystallisation occurs.

No new elements can be added within the rock. However, those already in the original minerals are re-arranged to make the new minerals. The new rock formed is called a **metamorphic rock**.

Slate is formed under high pressure, caused by movements in the Earth's crust or very deep burial under many layers of rock. The new minerals in slate are all lined up in one direction. The crystals grow at right angles to the pressure. As the mineral crystals grow, the increased pressure on them forces them to line up.

Slate is a metamorphic rock

AMAZING SCIENCE!

The outer part of the Earth is divided into huge slabs of rock called tectonic plates. These plates are still moving at a rate of a few centimetres each year (about the rate at which your fingernails grow).

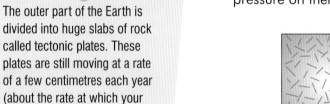

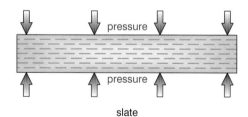

mudstone   slate

pressure

Q1 The new minerals in slate are made of the same atoms that were in the clay minerals. Explain this.

Slate is called a 'low grade' metamorphic rock. If mudstone and shale are subjected to higher pressures and temperatures, such as when mountains were formed, we get a rock called **schist**. This is 'medium grade' **metamorphism**. You can see bands of minerals running through the rock.

Then under even more extreme conditions, 'high grade' **gneiss** (pronounced 'nice') is made. Its bands of minerals stand out clearly.

Gneiss is a 'high grade' metamorphic rock made when mountains were formed

Baking rocks

Rocks can be heated up as they are buried. In general the temperature rises about 30°C for each kilometre we go down beneath the Earth's surface. But they are also subjected to more extreme heat from molten rock, called **magma**.

The magma rises towards the surface in areas where we find volcanoes. The Earth movements that build mountains also generate great heat. During metamorphism, the rocks may get very hot but they do not melt.

Marble can be formed by the action of heat on limestone or chalk.

Marble has 'sugary' like crystals as the calcite in limestone gets baked (without melting) and recrystallised.

Sandstones that are subjected to high pressure and temperature form metaquartzite, a very hard metamorphic rock.

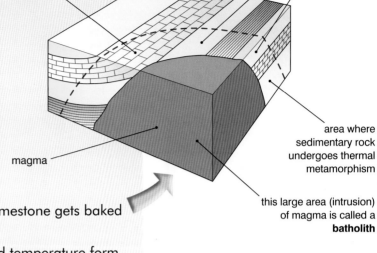

limestone changed to marble

sandstones changed to metaquartzite

magma

area where sedimentary rock undergoes thermal metamorphism

this large area (intrusion) of magma is called a **batholith**

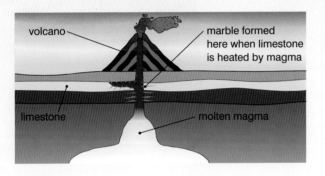

volcano

marble formed here when limestone is heated by magma

limestone

molten magma

Any type of rock can undergo metamorphism, but we see the greatest changes in sedimentary rocks.

The general characteristics of metamorphic rocks are:

- made of crystals that are often too small to see with the naked eye
- their crystals are usually interlocking, so the rocks are non-porous
- often have bands of minerals running through the rock
- no fossils, except distorted ones in 'low grade' metamorphic rock such as slate.

Why do you think there are 'streaks' running through some marbles?

The largest volcano in the Solar System is on Mars. Olympus Mons is 14 miles high and 341 miles across!

SUMMARY QUESTIONS

1 ☆ Copy these sentences. Complete them by filling in the gaps.

New rocks that have been formed by the action of . . . and/or heat (without . . . the rock) are called . . . rocks.

You can often see . . . of minerals running through the rock.

2 ☆☆ Draw a table showing sedimentary rocks in one column and the metamorphic rocks they form in the second column.

Key words

batholith
gneiss
magma
metamorphic
metamorphism
schist
slate

LEARN ABOUT
- how igneous rocks form
- the differences between igneous rocks

● Forming crystals

We looked at the hard rock, granite, in unit 8G. It is the hard, shiny rock you see on expensive kitchen worktops. It is also used sometimes for pillars and steps in buildings. Granite is an example of an **igneous** rock.

We saw on the previous page how molten rock, called magma, can rise towards the Earth's surface. Sometimes it actually escapes from the surface, as in a volcano.

The molten mixture of materials that breaks through the surface is called **lava**.

When molten rock (magma or lava) solidifies we get igneous rock formed.

As magma or lava cools down, the interlocking crystals which make up igneous rock form.

This lava contains a mixture of minerals and gas

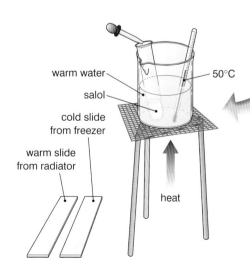

Why is granite used for kitchen worktops?

AMAZING SCIENCE!

Kilauea on Hawaii is the most active volcano in the world. It started erupting in 1983 and is still spewing out its runny lava today.

Crystal sizes

SAFETY

It is difficult to melt rock in a science lab. So in this investigation we will use a solid that melts at a suitable temperature. This will model what happens when molten rock **crystallises**.

The solid is called salol. You will investigate this question:

What effect does the rate of cooling have on the size of the crystals formed?

- Carry out the experiment shown opposite.
- Use the dropper to transfer a little molten salol to a warm and a cold microscope slide.
- You might have to add a small 'seed' crystal of salol to the warm slide.
- Use a hand lens to inspect the crystals carefully. What conclusion can you draw about the effect of temperature on the size of the crystals that grow?

warm water

salol

cold slide from freezer

warm slide from radiator

50°C

heat

Look at the two examples of igneous rock below:

The large crystals in **granite** were formed as molten rock cooled slowly under the ground, surrounded by thick layers of rock. It is called an **intrusive** igneous rock. (See the batholith on page 131.)

Gruesome science

A volcano on the island of Martinique in 1902 killed about 30 000 people in a nearby town as a cloud of hot gas, molten lava, chunks of rock and ash swept down its slopes.

The small crystals in **basalt** were formed as molten rock cooled quickly at or near the surface. The crystals are so small that you need a microscope to see them. Much of the ocean floor is made from basalt. It is called an **extrusive** igneous rock.

The slower the rate of cooling, the larger the crystals formed.

Q1 Why is granite called an 'intrusive' igneous rock and basalt 'extrusive'?

● Other types of igneous rock

Sometimes the lava that erupts from a volcano cools down so quickly that it doesn't have time to form crystals properly. They just have no time to grow. Then you get 'glassy' rock such as obsidian formed.

We also get a varying amount of gas in lava. Where there is a lot of gas ('frothy' lava), and the lava cools quickly, we get the rock pumice forming. It is riddled with holes where the gas bubbles get trapped.

Q2 Think of some factors that might affect how viscous (thick) and slow-moving lava is.

Obsidian has a 'glassy' appearance

A selection of igneous rocks

SUMMARY QUESTIONS

1 ☆ Copy these sentences. Complete them by filling in the gaps.

When molten rock (. . . or lava) cools down, it usually s. . . into crystals of . . . rock.

If the . . . cools down . . ., deep underground, then we get . . . crystals. Gr. . . is an example of such an . . . igneous rock.

If it cools down . . . at or near the surface, small crystals form. B. . . is an example of one of these . . . igneous rocks.

2 ☆☆☆ When an intrusion of magma cools down, the rate at which it cools differs the further you are from its edge. How do you think this affects the crystals forming in an intrusion? Draw a labelled diagram to show your ideas.

Key words

basalt
crystallise
extrusive
granite
igneous
intrusive
lava

LEARN ABOUT
- the minerals in igneous rocks
- the rock cycle

The minerals in igneous rocks

As well as texture, geologists also use chemical composition to classify rocks. In intrusive igneous rocks, with larger crystals, it is easy to see the different **minerals**.

Compare the granite and gabbro below:

Granite

Gabbro

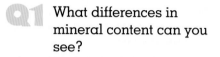

Q1 What differences in mineral content can you see?

Q2 Why will the mineral content of different igneous rocks vary?

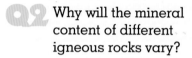

CHALLENGE

Test some other examples of igneous rock to see if they are more like granite or gabbro. Set up a spreadsheet to do your calculations in this experiment.

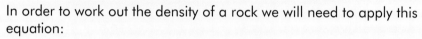

How dense are igneous rocks?

In order to work out the density of a rock we will need to apply this equation:

$$density = \frac{mass}{volume}$$

First of all work out the density of granite.

- Use a balance to find out the mass of your sample of granite rock.

- Measure its volume in a displacement can as shown.

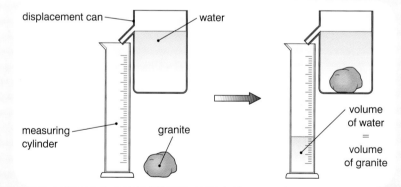

displacement can — water

measuring cylinder

granite

volume of water = volume of granite

AMAZING SCIENCE!

When Krakatau (a volcano near to Java) erupted in 1883 the sound of the blast could be heard over 4000 km away. It produced so much ash that the average temperature of the Earth fell by 0.25°C.

- Use the equation above to work out the density.

- Now repeat the process for another igneous rock called gabbro.
  a) Which of the two igneous rocks has the higher density?
  b) Explain why you think there is a difference in density between igneous rocks.

Iron content of igneous rock

Granite is a light coloured igneous rock. It is rich in the elements silicon and oxygen (present in **silicate** minerals). Granite is said to be a silica-rich rock, containing the mineral, **quartz**. On the other hand, **gabbro** is much darker in colour. It is rich in minerals that contain iron, called mafic minerals.

The minerals containing iron are more dense, so gabbro has a higher density than granite. Basalt is another igneous rock high in iron-bearing minerals. It is like gabbro in its mineral content. However, it was cooled down much more quickly when it formed. Its crystals are too small to see with the naked eye.

In general igneous rocks:

- are made of interlocking crystals
- are hard and non-porous.

However, if they are formed from a spray of lava, they can land as ash. We have also seen pumice and obsidian on page 133.

The rock cycle

The three main types of rock – sedimentary, metamorphic and igneous – are involved in a long cycle of change. Some changes happen rapidly but some can take thousands or millions of years.

The formation of igneous rocks on the Earth's surface is a quick process. Lava hitting cold sea water solidifies in seconds. However, the burial, compaction and cementation of sedimentary rocks is a very slow process. It can take millions of years.

The changes can be summarised in the **rock cycle**.

Some of the changes shown in the rock cycle happen continuously. These include the deposition of sediment on the seabed or lava pouring out from the ocean floor between continents. However, other changes have huge time gaps between them. An example is the mountain-forming Earth movements that happen over large areas, forming metamorphic rock.

Q3 Read the information above. Link the changes mentioned to the type of rock they form.

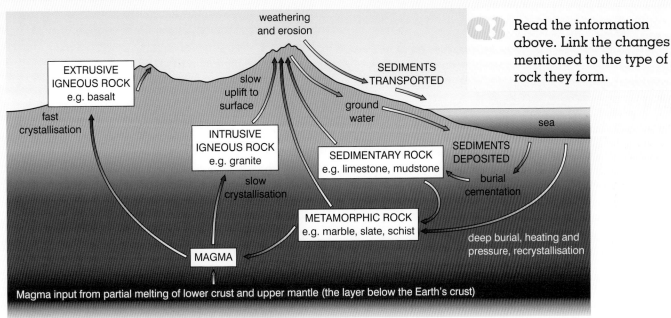

Magma input from partial melting of lower crust and upper mantle (the layer below the Earth's crust)

SUMMARY QUESTIONS

1 ☆ Copy the sentences below. Complete them by filling in the gaps.

Granite is a low ... igneous rock that is rich in ..., whereas gabbro is a ... density igneous rock rich in ... bearing minerals.

The rock ... shows how the processes that form igneous, ... and metamorphic rocks are linked together.

2 ☆☆ Get a blank copy of the rock cycle and fill in as much information as you can using the knowledge you have gained in this unit and in unit 8G.

Key words

gabbro
granite
minerals
quartz
rock cycle
silicate

IDEAS AND EVIDENCE

Drifting continents – the story of Alfred Wegener

The idea that continents are moving around on the surface of the Earth is difficult to believe. And it was in 1915 when Alfred Wegener first suggested his theory of continental drift. Few of his fellow-scientists took his ideas seriously. It took about 50 years for them to come around to his way of thinking. Unfortunately, Alfred had died many years before that happened.

Alfred was born in Berlin in 1880. He was the son of a minister who ran an orphanage. As a boy, he read everything he could about Greenland, and dreamt that one day he would get to explore there. He spent his youth studying in Germany and Austria and went on to get a PhD in astronomy.

Alfred decided to change his interests to meteorology. Studying the weather in a scientific way was quite a new branch of science. Then in 1906 he was asked to be an expedition's meteorologist on a trip to Greenland. He went again in 1912 and completed the longest crossing of the ice cap on foot.

Alfred was interested in many different areas of science. One day he was studying a scientific paper on fossils when he noticed how alike fossils found in Africa and South America were. This made him curious. Looking at an atlas of the world, people had already spotted that the coastlines of Africa and South America looked like two pieces in a jigsaw. But Alfred went further and suggested that at one time, millions of years ago, they had been joined together. He thought they had slowly drifted apart.

Alfred Wegener (1880–1930) on one of his expeditions to Greenland

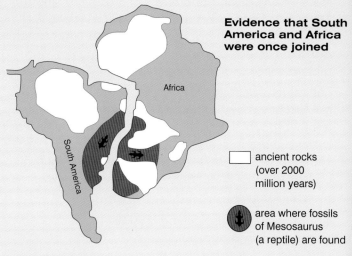

Evidence that South America and Africa were once joined

Africa

South America

☐ ancient rocks (over 2000 million years)

🦎 area where fossils of Mesosaurus (a reptile) are found

He could offer scientific evidence to support his idea. As well as the matching fossil evidence, he also used fossils of tropical plants found in the Arctic. They must have grown on land much nearer the equator millions of years ago. He argued that the land had drifted thousands of miles. He also noticed matches between the types of rock found in Africa and South America. There were also matching rocks across other continents, for example between Scotland and North America. This led him to think that millions of years ago all the continents had been joined together. He called this 'super-continent' Pangaea.

Pangaea

However, scientists already had a theory that could explain the similar fossils on different continents. They believed that in the past, bridges of land linked the continents to each other. But, they argued, the bridges must have sunk below the oceans by now. And Alfred couldn't explain how the continents had moved. So his ideas were never accepted in his lifetime.

In 1930 Alfred led his last expedition to Greenland and was never to return. He was lost in a snowstorm and died there. Over 20 years later scientists discovered direct evidence of Alfred's drifting continents. Exploring the ocean floor, they found new rock forming on either side of massive cracks that run between continents. Then the old 'land bridge' theory was dropped. A new theory, called plate tectonics, that could explain Alfred's ideas became accepted by the scientific community.

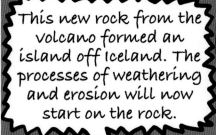

This new rock from the volcano formed an island off Iceland. The processes of weathering and erosion will now start on the rock.

- **Sedimentary rocks** form when layers of sediment are buried under more recent deposits. Under the pressure (**compaction**), and with the help of mineral 'cements' (left behind when water evaporates from between the particles of sediment – **cementation**), rocks are formed.
- **Metamorphic rocks** from when existing rock experiences high pressure and/or temperature (without melting). The original rock has its structure and possibly its minerals changed. Bands of minerals are often visible if the metamorphic rock is formed under high pressure.
- **Igneous rocks** form when molten rock solidifies. Slow cooling, inside the Earth's crust, produces rock with large crystals, such as granite. Faster cooling, at or near the Earth's surface, produces rock with small crystals, such as basalt.
- We can summarise the processes of rock formation in the **rock cycle** (see page 135).

Hold on, remember most rocks are mixtures... So they don't have a chemical formula like a compound.

But sometimes sedimentary rocks have really hard minerals joining their grains together, you know.

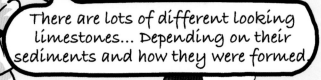

There are lots of different looking limestones... Depending on their sediments and how they were formed.

DANGER! AVOID THESE COMMON ERRORS

Some sedimentary rocks crumble easily when you rub them. However, there are also some that are hard because their mineral cement, such as quartz, is strong.

Metamorphic rocks don't all have bands visible in the rock. High pressure causes the banding. So if a rock is changed by only high temperatures, you will not see bands. The crystals in metamorphic rocks are often so small you need a microscope to see them. This is also the case with the crystals in extrusive igneous rock, such as basalt. In fact some igneous rocks, such as obsidian, form so quickly that crystals don't have time to form! However, most types of igneous rocks are made up of crystals.

The vast timescales involved in geological history are hard for anyone to imagine. But if the history of the Earth was represented by a 24-hour clock, then humans only arrived on Earth at about one second to midnight!

Key words

cementation
compaction
igneous
metamorphic
rock cycle
sedimentary

REVIEW QUESTIONS
Understanding and applying concepts

1 Identify the rocks below as igneous, metamorphic or sedimentary.

Rock X: It is made from plate-like crystals all lined up in the same direction. The rock fragment has parallel flat sides where it has been cleaved.

Rock Y: There are particles of sand visible held together by an orangey-brown mineral. Bits of sand crumble off the surface of the rock quite easily.

Rock Z: There are three different types of interlocking crystal arranged randomly in this hard rock.

2 Geologists believe that the continents have moved thousands of miles from their original positions. How do the coal mines in Britain provide evidence for this theory?

3 a Is limestone an igneous, metamorphic or sedimentary rock?
   b Explain how limestone is changed into marble.
   c Why are some types of marble almost pure white, but others have streaks of colour running through them?
   d Explain how slate is formed from mudstone.
   e Why is slate called a 'low grade' metamorphic rock, whereas gneiss is called 'high grade'?

4 a i) Name *two* igneous rocks made up of large crystals.
      ii) What do we call this type of igneous rock?
      iii) Under what conditions is this type of rock formed?
   b i) Name an igneous rock with very small crystals.
      ii) What do we call this type of igneous rock?
      iii) Under what conditions is this type of rock formed?
   c Explain the difference we find in the size of crystals in igneous rocks, using particle theory where necessary.

Ways with words

5 Write a story imagining you are a particle in a lump of granite. Describe your many adventures before arriving at your 'not-so final' resting place in the granite!

  You might like to present your story as a comic strip with a commentary.

Making more of maths

6 Look at the two graphs below showing the mineral content of granite and gabbro:

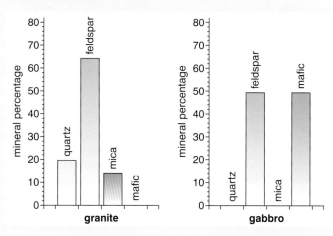

   a Show this information on pie charts for each rock.
   b Gabbro is more dense than granite. Deduce which is the dense mineral in gabbro.
   c A piece of the mineral quartz has a volume of $47\,cm^3$ and mass of $126.9\,g$. What is the density of quartz?
   d Which metal do mafic minerals contain?

7 The Earth is about 4600 million years old. You can represent this time on a time-line 92 metres long.

a The first bacteria appeared on Earth 3000 million years ago. Where would this appear on the time-line if zero is 4600 million years ago?

b Dinosaurs became extinct 65 million years ago. Where would this appear on the time-line?

c The first flowering plants have been put on the line at 90 metres. How long ago did they appear on Earth?

Thinking skills

8 Look at the rocks below:

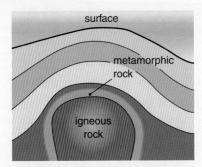

surface

metamorphic rock

igneous rock

From your knowledge of rock formation, suggest the order in which the events to form the rock structure above occurred.

Extension questions

9 Decide on a question to investigate on some aspect of volcanoes that interests you.

Use a variety of sources to gather information and present your findings as a poster.

10 Find out how the Himalayan mountains were formed.

SAT-STYLE QUESTIONS

1 Cath and Des were investigating how rocks can be worn down.

They made six cubes from plaster of Paris. They weighed the cubes then put them in a tin can with a lid. They shook them for 30 seconds then weighed the six largest blocks again, making sure no bits were lost from the can. They replaced the blocks in the can and repeated this several times.

Here is a graph of their results:

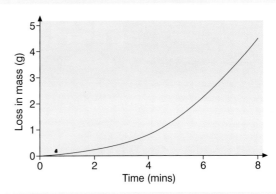

a Name the process Cath and Des were modelling. (1)

b Why did the blocks lose mass? (1)

c What happens to the edges of the cubes in their experiment? (1)

d If they weighed the tin can plus its contents before and after the experiment, what should they find?

A The mass had decreased after the experiment.

B The mass had increased after the experiment.

C The mass remained the same. (1)

e i) What do we call the rock formed from fragments of rock that settle in layers? (1)

ii) If these rocks are put under high pressure and baked at high temperatures, what type of rock forms? (1)

f When molten lava erupts into the sea, a glassy rock, called obsidian, forms. Explain why obsidian contains no crystals. (1)

g Which rock formed more slowly – basalt or chalk? Explain your answer. (2)

Key words

Unscramble these:

egtrain
sougine
teardesinmy
cocomatpin

81

Heating, cooling

What's it all about?

In unit 71 on energy resources, you learned about fossil fuels. If you hold a lump of coal, you are holding a store of energy that is hundreds of millions of years old. When you burn the coal, things get difficult.

Burning coal releases energy as heat. Heat energy is tricky – it tries to escape. You may want to warm your home, or have a barbecue. The heat energy from the burning fuel spreads out. Perhaps you boil a kettle and make a hot drink. The drink cools down as energy escapes from it. Even in an insulated cup, it will soon be cold.

In this unit, you will learn about how heat energy moves about, and why.

 What do you remember?

You already know about:
- keeping things warm.
- how materials change state.
- what happens when fuels burn.
- the particle model of solids, liquids and gases.

1   A material which helps to keep things warm is a good . . .

   conductor   indicator
   insulator   radiator

2   When fuels burn, they release their store of:

   electricity   **energy**   fossils   **oxygen**

3   Which of these is *not* a state of matter?

   gas   liquid   steam   solid

4   A liquid can change to a gas by (choose *two*):

   boiling   condensing
   evaporating   melting

Getting warm?

QUESTIONS

It's winter at Scientifica High. Do you agree with what the different characters have to say? How would you answer these questions?

a) If you leave the door open on a cold day, what comes in? What goes out?

b) Do warm clothes make you warm, or stop you from getting cold?

c) What happens to your temperature when you catch a cold?

d) Why is it colder at night than during the day?

Taking temperatures

LEARN ABOUT
- the Celsius temperature scale
- thermometers

No hiding place

Imagine that you are walking across the Arizona desert. A rattlesnake is after you. You hurry into a dark cave to hide. It's no good! A rattlesnake can see you in the dark. It has a special 'eye', which can see warm objects, and your body is warm.

Humans, like other mammals, are warm-blooded. Our bodies have a **temperature** close to 37°C (**degrees Celsius**). This means that, in the UK, we are usually warmer than our surroundings.

The police and other emergency services can make use of this. Suppose you are lost in the snow. It's night-time. A search helicopter flies overhead, equipped with a heat-sensitive camera. It can spot your warm body against the background of the cold snow. It swoops down to rescue you.

The police sometimes use heat-sensitive cameras to watch suspected criminals (and their cars) at night, without having to switch on any lights. People and cars are warmer than their surroundings. The car on the right has just turned off the road – you can even make out its track, because its tyres make the road warmer.

Q1 Look at the photo. How do colder and warmer objects appear in the photo?

Feeling warm

We can't 'see' warm objects the way a rattlesnake can, but our bodies are sensitive to temperature. When you go outside in the morning, you soon know if it's a freezing cold or boiling hot day. Our bodies are covered in nerve-endings, that detect temperature. They help us to judge how hot things are.

If you are unwell, the doctor or nurse may touch your forehead. They want to know if your temperature is 'above normal'. Because our nerves are **sensitive**, we can detect quite a small rise in temperature.

Am I getting warm?

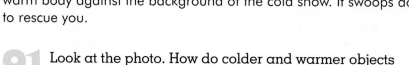

Getting in hot water

- Take two bowls of cold water. Add a little hot water to one. Try this:
  a) Put your right hand in one, then in the other. Can you tell the difference? Use a thermometer to check that your answer is correct.
  b) Now put a hand in each bowl at the same time. Can you tell the difference? Is this a better way to compare temperatures?

- Devise a test to find out how small a difference in temperature you can detect. Discuss how you would test whether some members of the class were more sensitive than others.

● Getting scientific

In science, we don't just rely on our nerves to detect temperature. We use **thermometers**. They show the temperature in °C.

There are many different types of thermometer. They all rely on something that changes as the temperature changes.

Liquid-in-glass thermometer: the alcohol or mercury expands as it gets warmer, and rises up the tube.
Electronic thermometer: the sensor's resistance changes, and the display shows the temperature.
Liquid-crystal thermometer: different colours show up as the temperature changes.

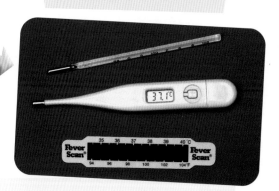

Bacteria have been discovered that can live in super-hot water at over 100°C!

Q2 Many cars have a thermometer which shows the temperature outside. Which type of thermometer would be best for this?

The drawing shows some important temperatures on the **Celsius scale** of temperature.

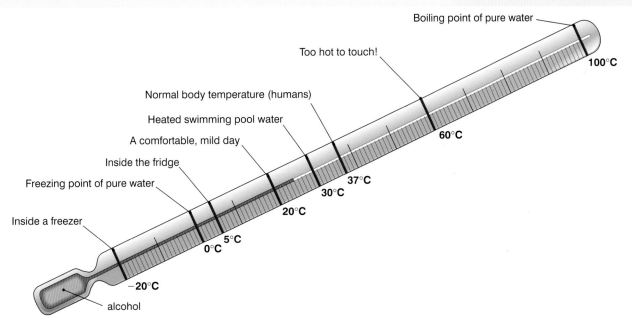

- Boiling point of pure water — 100°C
- Too hot to touch!
- Normal body temperature (humans)
- 60°C
- Heated swimming pool water
- A comfortable, mild day
- 37°C
- Inside the fridge
- 30°C
- Freezing point of pure water
- 20°C
- Inside a freezer
- 5°C
- 0°C
- −20°C
- alcohol

SUMMARY QUESTIONS

1 ☆ What instrument do we use to measure temperature?

2 ☆ What is the name of the temperature scale used in science? Can you name another temperature scale?

3 ☆ At what temperature does pure water boil? At what temperature does it freeze?

4 ☆☆ 'The temperature of ice is 0°C.' Do you agree?

5 ☆☆☆ Make a list of some different uses of thermometers. Find out the type of thermometer used in each case.

Key words

Celsius scale
degrees C (°C)
sensitive
temperature
thermometer

Getting hotter, getting colder

LEARN ABOUT
- why things cool down or warm up
- how heat energy flows

Cooling off

In the winter, you need more food than in the summer. Your body works hard to stay at 37°C, but, on a cold day, energy escapes from you more quickly. In very hot weather, you may not feel like eating at all.

Usually, we are warmer than our surroundings. Energy escapes from our bodies so, to remain at 37°C, we must release the energy supplied by our food.

Any object that is warmer than its surroundings loses energy like this. Think about what happens when you make a cup of tea. It starts off hot (close to 100°C), but soon cools down. Eventually it reaches the same temperature as the room.

LINK UP TO BIOLOGY

There's more about how we release the energy from our food in Unit 8B.

Sharing energy

In the past, people had an ingenious way of cooking. They heated stones in a fire until they were very hot. Then they put them in a pot with some food. Energy spread from the stones into the food and cooked it.

Energy moves from a warmer object to a colder one. Energy moving like this is called **heat energy**. The warmer object gets colder and the colder object gets warmer. The energy of the warmer object hasn't disappeared, it has been shared between the two objects.

Heat energy is moving around like this all the time. You just need to know the temperatures of different objects, and you will be able to predict which way the heat energy will flow.

Q1 Look at the picture of the lab. What is the hottest thing you can see? How is Molly making use of the heat energy that spreads out from this very hot object?

AMAZING SCIENCE!

The giant freezers where manufacturers store frozen food for a long time are at −60°C.

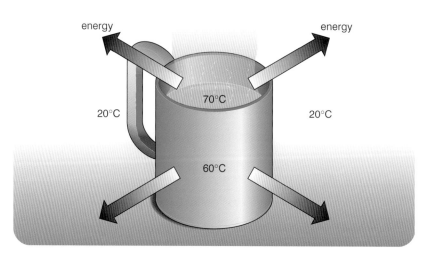

energy   energy

70°C

20°C   20°C

60°C

● Warming up

Hot drinks cool down and cold drinks warm up. We say that heat energy escapes from hot objects, so does 'cold energy' escape from cold objects?

That's not the scientific way of explaining things. There's only heat energy. A cold object warms up because heat energy spreads into it from its surroundings.

A fridge is a clever way of making things colder than their surroundings. It has very cold shelves; heat energy spreads from food and drinks into the cold shelves. Then the fridge pumps the heat energy out. You can feel the heat coming from the back of the fridge.

Q2 You take a cold can of drink from the fridge and put it on the table. Draw a diagram to show how heat energy flows. What happens to the temperature of the can?

In this special photo, the colours tell you how cold things are. Purple and blue show the lowest temperatures; red is the warmest.

The flow of heat

● Sketch a room. It could be a lab, a kitchen, or some other room. Include hot things and cold things.
  a) Use colours to show the different temperatures. (The photo of the fridge may give you some ideas.)
  b) Add arrows to show how heat energy is flowing in the room.

Close the door. You're letting the cold in!

But there's no such thing as cold!

SUMMARY QUESTIONS

1 ☆ Copy and complete this sentence:

Heat energy flows from a . . . object to a . . . one.

2 ☆☆ Look at the photo of the fridge. Which shelf is the coldest? Name an item that has just been put in the fridge. How can you tell?

3 ☆☆ Look at the picture of the lab on the opposite page. Name an object that is colder than its surroundings. Use the idea of heat energy to explain what will happen to this object's temperature.

4 ☆☆☆ You make a hot drink, and leave it on the table.
  a) Choose the graph that shows how the drink's temperature will change.
  b) Describe an experiment you could do to check your answer.

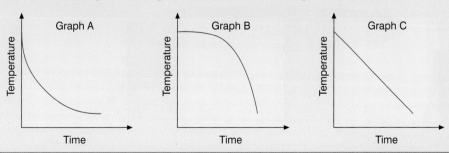

Graph A — Temperature / Time

Graph B — Temperature / Time

Graph C — Temperature / Time

Key words

heat energy

Conduction, insulation

8B

LEARN ABOUT
- thermal conductors
- thermal insulators

Slowing the flow

Heat energy is always escaping from our bodies – about 100 joules (J) every second. In cold weather, we try to slow down this flow by wearing suitable clothes – coats, hats, scarves, etc. Perhaps you think of these as 'warm clothes', but they aren't necessarily warm. In fact, when you wear them out-of-doors on a cold day, they are 'cold clothes'.

Clothes for cold weather are made of materials like wool. Wool is a good insulating material – a **thermal insulator**. If you wear a woollen jacket on a cold day, its temperature is about 37°C on the inside, because it is warmed by your body. It is perhaps 30°C colder on the outside. Although that's a big temperature difference, heat energy flows only slowly.

Insulating clothing keeps your body heat in on a cold day. A hat can save up to 50% of the heat loss from your head.

Q1 Explain why knights in shining armour wore thick linen undergarments beneath their armour.

This experiment can show which metal is the best thermal conductor. The temperature sensor detects the increasing temperature at the cold end of the rod.

Faster flow

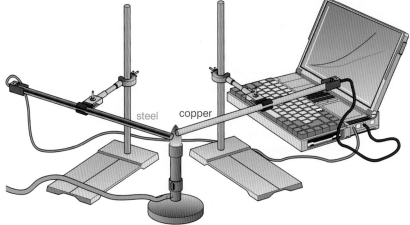

steel   copper

Metals are good **thermal conductors**. Heat energy can flow through them easily. That's why radiators are made of steel – energy can spread out from the hot water inside them into the room.

Some metals are better at conducting than others. Copper is twice as good as aluminium, and steel is a poorer conductor than both copper and aluminium.

Other materials, such as plastic and glass, are good insulators.

Seeing where the heat goes

- Thermocolour film is a sheet of special plastic. If you warm it, it changes colour.
  a) The photo shows an experiment. The student wore a glove on one hand, and then pressed on the sheet with both hands. Can you explain what he observed?
  b) Try out some other experiments using thermocolour film.

Hot to handle

Our senses sometimes deceive us. A metal ruler feels cold when you touch it; a plastic one feels warm, even though a thermometer would show that both are at the same temperature.

- The metal ruler is at room temperature. When you touch it, heat energy flows quickly out of your finger. Your nerve endings get cold, and tell your brain that the metal is cold.
- Plastic is different. When you touch the plastic ruler, heat can't flow from your finger, so your nerve endings stay warm.

Wool is a good insulator because, mostly, it isn't wool! Most of the volume of a woolly jumper is air. And air is a good insulator.

Solids are better thermal conductors than liquids. Gases are very bad thermal conductors.

A misunderstanding

Benson took a can of cold drink from the fridge. He wanted to warm it up. He said, 'I'll wrap the can in this warm blanket! It will be warm enough to drink!'

Q2 Benson was wrong! Explain why the can would warm up more quickly *without* the blanket. Explain how he could have warmed the can even more quickly.

If you wrap a cold *person* in a blanket, they will warm up. Our bodies are constantly producing heat, and the blanket prevents it from escaping. We're different from a cold can of drink.

SUMMARY QUESTIONS

1 ☆ a) A material which allows heat to flow through easily is called a thermal . . .
   b) Heat cannot flow easily through a material which is a . . . . . .

2 ☆ Put the following words in the correct boxes:

plastic   air   copper

good thermal insulator				good thermal conductor

Key words

thermal conductor
thermal insulator

Expanding and explaining

LEARN ABOUT

- solids, liquids and gases expanding
- using the particle theory to explain expansion
- using the particle theory to explain conduction

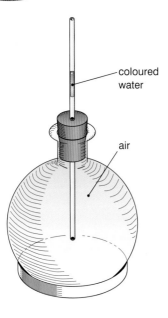

coloured water

air

● The oldest thermometer

Over 2000 years ago, the Greek scientist Archimedes ('Eureka!') invented a thermometer. You can see it in the picture.

On hot days, the air in the flask expanded and pushed the water up the tube. On cold days, the air contracted and the water moved down again.

Archimedes had noticed that air expands when it is heated. It only expands a little. That's why he designed his thermometer with a big flask containing a lot of air, and a thin tube so that the water would move further when the air expanded.

● Expanding solids

Railway lines are designed to survive temperatures as high as 40°C, but recent hot summers have caused some to expand and buckle

Most materials **expand** when they get hotter, and **contract** when they get colder. Solids, liquids and gases all behave like this. Sometimes, it can be a problem.

On very hot days, railway lines may expand so much that they buckle. Then the trains have to stop running. In Australia, electricity cables between pylons expand and droop down. When they touch vegetation, sparks fly and a bush fire may start.

Experimenting with expansion

- Watch some demonstrations of solids expanding.

● Particle explanations – expansion

You have studied the **particle model** of matter. Remember that everything is made of particles, too small to see. In a solid, the particles are packed closely together. They vibrate about their fixed positions.

● When a solid is cold, its particles vibrate a little.
● When the solid gets hotter, its particles have more energy, so they vibrate more. Each particle pushes on its neighbours, and takes up more space, and so the solid gets bigger – it expands.

Take care! The particles don't get bigger, they just take up more space.

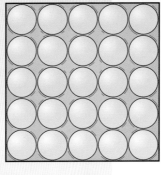
cold

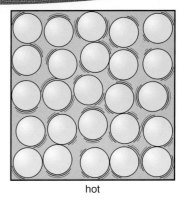
hot

● Particle explanations – conduction

We can use the same model to explain how heat energy spreads through a solid material.

● At the hot end, the particles vibrate a lot. They jostle their neighbours and share their energy.
● Gradually the vibration spreads along the solid. The particles at the cold end begin to vibrate more – they have more energy.

You can see that heat energy spreads through a solid just by **random** bumpings of one particle with another.

In a liquid, the particles are less tightly packed, so they don't share their energy so easily. In a gas, the particles are far apart, so they share their energy even less. So gases are the worst thermal conductors, solids are the best.

heat energy spreading

hot   cold

SUMMARY QUESTIONS

1 ☆ Copy these sentences and replace the words in italics with the correct scientific words.

When a steel bar is heated, it *gets bigger*. When it cools down, it *shrinks*.

2 ☆☆ Explain how a liquid-in-glass thermometer makes use of expansion.

3 ☆☆☆ The drawing shows a glass rod. It is hot at one end, cold at the other.
 a) Imagine that you have a powerful microscope and you can see the particles of the glass. Draw what you would expect to see in the areas circled.
 b) If no heat escaped from the rod, how would the movement of the particles change? Explain your answer.

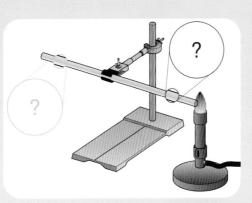

ICT CHALLENGE

Search the Internet for an animated (moving) diagram that shows how the particles move as a solid is heated.

Key words

contract
expand
particle model
random

LEARN ABOUT
- radiation of heat energy
- convection of heat energy

Heat energy spreading out

Do you remember the rattlesnake on page 142? It could see in the dark. It has a special 'eye', which can detect heat energy coming from its prey.

infra-red radiation

Heat energy radiates in straight lines, just like light

Heat energy from a warm prey reaches the snake's eye, but this isn't another example of conduction. **Radiation** is another way in which heat energy leaves a warm object. Every object which is warmer than its surroundings loses energy by radiation, because of the difference in temperatures. When heat energy travels as radiation, we call it **infra-red radiation**.

The Sun is a very large, very hot object, and so it radiates energy at a great rate. We are used to feeling the heat energy radiated by the Sun, warming our skin on a sunny day.

Q1 How do we know that heat radiation can travel through a vacuum (empty space)? (Think about radiation from the Sun.)

Heat moving upwards

The vultures in the photograph can't take off first thing in the morning. They are waiting for the wind to blow. What makes the wind blow? No, it's not the trees waving their leaves. (You knew that.)

Everyone knows that hot air rises. This gives us a clue to the wind. Wind is moving air, and moving air carries energy. Like most energy on Earth, the energy of wind comes from the Sun.

Heat and light energy from the Sun warms the air. Warm air rises, and colder air flows in to replace it. This is called a **convection current**.

Ready for lift-off – these vultures make use of rising air

Seeing and using convection currents

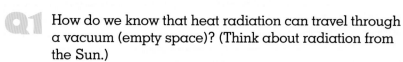

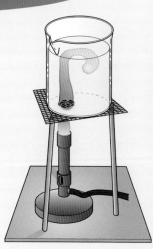

You can have convection currents in liquids as well as gases. The picture shows one way to see how water moves when it is heated.

- Try out this experiment, and some ways of using convection currents in the air.

Safety: Use forceps to handle the coloured crystals.

The colouring in the water shows how the convection current flows when the water is heated

● Explaining convection

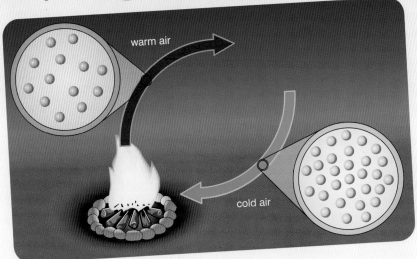

warm air

cold air

Convection is a way in which heat energy can move around in air or water (or anything else which can flow). We can explain it using the particle model, together with what we know about forces.

● When air is heated, it expands. Its particles move slightly further apart, so it becomes less dense. (Its **density** has decreased.)

● Because it is less dense than the surrounding air, it floats upwards like a cork in water. (The **upthrust** force on it is greater than the downward force of gravity.)

● Now colder air moves in to replace it. When this air is heated, it too floats upwards.

Weather forecasters need to understand convection currents in air. They try to predict which way the wind will blow, so that they can tell us if warm or cold air is on its way.

The ocean currents are also caused by convection. They carry large amounts of heat energy around the world.

LINK UP TO
SCIENCE

When you studied the water cycle, you learned how rising air carries water vapour upwards.

Clouds like these are carried along by convection currents in the air

SUMMARY QUESTIONS

1 ☆ What processes are being described here?
   a) Heat energy travelling along a metal rod.
   b) Heat energy spreading out from a hot object, travelling through a vacuum.
   c) Heat energy being carried by a current of water or air.

2 ☆☆ Why are convection currents important for people who enjoy hang-gliding or hot-air ballooning?

3 ☆☆ Explain how a convection current makes the smoke from an open fire go up the chimney. Include a diagram in your answer.

4 ☆☆☆ Every object radiates energy. Use this idea to explain why it is coldest just before dawn.

Key words

convection
convection current
density
infra-red radiation
radiation
upthrust

Conserving energy

● Weather worries

The Gulf Stream is a giant ocean current. It carries heat energy from tropical areas and helps to give the British Isles a mild climate.

Some scientists are concerned that global warming may change the flow of the Gulf Stream, so that we will no longer be warmed by its waters. Then our climate will be colder, and we will have to adjust the way we live. We will have to redesign our houses so that we can survive colder winters.

People who live in cold countries need houses designed to keep energy in

● Switching off

You can tell from this photo where energy is escaping from the houses. Yellow and orange are hot; purple and blue are the coldest.

If you turned off the heating in your house, it would gradually cool down. It might not be cold in the summer, but in the winter, it would be as cold as the outside, and you would feel very chilly.

Heat leaves a house in all of the ways you have been learning about:

- Heat escapes by **conduction** through the floor into the ground below. It conducts through the walls, windows and ceilings.
- Because the house is warmer than its surroundings, heat escapes by **convection**. Warm air rises above the house, and cold air replaces it. Draughts are convection currents, too.
- Some energy also escapes by **radiation**, because the outer walls are a little warmer than the surroundings.

All of the energy that escapes is energy that has been paid for. Fuel and electricity cost money. It makes sense to **conserve** energy, because that saves money. There is another reason, as you saw when you studied energy. Our use of energy damages the environment.

Q1 Describe as fully as you can how our use of energy is damaging the environment.

● Keeping it in

There are lots of ways of making sure a house loses less energy.

- Add **insulation** to the walls and floor. Then heat energy won't conduct away so quickly. Thick carpets and double-glazed windows help, too.
- If the loft is insulated, the roof will be colder, and less energy will be lost by convection currents.
- Stopping draughts that come in through doors and windows saves energy. Fill any gaps, and use thick curtains.

Turning down the thermostat for the central heating so that the house is a little cooler helps a lot, too. You might need to wear warmer clothes. Turn the temperature down by 1°C and you could cut fuel bills by 10%.

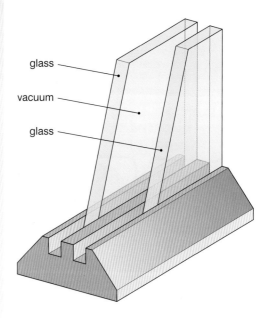
glass
vacuum
glass

A double-glazed window has two sheets of glass with a vacuum in between. Heat energy cannot escape through a vacuum by conduction or convection.

Q2 Look at the 'thermogram' of the houses on the opposite page. How can you tell that they are losing heat quickly through their windows? Do you think that any of the houses has an insulated loft?

Ideal homes

- Use a model house with a small light bulb inside, to heat it. Switch off the heating and investigate the pattern of the temperature inside the house as it gets colder.
  Investigate how you can reduce the rate at which energy escapes. Your teacher must check your plan before you start.

SUMMARY QUESTIONS

1 ☆ Give two reasons why it is a good idea to reduce the amount of energy we use to heat our houses.

2 ☆ Fitting thick carpets can help stop heat escaping through the floor. Does this reduce conduction, convection or radiation?

3 ☆☆ Explain why heat cannot escape through a double-glazed window by either conduction or convection. (See the picture at the top of this page.)

Key words

conduction
conserve
convection
insulation
radiation

LEARN ABOUT
- particle explanations of changes of state
- finding melting and boiling points

Professor Plum, in the kitchen, with the deadly ice-cube.

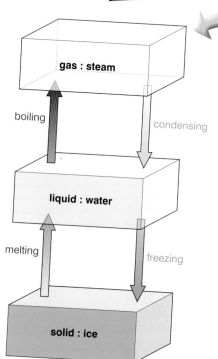

Murder in the kitchen

A body lies dead on the floor, stabbed through the heart. There is no sign of the weapon, but the victim's clothes are damp. The detective suddenly realises how the dreadful deed was done – with a knife made of ice.

Ice is very hard, and can have sharp edges. The murderer hoped that the ice would melt and then evaporate, leaving no trace of the weapon. The detective arrived on the scene too soon.

Ice is just frozen water. However, if you weren't familiar with it, you might be very surprised to find that a runny liquid can turn into a hard, brittle solid. And it can disappear completely when it boils and becomes steam.

Melting and freezing, boiling and condensing – you already know about these **changes of state**.

Particle explanations

We can use the particle model to explain what happens when a substance changes state.

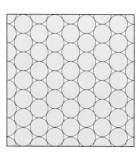

In a solid, the particles are closely packed together. Each particle sticks tightly to its neighbours, so that all the particles are held firmly in place.

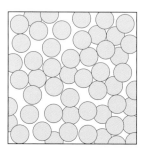

In a liquid, the particles are less tightly packed. They have started to break away from each other. It is easier for particles to slip past each other.

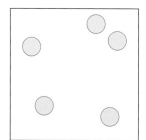

In a gas, the particles are far apart, so they can move around easily. The particles in a gas have more energy than those in a solid or a liquid.

Q1 Try to picture a liquid freezing so that it becomes a solid. Describe what happens to the particles of the liquid. Now do the same for the particles of a gas as it condenses to become a liquid.

Imagine heating a solid. Its particles vibrate more and more strongly. Eventually the vibrations are so strong that the particles start to break apart. They are more free to move about – the solid has become a liquid.

Now imagine heating the liquid. Its particles gain more energy, and eventually they fly apart – the liquid has become a gas.

Meanwhile, back in the kitchen . . .

If you put a pan of water on the stove, it will soon come to the boil. Leave it there for a while, and the water boils away. This can take a long time; the energy you are supplying is needed by the water particles, so that they can break free and become steam. The graph shows that, while the water is boiling, its temperature stays at 100°C – that's its **boiling point**.

If you want to make ice cubes, you put water in the freezer. It takes a while for the ice to form, because the freezer has to remove energy from the water, so that its particles will slow down and bond tightly together. While the water is freezing, its temperature stays at 0°C – its **freezing point**.

Q2 Sketch a graph to show how you think the temperature of water changes when you put it in the freezer.

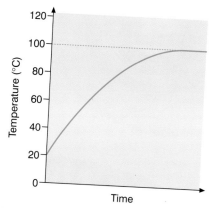

When you heat water on the stove, its temperature rises until the water boils. Then it remains steady – that's how you can find the boiling point of water.

Freezing hot

SAFETY

Salol is a kind of wax. If you warm it up in a beaker of warm water, it melts. When it cools down, it freezes again. It's still very hot when it freezes.

Safety: Wear eye protection

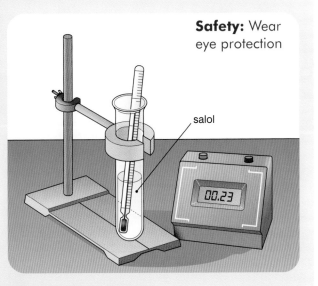

salol

● Carry out an experiment to find the freezing point of salol. Start with some liquid salol, and measure its temperature as it cools.

SUMMARY QUESTIONS

1 ☆ Which change of state is the opposite of boiling?

2 ☆ What is another name for melting point?

3 ☆☆ If you put a bottle of cooking oil in the fridge, it will go solid. What does this tell you about the freezing point of cooking oil?

4 ☆☆☆ When a solid melts, some of the bonds between its particles break. That takes energy. More bonds break when a liquid boils. Which do you think needs more energy, melting or boiling? Use the particle model to support your answer.

Key words

boiling point
change of state
freezing point

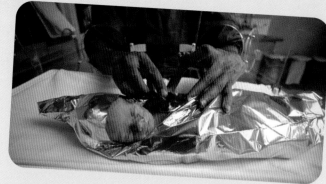

IDEAS AND EVIDENCE

This baby was born prematurely. She doesn't have much body fat to keep her warm, and she would die quickly if she had not been transferred to an **incubator**. You can imagine how quickly heat would escape from such a thin little arm. The temperature, humidity and oxygen level inside the incubator are all monitored electronically and kept at the ideal levels for the baby to survive.

This baby is also wrapped in a sheet of aluminium and plastic – a space blanket. Heat energy **radiating** from the baby's body is reflected back, another important way of helping to keep her warm. The doctor is checking her heart.

Even very tiny babies like this one have a good chance of survival provided they are kept warm, fed, and protected from infection.

Using science today

Have you ever eaten Baked Alaska? It's a surprise pudding. When you take it out of the oven, it has hot meringue on the outside, and frozen ice-cream on the inside. How can that be?

The cook puts a block of ice-cream on a cold dish, and then heaps the meringue mixture on top. Meringue is made from beaten egg whites and sugar – it's mostly air.

When the meringue goes in the oven, it cooks quickly. It's mostly air, so:

● it doesn't take much energy to cook it.
● it's a good **insulator**, so heat can't get through to the ice-cream.

A scientist recently invented another surprise pudding, ice-cream with hot jam inside. You put runny jam inside the ice-cream, and cook it in a microwave oven. The jam absorbs the microwaves and melts; the ice-cream doesn't absorb any of the energy of the microwaves.

Cooking chips

Computer chips like this need constant cooling to ensure they do not over-heat

Why does your computer hum? Doesn't it know the words? No, that constant hum is the fan blowing cool air over the chips which do all the work in a PC.

Chips get hot because electric currents flow through them as they operate. The silicon from which they are made has **resistance**, so energy is lost. If this energy were not removed, the chips would over-heat.

Blowing away hot air is known as '**forced convection**'. It's what you do when you blow on a hot drink to cool it down. As computer chips get smaller and faster, more energy is concentrated in a smaller volume and engineers are looking for new ways to make sure they don't over-heat.

DANGER! AVOID THESE COMMON ERRORS

Don't get confused between heat energy and temperature.

Temperature tells you how hot something is. If it is cold, its particles will not have much energy. They will be moving around slowly, and they will be close together. If it is hot, they will be moving faster, and they will be farther apart. If you put a thermometer into a hot object, it will detect the fast-moving particles and tell you that the temperature is high.

Heat energy is energy transferring (moving) from one place to another. It moves from a hotter place to a colder one.

So the *temperature* tells you about a place where the particles have energy; *heat* is what moves from that hot place to a colder one.

Key words

forced convection
incubator
insulator
radiating
resistance

REVIEW QUESTIONS
Understanding and applying concepts

1   Look at the 'thermogram' photo of someone making a pot of tea. Say as much as you can about what the photo tells you.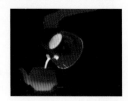

2   A saucepan is usually made of metal, but its handle is made from plastic. Explain why these are good choices of materials.

3   You have previously learned about the water cycle. Explain the part played by heat energy in the water cycle. You should mention convection and radiation.

Ways with words

4   You have learned about thermal conductors and insulators. Explain what is meant by 'thermal clothing'.

5   We talk about the Celsius **scale** of temperature. A mountaineer might **scale** a mountain. A pianist might play a musical **scale**. Explain what these different scales have in common with each other.

Making more of maths

6   The table shows the melting and boiling points of four different substances, W, X, Y and Z. (To answer the questions, it may help to draw a diagram or graph.)

Substance	Melting point (°C)	Boiling point (°C)
W	0	100
X	−117	79
Y	−39	357
Z	44	125

a   Which substance has the highest boiling point?
b   If you cooled all of the substances down, starting at 200°C, which would be the last to become solid?
c   In what state is substance W when the temperature is 80°C?
d   Which substances are gases at 110°C?

7   You will sometimes hear temperatures given using the Fahrenheit scale (°F) instead of the Celsius scale (°C). You can make a graph to help you convert between the two.

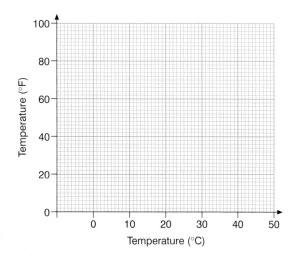

a   On a piece of graph paper, copy the axes.
b   Mark two points to show these:
   i)   When it's 0°C, it's 32°F.
   ii) When it's 40°C, it's 104°F.
c   Join the two points with a straight line. Extend the line in both directions.
d   Now use your graph to work out what is 50°F in °C.
e   When people say, 'The temperature is over 100°F!', just how hot is it in °C?

Extension question

8   Copper is a good conductor of heat and electricity. However, it's not the best thermal conductor. Do some research to find out the material which is the best thermal conductor, but which is also a very bad electrical conductor.

SAT-STYLE QUESTIONS

1 Tess was investigating how a beaker of hot water cooled down. The drawing shows her apparatus.

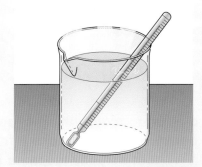

a Name the instrument she used to measure the temperature of the water. (1)

b Heat energy escaped from the beaker of water in several different ways. The table shows some of the ways heat energy escaped from the water. Copy and complete the table by filling in the last column. Choose from:

conduction   convection

insulation   radiation

How the heat energy escaped	Name for this
Heat energy passed through the glass of the beaker and spread into the top of the table.	
Heat energy was carried away by warm air rising above the beaker.	

(2)

c After a while, Tess measured three temperatures:

temperature of water in beaker = 20°C
temperature of air near beaker = 20°C
temperature of table under beaker = 20°C

Predict whether the water would continue to get colder.
Give a reason to support your answer. (2)

2 Benson was investigating the freezing of sea water. He put a plastic beaker of sea water into a freezer, together with a temperature sensor connected to a computer to record the temperature of the water.

The graph shows how the temperature of the water changed.

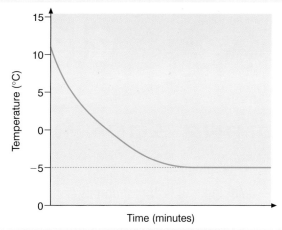

Use the graph to help you answer these questions:

a What was the temperature of the water when Benson put it in the freezer? (1)

b At what temperature did the water freeze? (1)

The sea water froze at a different temperature to pure water.

c At what temperature does pure water freeze? (1)

d Benson repeated the experiment with pure water instead of sea water. On a copy of the graph, show how you think his results would appear. (1)

3 In Pete's room, there is an electric heater. Heat energy is carried around the room by convection currents.

Air close to the heater is heated.

a How does the temperature of the air change? (1)

b How does the density of the air change? (1)

When the air is heated, the speed and separation of the particles of the air change.

c How does their speed change? (1)

d How does their separation change? (1)

e What happens as the warm air rises? (1)

Key words

Unscramble these:
remothertem
inourlast
venscore
prematurete
daniatior

8J

Magnets and electromagnets

My big brother THINKS he's got a magnetic personality!

That explains why he repels everyone!

What's it all about?

Magnets are fun to play with. They seem slightly magical, because they can make a force act on something without actually touching it. They can attract and repel another magnet.

The ancient Chinese were lucky, because they found rocks that contained naturally-magnetic materials. Then they learned to make new magnets, so that they had compasses, which helped them navigate around the seas. In Europe, magnetic rocks are rare, and it took a long time for Chinese knowledge to spread westwards.

In this unit, you are going to extend what you already know about magnets and magnetic materials. You may have learned about Michael Faraday, the scientist who did most to explain how electricity and magnetism are linked. Now you can learn about how electricity can make a magnet. Later in your studies of science, you will find out about the other half of Faraday's idea, how magnetism can make electricity.

What do you remember?

You already know about:
- How magnets are used.
- Magnetic and non-magnetic materials.
- How to represent forces using arrows.

1 Which *two* of these are magnetic materials?

copper   **iron**   plastic   **steel**

2 Which word is the opposite of *attract*?

contract   **distract**   retract   **repel**

3 Magnets are useful in recycling. How could you use a magnet to decide between an aluminium can and a tin can?

4 What happens if you put a magnet on a small dish floating on water?

Ideas about experimenting with magnets

You already know quite a lot about magnets and magnetic materials.

a) What can you say about the magnets which Pip and Molly are trying to pull apart?

b) Can you help Pete with his problem? Has Reese got the answer?

c) Mike and Benson have a strange idea of what magnets can do. What do you think?

What magnets do

8J1

LEARN ABOUT
- magnets
- magnetic materials

I spy magnets

Magnets keep the fridge door shut. Magnets are a handy way of pinning up notices. There are magnets in electric motors and in headphones. They're all around.

Q1 List some places where magnets are used. Try to think of some unusual examples.

Magnetic materials

A magnet can attract a piece of steel – a paper clip, for example. This tells us that steel is a **magnetic material**.

- Magnetic materials include **steel**, iron, **nickel** and cobalt. These are all metals.
- Non-magnetic materials include aluminium, copper, gold and many other metals. Many other materials are also non-magnetic – paper, wood, water, plastic, air, etc.

Take care! Some metals are magnetic, others are non-magnetic. And magnets can attract magnetic iron oxide, which is not a metal.

Q2 Have a guess. Is silver magnetic or non-magnetic? Give a reason to support your idea. How could you check it?

All magnets are made of magnetic materials. Many cheap magnets are made of a non-metallic material, which contains iron oxide.

Magnetic all over?

- Examine some magnets. Test each one with a paper clip. Does every part of the magnet attract the clip?
- Draw a diagram of a bar magnet. Think of a way of showing where the magnet's attraction is strongest, and where it is weakest.

Pairs of poles

A bar magnet has two ends. It is strongest at the ends, and we call these its north and south **poles**. Usually, a magnet is marked so that you can tell which is its north pole and which is its south pole.

Two magnets can **attract** each other, or they can **repel** each other. It depends which poles are facing each other. The picture shows how we can represent these forces, using arrows.

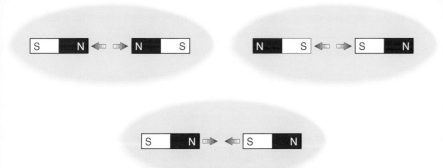

When two magnets are repelling each other, we draw the arrows pushing away from each other. From the picture, you can see that the rule is:

- Two north poles repel each other. Two south poles repel each other.
- A north pole and a south pole attract each other.

This is usually summarised like this:

'Like poles repel, opposite poles attract.'

The magnet test

A magnet can attract another magnet. It can also attract a piece of magnetic material that isn't a magnet.

- Suppose you have several pieces of metal. They all look identical, but some are magnets, others are not.
  Devise a method to find out which of the pieces of metal are magnets. No cheating – you are *not* allowed to use any other materials!

SUMMARY QUESTIONS

1 ☆ Copy and complete these sentences:
   a) Two north magnetic poles will . . . each other.
   b) A north magnetic pole will . . . a south pole.

2 ☆☆ The rule says 'Like poles repel.' What do we mean by *like poles*?

3 ☆☆ Copy the square table. Write the name of at least one material in each square.

Metal, magnetic	Metal, non-magnetic
Non-metal, magnetic	Non-metal, non-magnetic

4 ☆☆☆ Read this description of what happens when the north pole of a magnet attracts an unmagnetised steel pin. Then draw a strip cartoon to show the same information.

At first, the pin has no poles. When the north pole gets close to the pin, it makes a south pole at that end of the pin. A north pole appears at the other end of the pin. Now the north and south poles attract each other, and the pin and magnet move closer together. If you pull the pin away from the magnet, its poles disappear.

Key words

attract
magnetic material
nickel
pole
repel
steel

Making and testing magnets

LEARN ABOUT
- making a magnet
- testing its strength

Through thin air

Small children find magnets very surprising. We are used to making things move by touching them. Magnets can work through thin air. When you are very little, it seems like magic.

The force of a magnet can work through many different materials. The picture shows one way of finding out about this.

The magnet attracts the paper clip, but the thread stops them from touching. If you pass a piece of cardboard into the gap, the clip is still attracted. If you use a thin sheet of steel instead, the clip falls down. It is no longer attracted. This shows that the magnetic force can pass through cardboard but not through steel.

Q1 Your teacher says, 'The magnetic force can pass through all non-magnetic materials, but is stopped by all magnetic materials.' Can you devise a way of testing this idea?

Getting magnetised

As the north pole of the magnet moves away from the iron, it leaves a south pole behind

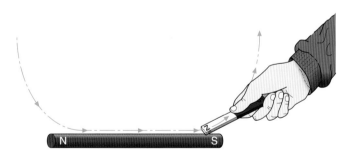

You can use one magnet to make another. Here's how to magnetise a piece of iron.

- Stroke the piece of iron from one end to the other, using the north pole of the magnet.
- Repeat this several times.
- Make sure you always stroke the iron in the *same* direction, using the *same* pole of the magnet.

Q2 What do you think will happen if you stroke the iron in the opposite direction, or with the opposite pole of the magnet?

Evaluating strength tests

There are many ways to test the strength of a magnet. The pictures show some. You may be able to think of others.

Hang paper clips end-to-end from the magnet.

Hang weights on a paper clip attached to the magnet.

Put layers of cardboard between the magnet and the paper clip.

Use the magnet to pull on a spring; see how long the spring gets before it breaks free.

Push the magnet towards a pin; watch for when the pin moves.

Move the magnet towards the compass; watch the needle change direction.

- Your task is to try out some of these methods. Use them to compare some magnets. Which magnet is the strongest? Which is the weakest?
- Then you have to decide – which is the best method for comparing magnets? In other words, you have to **evaluate** the methods.
- You should also try to decide – which method is best for detecting a very weak magnet? In other words, you must decide which method is the most **sensitive**.
- Can your ideas help you to improve any of the methods?

SUMMARY QUESTIONS

1 ☆ Which type of material will a magnetic force *not* pass through?

2 ☆☆ Some coins are made of a steel disc covered in copper. Explain why a magnet can pick up a coin like this.

3 ☆☆☆ How could you turn an iron rod into a magnet with south poles at both ends?
How could you show that the rod had south poles at both ends?

4 ☆☆☆ The skin on your top lip is very **sensitive** to temperature and to touch. (Try touching it gently with something made of cold metal.)
How could you investigate how sensitive it is?

Key words

evaluate
sensitive

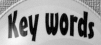

8J3 Magnetic fields

Compasses

The needle of a compass is a magnet. It is free to turn round – its north pole points north and its south pole points south. Of course, this is why we call them north and south poles.

A more formal name is **north-seeking pole** and **south-seeking pole**. These are better names because they remind you why we call the poles north and south. A north-seeking pole seeks the north, where the polar bears are. A south-seeking pole seeks the south, where the penguins are.

The magnetic Earth

People have used magnetic compasses for centuries to help with navigation. When you are out of sight of land, it is useful to know which way is north. At night, there are the stars, but a compass works during the day, too.

The Earth is like a giant magnet, and compass needles are attracted to the poles of this magnet. (So if you thought that compass needles were attracted to polar bears and penguins, you were wrong.)

The north pole of a magnet is attracted towards the Earth's north pole. This means that there must be a south magnetic pole up there, close to the north pole, because opposite poles attract.

Q1 What kind of magnetic pole must there be near the Earth's south pole? Explain your answer.

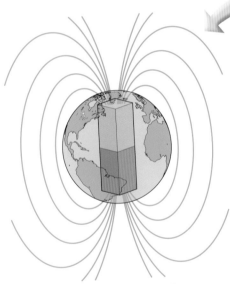

The Earth behaves as if it has a giant magnet inside it

Field lines

The force of a magnet is strongest near the poles. It gets weaker as you go further away. We say that the magnet is surrounded by a **magnetic field**. If you put a piece of magnetic material anywhere in the field, there will be a force on it.

The diagram shows a way of representing the magnetic field around a magnet. We draw **magnetic field lines**. These come out of the north pole of a magnet and go round to the south pole. They are close together at the poles, where the field is strong, and further apart where the field is weak.

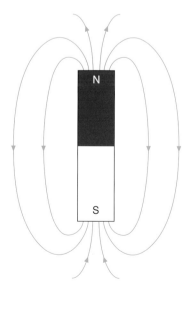

The Earth's field

The pictures on the opposite page show the Earth's magnetic field and the field around a bar magnet. The two fields look very similar.

Q2 Compare the two pictures. In what ways are they similar?

AMAZING SCIENCE!

Pigeons can detect the Earth's magnetic field. That's how racing pigeons can find their way home.

Field plotting

You can find out about the Earth's magnetic field using a compass. You can also use a compass to find out about the field around a magnet.

- Place a bar magnet on a piece of paper. Mark its position.

- Put a plotting compass on the paper, near the magnet. Move it around. Does it always point straight towards the pole of the magnet?
  Your teacher will show you how to use the compass to make a drawing of the magnet's field.

Q3 Draw a diagram to show the field lines around a horseshoe magnet. The photo will give you a clue.

The iron filings help to show up the magnetic field around this horseshoe magnet

SUMMARY QUESTIONS

1 ☆ Copy and complete this sentence:

If a magnet is free to turn around, the end which points north is its ... ...

2 ☆☆ Look at the diagram of the magnetic field lines around two magnets.
   a) Is pole X a north pole or a south pole? How do you know?
   b) Is pole Y a north pole or a south pole? How do you know?

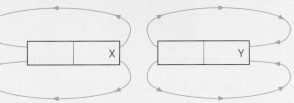

   c) How can you tell from the field lines that the magnets are repelling each other?

3 ☆☆☆ In the past, a ship's compass was often mounted in a brass box. Give as many reasons as you can why brass was a good choice for this.

Key words

magnetic field
magnetic field line
north-seeking pole
south-seeking pole

Making an electromagnet

A magnet with a switch

The photograph shows a very large magnet. It is being used to pick up scraps of iron. It will move the iron to where it is needed, then let it fall. This is a magnet which can be switched on and off – it is an **electromagnet**. The operator switches on the electric current to the magnet, and it attracts the iron. He switches the current off, and the magnet no longer attracts the iron.

Electromagnets are used in many different places – in bells, buzzers, loudspeakers, headphones, motors, circuit breakers. A bar magnet is not an electromagnet; it is a **permanent magnet**.

An electromagnet at work in a steelworks, lifting iron

Q1 Why is an electromagnet better than a permanent magnet for lifting iron at a steelworks?

Inside an electromagnet

Every electromagnet is made from a coil of wire, called a **solenoid**. When an electric current flows through the wire, a magnetic field is produced. When the current stops, the field disappears.

Most electromagnets also have a **core** inside the coil. In your experimental electromagnet, the iron nail was the core.

Q2 Suggest a reason why iron is a good material for a core, but wood is not.

Making an electromagnet

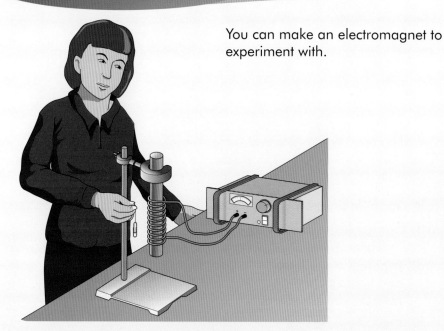

You can make an electromagnet to experiment with.

- Wind a coil of insulated wire around a wooden rod. Connect the ends of the wire to a power supply.
- When your teacher has checked your circuit, switch on.
- Will your electromagnet attract a paper clip?
- Replace the wooden rod with an iron nail. What effect does this have?

Investigating an electromagnet

You have learnt how to make an electromagnet. Your task now is to discover the factors that affect the strength of a magnet.

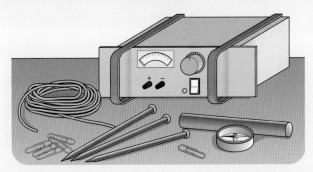

 Make a list of the factors which you think might make a magnet stronger.

● Decide how you are going to test your ideas.

● What will you measure? (Remember that you evaluated several methods for testing the strength of a magnet – look back to page 165.)

● When you have planned your investigation, check your ideas with your teacher and carry out your plan.

● Electromagnets at work

Does your doorbell go 'ding-dong'? Inside, there's a solenoid. When the button is pushed, a current flows through the coil. This attracts an iron rod, which moves through the coil and strikes the 'ding' chime. When the current stops, a spring pulls the iron rod back so that it strikes the 'dong' chime.

Q3 Why is the rod made of iron?

Gruesome science

Eye surgeons use an electromagnet to pull metal splinters out of the eyes of patients who have been in car accidents.

LINK UP TO TECHNOLOGY

In control circuits, many automatic switches make use of electromagnets.

SUMMARY QUESTIONS

1 ☆ What is another name for the wire coil of an electromagnet?

2 ☆ What is the piece of iron inside the coil called?

3 ☆☆ Why must insulated wire be used to make an electromagnet?

4 ☆☆ What is the difference between a permanent magnet and an electromagnet?

5 ☆☆☆ The photo shows the inside of an electric doorbell. Which part is the electromagnet? Find out how a doorbell like this works.

Key words

core
electromagnet
permanent magnet
solenoid

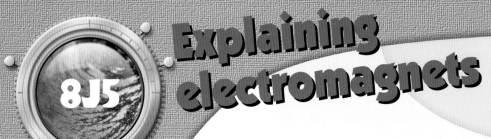

Explaining electromagnets

LEARN ABOUT
- electric current and magnetism
- the magnetic field of an electromagnet

A stronger magnet

An electromagnet is a coil of wire. It only becomes **magnetised** when an electric current flows through it. It must be connected up to a power supply or a battery, so that there is a complete circuit.

Q1 Which terminal of the supply does the current flow out of, positive or negative?

There are several ways to make an electromagnet stronger. You can:

- Wind more turns of wire.
- Squash the turns of wire more closely together.
- Make a bigger current flow.
- Add an iron core.

You probably investigated these on page 169.

Q2 How can you make a bigger current flow?

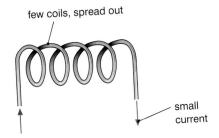

few coils, spread out

small current

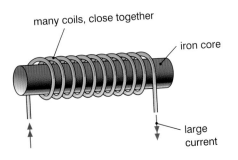

many coils, close together

iron core

large current

To coil or not to coil?

An electromagnet is a coil of wire with a current flowing through it. The wire is made into a coil, because that helps to concentrate the magnetic field. However, any wire with a current flowing through it produces a magnetic field – but it will be weaker than the field of a coil.

Q3 How could you show that, when a current flows in a wire, a magnetic field is produced?

The field of an electromagnet

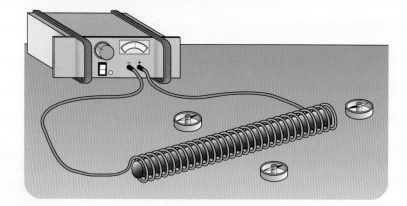

Use a plotting compass to investigate the magnetic field around an electromagnet. Try to answer these questions:

- Does an electromagnet have poles like a bar magnet?
- What happens if you swap over the connections to the power supply?
- Is there still a field around the electromagnet if you remove the iron core?

● Current ideas

Here's how we explain how an electromagnet works:

● If a current flows in a wire, a magnetic field is produced. It's not the wire that matters, it's the current. (A flash of lightning is an intense electric current. It produces a magnetic field, but there isn't any wire.)

● The bigger the current, the stronger the field. Twice as many amps make a field that's twice as strong.

● The magnetic field produced by a current is weak, so we make the wire into a coil. That concentrates the field, so it's stronger. Squash the turns of the coil closer together and that concentrates it a bit more.

● The more turns of wire you have in the same space, the stronger the field is. The current spends longer flowing through the coil if the coil is made from a longer piece of wire.

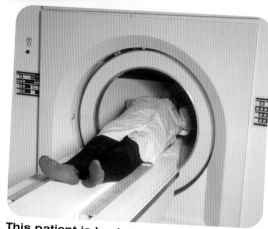

This patient is having a scan. He has to spend several minutes inside a giant electromagnet. He won't feel a thing!

 We say that the strength of the field is **proportional** to the number of turns of wire.

What other factor is the strength of the field proportional to?

● The core question

An iron **core** makes an electromagnet much stronger. How does this happen?

Remember that iron is a magnetic material. The electromagnet produces a magnetic field, and this magnetises the iron so that it becomes a magnet, too. Its magnetic field is much stronger than the field produced by the electromagnet on its own. When the electromagnet is switched off, the iron is demagnetised. It is no longer a magnet. (In fact, if you test the iron core with a compass, you may find that it is still a little magnetised.)

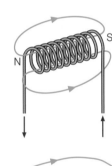

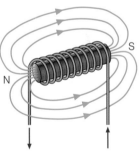

SUMMARY QUESTIONS

1 ☆ Copy and complete the sentences below:
   a) You can make an electromagnet stronger by increasing the ... flowing through it, or by adding an iron ...
   b) An electromagnet has a magnetic field similar to that of a ... ...

2 ☆☆ Make a prediction: How will the magnetic field of an electromagnet change if you reverse the current flowing through it? How could you test your prediction?

3 ☆☆ Explain what's wrong with this statement:

'When an electric current flows through a coil of copper wire, the wire becomes magnetised.'

Key words

core
magnetised
proportional

IDEAS AND EVIDENCE

Getting around

There is a type of rock called **lodestone**, which is naturally magnetic. (It contains iron oxide.) This was discovered in China 2500 years ago, and used to make a compass. A piece of lodestone floating on a cork would turn towards the south. That was important, because many Chinese ships sailed south to trade.

By 1000AD, the Chinese had discovered how to make magnetic compass needles by stroking steel wire with a piece of lodestone. They discovered other ways of making magnets – by heating iron and cooling it, or by hammering it. The iron had to be placed north–south, so that it became magnetised by the Earth's field.

European sailors learned about compasses from Chinese sailors, but they didn't really understand how they worked. For a long time, people thought that a magnetic compass needle was attracted to the Pole Star, the star that is always due north. But then compass makers noticed that compass needles tend to tip downwards slightly – they point into the Earth, not into the sky.

William Gilbert, an English doctor in the 16th century, was interested in magnets because they seemed to have magical properties. He realised why compasses behave as they do. The Earth is itself a giant magnet. He was 600 years behind the Chinese, who had realised that it was the magnetism of the Earth that helped them to magnetise their compass needles.

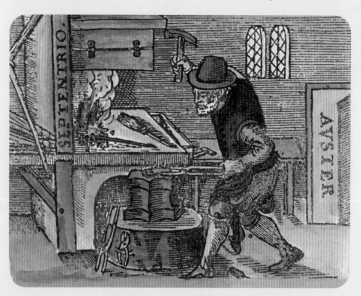

This picture is from William Gilbert's book about magnetism, published in 1600. It shows a blacksmith hammering an iron rod to magnetise it. The rod must be pointing north–south, so that it is magnetised by the Earth's field.

The Earth's magnetism

Scientists are **uncertain** about the Earth's magnetic field. We know that, deep inside, there is a core made mainly of iron and nickel. These are magnetic materials. But the mystery is, why do the Earth's magnetic poles keep moving about? And why do they sometimes change over completely, so that north becomes south and south becomes north?

One theory is that an enormous electric current flows in the metal core. This circulating current changes position slowly over the years, so that the poles wander about. The current may die down and even go into reverse. So it's wrong to think that there's a permanent magnet inside the Earth – it's better to say that there's an electromagnet in there.

Today, satellites orbit the Earth, measuring its magnetic field. Scientists **publish** their ideas about the Earth's field in **scientific journals**, so that anyone can read them. A thousand years ago, there was little communication of knowledge from one part of the world to another, and that's why it was possible for the Chinese to know about compasses and the Earth's magnetism for centuries before Europeans discovered it for themselves.

These are the four Cluster satellites which monitor the Earth's magnetic field. This is a European space project to warn us of magnetic storms from the Sun, which might affect our electricity supply.

- Magnetic materials are those which are attracted by a magnet.
- To test a magnet, see if it is repelled by another magnet.
- Opposite poles attract, like poles repel.
- Around a magnet is its magnetic field, where magnetic materials feel a force.
- We draw magnetic field lines to represent a magnetic field.
- An electromagnet is a coil of wire with a current flowing in it.
- More current, more turns of wire and an iron core make a stronger electromagnet.

DANGER! AVOID THESE COMMON ERRORS

Don't forget that the north pole of a magnet is a north-seeking pole. At the Earth's north pole, there is a south magnetic pole which attracts the north pole of a magnet.

Don't get confused about the Earth's magnetism. It's nothing to do with gravity.

- The Earth has a magnetic field because of its magnetic core. The field makes compass needles point north–south.
- It has gravity because of its enormous mass. That's what gives us our weight.

So it isn't magnetism that makes us stick to the Earth.

Key words

lodestone
publish
scientific journals
uncertain

REVIEW QUESTIONS
Understanding and applying concepts

1   The diagram shows three magnets. Think about how their poles are attracting and repelling each other.

   Make a copy of the diagram and add an arrow to each pole to show the force acting on it.

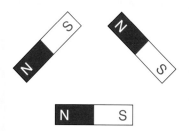

2   Pip made an electromagnet like this:
   She wound ten turns of wire onto an iron core. Then she wound ten more turns, in the opposite direction. She connected it up to a power supply and switched on.

   a   Pip said, 'I predict that my electromagnet will not produce a magnetic field.'
       How could you check Pip's prediction?
   b   Pip was right. Can you explain why her electromagnet produced no magnetic field?

Ways with words

3   You have been studying magnetism – everything to do with magnets and magnetic fields. You will have used several words that sound very similar – don't get them confused!
   Can you explain the difference between *magnetic* and *magnetised*? For example, what is the difference between saying that iron is a magnetic material, and that a piece of iron is magnetised?

Making more of maths

4   A graph can help to show a relationship between two quantities that you have measured. Look at the three graph shapes, and decide which one would help to show each of these relationships:
   a   The more turns of wire on an electromagnet, the greater its strength.
   b   As you increase the current through an electromagnet, its strength increases.
   c   As you push one south pole towards another south pole, the force between them increases.

   For each example, copy the graph and label the x and y axes with the quantities each represents.

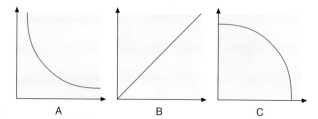

A   B   C

Thinking skills

5   Here's a test of systematic thinking. The statements that follow are about the four metal bars shown in the picture. Each bar might be a magnet, or it might not. Your task is to decide which bars are magnets, which are not magnets, and which you can't be sure about.

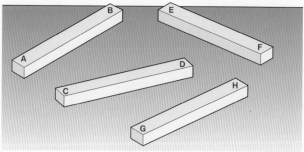

A attracts C.   B attracts C.
D attracts E.   E repels B.
G attracts F.   H attracts E.
(Hint: Look at the evidence. Is there anything you can be sure of, to start off with?)

SAT-STYLE QUESTIONS

1 Reese is investigating the magnetic field of a bar magnet. She places a small plotting compass near one of its poles, B, as shown in the diagram.

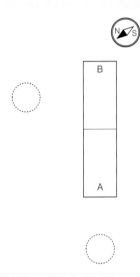

a Is Pole B a north magnetic pole or a south magnetic pole? (1)

b The diagram shows two other positions in which Reese placed the compass. Copy the diagram and mark on it the direction of the plotting compass needle in these two positions. (2)

c Reese hangs the magnet up using a length of string. The magnet is free to turn around. In which direction does Pole A point? (1)

d Explain why the magnet points in this direction. (1)

2 Molly made a coil of wire, which she connected up to a power supply and a switch to make an electromagnet. She placed two iron bars inside the coil, end-to-end.

She held the ends of the iron bars. With the switch closed, she found it difficult to pull the two bars apart.

a Explain why the iron rods were attracted to each other. (2)

b What would Molly notice if she switched off the current and then tried to pull the bars apart? (1)

c If Molly repeated the experiment using two brass bars, instead of iron ones, what difference would she observe, if any? (2)

3 Benson has been experimenting with electromagnets. He has invented a way of using electromagnets to compare two electric currents.

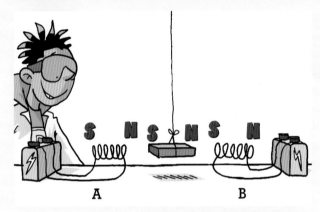

The picture shows what he did. He made two identical coils of wire, and hung a bar magnet half-way between them. Then he made the same current flow through both coils.

a Explain why the magnet hung straight down, between the two coils. (1)

Benson increased the current through coil A.

b How would the magnet move? (1)

Benson swapped over the connections to coil A, so that the current flowed the opposite way through it.

c How would the magnet move? (1)

Key words

Unscramble these:
cemating
investise
grantmecleet
dolonise
menparent

8K

Light

Never buy a cheap laser!

What's it all about?

Our eyes are important to us. They gather the light that allows us to see the world around us. Roughly 80% of the information that comes into our brains is sensed by our eyes. If our eyes don't work well, our other senses try to take over.

Our eyes can tell us lots of things about what we are looking at. What colour is it? Does it have straight edges? Is it smooth and shiny or rough and dull? Is it transparent or does it block light? Does it have a shadow?

Young children, and people who don't think scientifically, think that our eyes can just do this. But if you are prepared to think like a scientist, you can understand just how the light entering our eyes can tell us all this information about the world out there.

What do you remember?

You already know about:

● how shadows are formed.

● how light is reflected by surfaces.

● how we see things.

1 What word describes an object that blocks light?

luminous   **opaque**

shadow   **transparent**

2 Which surface would reflect light best?

black   **dull**   **rough**   **smooth**

3 When you look at a shiny surface, you see:

a bright light   **a reflection**

a shadow   **straight through**

4 When you read this book, your eye:

shines light onto it

collects light reflected from it

touches the letters on the page

reflects light onto it

5 Draw a diagram to explain your answer to question 4.

Seeing the light

Look around you. Do you feel as if your eyes are like searchlights, scanning the room? Perhaps you have seen the eyes of animals at night, seeming to glow in the dark as you drive by. You already know about how we see things.

a) How do we see luminous objects?

b) How do we see non-luminous objects?

You can see your eyes if you look in a mirror.

c) Can you draw a diagram to explain this?

And here's another puzzle: When you look at the stars in the night sky, you are looking into the past.

d) Can you explain that?

8K1 How light travels

LEARN ABOUT
- light rays
- the speed of light

● Laser light

You may have seen a laser light show at a pop concert or in the theatre. A **laser** is a useful **source** of light because it gives a narrow, bright **beam**.

The photo shows another use for lasers: monitoring pollution. We can see the laser beam because the air is polluted with gas and dust, and this reflects some of the light towards us. If the air were clean, the laser light would not show up. The photo shows an important thing about light: it travels in straight lines. You would be very surprised if the laser light in the photograph went round in a circle.

Q1 Where else have you seen straight beams of light like this?

A beam of light from a laser being used to monitor pollution near an American city. The more dust there is in the air, the more the beam shows up.

Lines of light

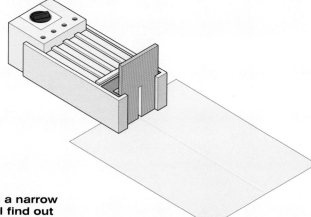

A ray box produces a narrow beam of light. You'll find out how to use one in this unit.

Try out some simple activities with light. For each one, try to explain why 'light travels in straight lines' is part of the explanation.

- Take a length of rubber tubing. Try to look through it, from one end to the other.
- Make a pinhole in the middle of each of two pieces of paper. Can you line them up so that you can see light through them?
- Make the light from a ray box travel along the edge of a ruler.
- Use a piece of wood to block half the light from a ray box. Does the shadow have a straight edge?
- Reflect the beam of light from a ray box off a mirror. Does the beam remain straight?

Invisible light

- A TV remote control produces a beam of **infra-red radiation**. How could you show that infra-red travels in straight lines, just like light?
  Be prepared to explain your method to the class, and to evaluate all of the proposed methods.

Seeing the light

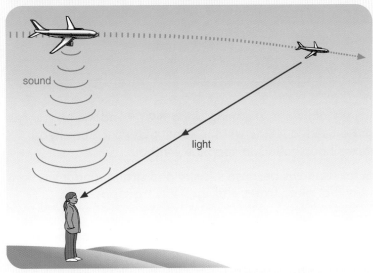

Here's an odd thing you may have noticed. You hear an aircraft flying overhead. You look above you, but it's nowhere to be seen. Then you spot it, far off in the distance – not where you expected to see it at all. What's going on?

Here's another example. You see a flash of lightning, and you hear the rumble of thunder a few seconds later. This happens because light travels much faster than sound. They set off towards you at the same time, but the light of the flash gets to you first, before the sound of the thunder.

Light travels very, very fast – about a million times as fast as sound. Lightning flashes one kilometre away, the light reaches you in a tiny fraction of a second, but the sound takes three seconds.

Can you explain the aircraft mystery? The picture might help.

As fast as can be

Switch on a torch, and the darkness is lit up in an instant. Light travels so quickly, it seems to happen in no time at all. In fact, it takes a tiny fraction of a second for light to travel out from the torch and reflect back to your eyes. Usually, we don't have to worry about this. However, it does matter sometimes – to astronomers, for example.

Astronomers measure the distance to the Moon by shining a laser beam at it. The beam reflects off it, and the light takes 2.7 seconds for the round trip. The Sun is so far away (150 million kilometres) that it takes light over 8 minutes to get here. And the next star is so distant that it takes light four years to reach us here on Earth.

So when they look at other stars, astronomers can't tell what's going on there now. They can only say how the star looked years ago.

 AMAZING SCIENCE!

Light travels at a speed of 300 000 000 m/s.

SUMMARY QUESTIONS

1 ☆ Copy and complete these sentences:
a) Light travels in ... ...
b) Light travels very ...

2 ☆☆ As you are driving along, you come to a road tunnel. You cannot see daylight at the other end. What does this tell you about the tunnel?

3 ☆☆☆ When a cricket match is shown on TV, the cameras are on the edge of the pitch, far from the batsmen. However, there is a microphone buried in the grass in the middle of the pitch. Why can the cameras be far from the action, but the microphone must be close up?

4 ☆☆ Imagine that light travelled at just 1 metre per second. Why would this make driving dangerous?

Key words
beam
infra-red radiation
laser
source

Passing through

LEARN ABOUT
- how light is transmitted, reflected and absorbed

Glass eyes

'Window' is a very old word, meaning 'wind eye'. Windows let you see out, but they also used to let the wind in. Until glass became cheap enough, windows had shutters to keep the wind out.

Glass is great for windows because it is stiff and strong, and it lets light through. We say that glass **transmits** light. It is **transparent**.

There are different types of glass. Some glass is coloured, so that the light, which it transmits, is coloured – think of stained glass windows. Other glass is frosted, so that some light is transmitted, but you cannot get a clear picture of what's on the other side. A material like this is called **translucent**.

Q1 If you write on one side of a sheet of paper and then hold it up to the light, you may be able to read the writing from the other side. What does this tell you about paper?

Transmitting light

If you look through a window, you may see the sky. If you open the window, does the sky seem any brighter? Does the glass of the window let through all of the light from the sky?

- Devise a way of testing this. You can use an electronic light sensor to measure the brightness of the light. Does glass let through all of the light which falls on it? Can you be sure that 100% of the light gets through?

- Investigate some other pieces of transparent and translucent materials. How much of the light gets through?

Reflections

Shop windows can work like giant mirrors. That's because the glass **reflects** some of the light that falls on it.

As you already know, we see non-luminous things because they reflect light into our eyes. Glass seems almost invisible because it doesn't reflect very much light.

Absorption

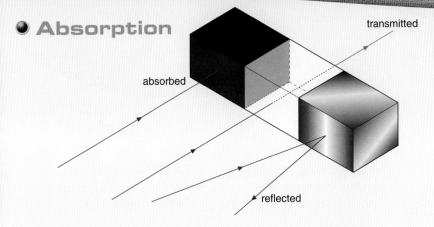

transmitted

absorbed

reflected

Now you know two things that can happen when light falls on something:

- It can pass straight through – that's **transmission**.
- It can bounce off it – that's **reflection**.

Sometimes something else happens. Think about a dull, black object. It doesn't let light through, so we describe it as **opaque**. It doesn't reflect light either. The light that falls on a dull black object disappears – it has been **absorbed**. So that's the third thing which can happen to light when it falls on something:

- It disappears, because it isn't transmitted or reflected – that's **absorption**.

Q2 How could you find out which materials are best at absorbing light? (Think about how you could use a light sensor for this.)

Reflecting light

- Extend your study of what happens when light hits different materials. Can you use a light sensor to detect reflected light?

- Does a mirror reflect 100% of the light that falls on it? What about other materials, such as aluminium foil, white paper and coloured paper?

SUMMARY QUESTIONS

1 ☆ Give some examples of materials which are:
a) good at transmitting light
b) good at reflecting light
c) good at absorbing light.

2 ☆☆ Copy the table and complete the first column using words from the list:

absorption   reflection   transmission

	Light bouncing off the surface of an object.
	Light passing through an object.
	What happens to light which isn't reflected or transmitted.

3 ☆☆☆ You should remember that light is energy on the move, and energy can't just disappear. Think about what happens when light is absorbed. What do you think happens to the temperature of an object that absorbs light? How could you test your idea?

Key words

absorption
opaque
reflection
translucent
transmission
transparent

Seeing things

- how we see things
- drawing ray diagrams

◉ Seeing in black and white

You may have black skin, brown skin or white. But we all have something blacker than any skin, and something whiter. Look at your eye in a mirror. The white of the eye is very white, and the pupil in the centre is very black.

The pupil of your eye is the hole through which light enters. It is black because it lets light in, but none comes back out. If you are going to see anything, light must reach the sensitive cells at the back of your eye.

When light reaches the back of your eye, a tiny **image** is formed of what you are looking at. The cells detect the light and send messages about the image to your brain. What goes on inside your brain is much harder to explain!

Q1 Does the eye absorb, reflect or transmit light? Does the pupil absorb, reflect or transmit light?

◉ Believing about seeing

People have had different ideas about how we see. When you look at something, it seems as though you are doing something very active – almost pointing at it. So people once thought that your eyes produced invisible 'feelers' which touched things, and that was how you saw. When you closed your eyes, the feelers came back inside.

Now we know it's not like that. You move your eyes around so that the light from the thing you want to look at will enter your pupils. The drawing shows this, using **rays** of light.

- We see a **luminous** object because rays travel directly from the object into our eyes.
- We see a **non-luminous** object because it reflects rays of light, and they enter our eyes.

The eyes of creatures which hunt at night have large pupils, to collect as much light as possible

ICT CHALLENGE

Search the Internet or a CD-ROM encyclopaedia to find out what an optician looks for during an eye examination.

Drawing rays of light

The picture on the opposite page shows how we see things. Of course, light comes out of the light bulb in all directions, and reflects off the ship in all directions. However, we don't draw the light like that. We only show the rays that tell the story of how we see these things:

- We show the ray that travels straight from the light bulb to the eye.
- We show the ray from the light bulb that reflects off the ship to the eye.

These tell us all we need to know. They make up a **ray diagram**.

Ray Diagram? Sounds like he should join the Scientifica crew!

Drawing rays of light

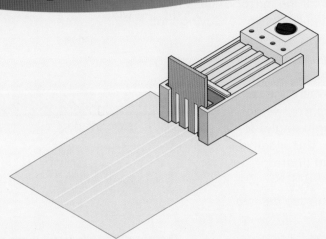

Use a ray box to make different patterns of light on a piece of paper.

- Make a single ray travel across the paper. Use a pencil to mark three dots along the ray. Use your ruler to draw a line through the dots, showing where the ray went.

- Adjust your ray box so that it makes three rays. Mark their positions and draw the rays. Are the three rays exactly parallel?

- Make a single ray bounce off a mirror. Mark the position of the ray before and after it has been reflected, and draw the ray.

- Try again with three rays. What pattern do you see?

Q2 Why is it better to mark the ray with three dots, rather than just two?

SUMMARY QUESTIONS

1 ☆ Which word means the picture that is formed at the back of your eye?

diagram   image   pupil   retina

2 ☆☆ Draw two ray diagrams:
   a) to show how, on a sunny day, you can read a book
   b) to show how you can see a TV programme.

3 ☆☆ Think about the 'feeler' theory of how we see. What's good about this theory, and what's bad?

Key words
image
luminous
non-luminous
ray
ray diagram

LEARN ABOUT
- how mirrors reflect light
- how images are formed
- predicting where reflected rays go

● Back-to-front

Why does an ambulance have ƎƆИALUBMA on the front? A driver in front will see this in the rear-view mirror, and it will appear the right way round. An image in a mirror (a reflection) is **inverted**.

To understand how mirrors work, you need to find out what they do to light. It's simplest to start with a single ray of light striking a flat mirror. It bounces off the mirror at the same angle as it strikes it. Here's a rather complicated way of saying that:

There are two rays, which we call the **incident ray** and the **reflected ray**. At the point where the rays meet the mirror, we draw a line at right angles to the mirror. This is called the **normal** ('normal' means 'at 90°').

Look at the backwards writing on the front of this ambulance. Could we have printed this photo the wrong way round? Can you tell?

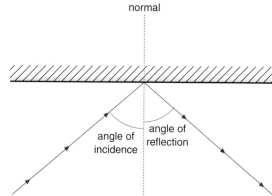

The shading tells you which side of the mirror reflects light.

Now we can see the two angles:

- the **angle of incidence** (the angle between the incident ray and the normal)
- the **angle of reflection** (the angle between the reflected ray and the normal).

Because the ray reflects off at the same angle, we can say:

- the angle of incidence = the angle of reflection.

This rule allows us to predict what will happen to any ray of light when it strikes a flat mirror.

● Modelling light

Snooker balls bounce off the side of the table just like light off a mirror. Players use this idea when they are working out where a ball will go.

So, in some ways, light behaves like snooker balls. Light travels in straight lines, and so do snooker balls. Light and snooker balls show the same pattern when they reflect. We can say that snooker balls are a **model** for the way light behaves.

(Of course, this doesn't mean that light is just a lot of snooker balls. It's very different in some ways, but if we think about how snooker balls move, it can help us to understand how light behaves.)

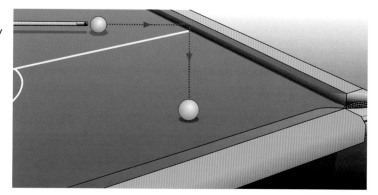

Reflecting rays

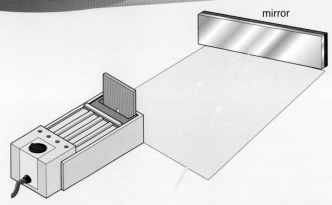

mirror

You can investigate how light rays are reflected by shining a ray of light from a ray box at a small mirror.

- Mark the incident ray and the reflected ray.
- Mark the position of the mirror's reflecting surface.
- What angles will you measure and record? What will you alter?
- Present your results as a graph.

● Explaining images

When you see something in a mirror, its image appears to be behind the mirror. The diagram will help you see why.

The light from the candle flame reflects off the mirror. The dashed line shows that it appears to be coming from behind the mirror, so your brain tells you that that's where the candle is.

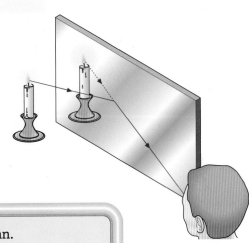

SUMMARY QUESTIONS

1 ☆ Copy the table and complete it by filling in the first column.

	The ray of light which strikes a mirror.
	The line at right angles to a mirror.
	Describes a back-to-front image.

2 ☆☆ Draw an accurate diagram to show this:

A ray of light strikes a flat mirror and is reflected. The angle of incidence is 60°.

Mark the angle of reflection, and give its value.

3 ☆☆ Set up two mirrors at right angles, as shown. Look at yourself in this double mirror.

Try winking your right eye. What do you notice? Try to explain this observation.

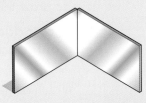

Key words

angle of incidence
angle of reflection
incident ray
inverted
model
normal
reflected ray

8K5 Refracting light

LEARN ABOUT
- bending light rays
- making a spectrum

Not so straight lines

You have learned that light travels in straight lines. You have also learned that rays of light change direction when they are reflected by a mirror, so they're not such straight lines after all.

Now you can find out another way of making light rays bend. This time, you have to make them pass through a glass block.

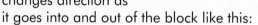

Changing direction

Use a ray box and a glass block. Place the block as shown, and shine a ray of light through it. Turn the block to different angles.

The ray of light changes direction; this is called **refraction**. You can find out how the ray changes direction as it goes into and out of the block like this:

- Lay the block down flat, and draw around it.

- Mark the ray before it goes into the block, and after it comes out.

- Now remove the block and draw in the complete path of the ray.

The diagram on the left shows two important angles.

- Investigate how the angle of refraction changes as you change the angle of incidence.

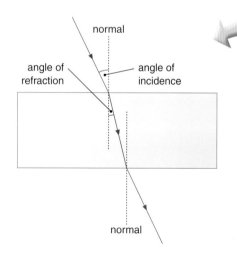

Two angles

A ray of light doesn't change direction when it is going through glass or plastic. It changes direction just when it goes in, and when it comes out.

To measure this change, we look at two angles. Just as with a mirror, we have to draw the **normal** line. Then:

Angle of incidence = angle between incident ray and normal.
Angle of refraction = angle between refracted ray and normal.

Q1 Which angle is bigger when a ray of light goes *into* a glass block? And when it comes out?

● A trick of the light

There are lots of weird effects caused by refraction of light. Fill a glass tumbler with water and look at the world through it. Everything becomes distorted. It makes you glad that you're not a goldfish in a bowl.

You brain thinks that light travels in straight lines; it doesn't realise that the rays of light may have been bent before they reached you.

● Colours from nowhere

If you look at a beautiful diamond in a ring, you may notice that the diamond sparkles with different colours. The diamond is colourless. So where do these wonderful colours come from?

It's refraction again. You may have noticed that, when you shone a ray of light into a glass block, it tended to split up into different colours. These are the colours of the rainbow:

red   orange   yellow   green   **blue**   **indigo**   **violet**

When light is split up like this, we say that a **spectrum** has been formed.

Looking at a spectrum

Use a triangular block (a prism) to split a ray of white light into a spectrum. Which colour of light is refracted (bent) the most?

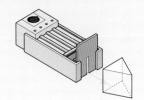

SUMMARY QUESTIONS

1 ☆ A ray of light changes direction when it goes into glass. This is called

the normal   **reflection**   **refraction**   **a spectrum**

2 ☆☆ Which of these diagrams shows correctly how a ray of light is refracted by a glass block?

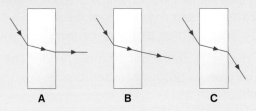

A   B   C

3 ☆ a) Which colours are at the two ends of the spectrum?
   b) Which colour comes between orange and green?

Key words

angle of incidence
angle of refraction
normal
refraction
spectrum

Changing colours

8K6

Shades of colour

If it's a bright day, you may wear sunglasses. The lenses may be coloured, and that can make everything you see change colour. (Your brain soon gets used to the strange colours of things.)

The coloured lenses of sunglasses stop the bright light from getting to your eyes, by absorbing some of it. But how do they change its colour?

It's better to say that the 'lenses' are **filters**. A filter is a device that lets some things through but stops others. So what does a coloured filter let through? Find out with the activity that follows.

Getting through

- Look through some coloured filters at a white light. What colour is the light that comes through each one?

- Now set up a ray box, and shine a ray of light through each filter in turn. Use a prism to split the light up into a spectrum *before* it goes through the filter. What colours come through, and which are filtered out?

- Try using the prism to split up the light *after* it has passed through the filter.

AMAZING SCIENCE!

Supermarkets have special lighting to make the fruit and vegetables look bright and colourful.

Adding and subtracting colours

White light is made up of all of the colours of the spectrum. When you shine it through a coloured filter, some of the colours are **absorbed**. The light that comes through is coloured because it is made up of only part of the spectrum. You can think of this as subtracting colours from the white light. A red filter lets red light through but absorbs all the other colours. It **transmits** red light.

We can also add different colours of light together. You see this happening every day, but you may not realise it. A television picture is made up of thousands of dots, which are coloured red, green and blue. (You can see them if you look at the screen with a magnifying glass.) These are the three **primary colours** of light.

Red, green and blue dots together make white. The diagram on the left shows the colours produced when a pair of primary colours are mixed together.

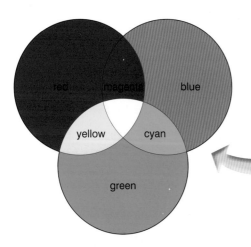

Q1 What colour is produced when blue and green light are mixed together?

Cats at night

There is a saying: 'At night, all cats are grey.' That's because, in the dark, there isn't enough light to show up their true colour (the colour they would have if you saw them in daylight). The colour of something may change, depending on the light that is falling on it.

When choosing new clothes, you may have taken them to the door of the shop to see what they look like in daylight, when white light falls on them. The lighting in the shop may be yellowish, so the clothes don't show their true colours.

- A red object looks red when white light falls on it, because it reflects only red light; it absorbs all the other colours. (That's subtraction again.)
- If you shine blue light on a red object, it will look black, because it absorbs the blue light and no light is reflected.

To work out what colours will be seen, first decide what colours of light are being shone on an object. Then decide which colours will be absorbed, and which will be **reflected**.

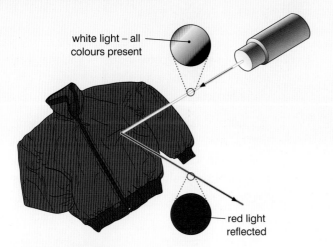

white light – all colours present

red light reflected

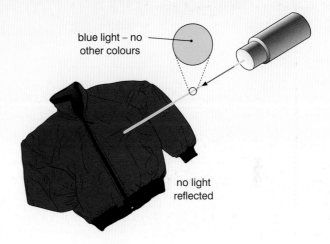

blue light – no other colours

no light reflected

Coloured views

- Try shining different colours of light, including white light, onto different objects. Can you explain the colours you see?

- Now repeat the experiment, but look through a coloured filter.

- Try drawing a multicoloured picture with felt pens, and then look at it through filters. Can you make a game or puzzle using these ideas?

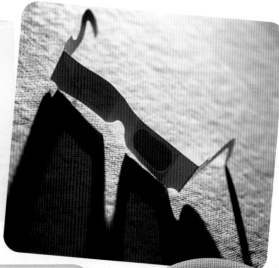

These spectacles have filters of different colours. What might they be used for?

SUMMARY QUESTIONS

1 ☆ Which of these is *not* a primary colour of light?

   blue   green   red   yellow

2 ☆ Which two primary colours of light must be mixed to give yellow?

3 ☆☆ What colour will a blue book appear if you shine these different colours of light on it?

   white   blue   red

Key words
absorb
filter
primary colours
reflect
transmit

IDEAS AND EVIDENCE

In science, we often explain things by using models. You have studied the particle model of matter, and you will learn about many different things that can be explained by this model.

On page 184, you saw a model for light. We explained reflection by saying that light behaves a bit like snooker balls. It bounces off a mirror in the same way that a snooker ball bounces off the side of a snooker table.

Here is another model for light. You may have noticed that, when you look at things in water, they seem much closer than they really are. Perhaps you have worn goggles at the swimming pool and seen this effect when looking at things underwater. It's to do with refraction.

Light waves are more squashed up in water than in air, so that things look closer when they are under water

The drawing shows an explanation of this. We imagine that light is made of waves. In water, they travel more slowly than in air, so they are squashed up. The part of the person which is under water looks closer than the part which is above the water, in the air.

So our model of light is that it behaves like waves. This doesn't mean that light is made of waves (or snooker balls). But these models can help us to explain things. The wave idea of light can explain many other things about light.

Using science today

A laser is an unusual source of light. It is different from a light bulb in two ways:

● its light comes out in a narrow beam
● its light is of just one colour.

If you shine a laser beam through a prism, it won't be split up into a spectrum because there is just one colour there.

Supermarket check-outs use lasers in two ways. One is in the bar-code reader – you may have noticed the bright red light which reflects off shiny objects as they are scanned.

The other use of a laser is to stop the moving belt as your purchases are carried along it. At one side of the belt there is a small hole. A beam of laser light shines through this, across the belt to a detector at the other side. When an item breaks the beam, the belt automatically stops.

The following text appears projected (mirror-reversed) on the screen in the image:

- Light travels very fast, in straight lines.
- Objects may reflect, absorb or transmit light.
- We see non-luminous objects when they reflect light into our eyes.
- A ray of light is refracted when it passes into or out of a transparent material.
- When white light is refracted, it is split up into a spectrum, showing all of the colours of which it is made.

DANGER! AVOID THESE COMMON ERRORS

It's easy to think that, when light passes through a coloured filter, some colour is *added to* the light, but that's wrong. White light is made up of all the colours of the spectrum. The filter *subtracts* some of these colours, leaving coloured rays of light.

In the same way, a red object doesn't add redness to the light. It looks red because it reflects red light and absorbs all of the other colours that fall on it.

Key words

laser
model
particles
prism
waves

REVIEW QUESTIONS
Understanding and applying concepts

1 You have learned about what happens when a ray of light strikes different objects – glass blocks, mirrors and so on. Look at the diagrams below, and decide what object might be hidden in each. Copy and complete each diagram. (In some cases, there might be more than one correct answer.)

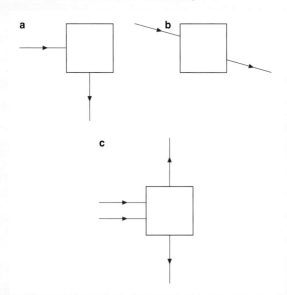

2 Imagine that you are looking at the cover of a blue book through a yellow filter.

- The filter lets through orange, yellow and green light.
- The book reflects green, blue and indigo light.

What colour will the book appear when you look at it?

3 Someone says, 'If you see something yellow, then yellow light must be entering your eyes.' Are they right? (Hint: Think about mixing the primary colours of light.)

4 Does the spectrum of white light contain all possible colours?

Ways with words

5 The word *refraction* means the bending or breaking of a light ray. Can you guess how this is related to the word *fraction* (those things you study in maths)?

Find out what an *infraction of the law* is.

Making more of maths

6 Pete and Benson carried out an experiment on refraction. They shone a ray of light into a glass block (like the experiment on p. 186). They altered the position of the glass block, and for each position they measured the angle of incidence and the angle of refraction. The table shows their results.

Angle of incidence	Angle of refraction
10°	7°
20°	14°
40°	27°
60°	38°
80°	45°

At first, they thought that double the angle of incidence always gave double the angle of refraction. Then they weren't so sure.

Draw a graph to show their results, and help them to decide: is the angle of refraction proportional to the angle of incidence? Why is drawing a graph a better way of looking at this data than simply using a table?

Thinking skills

7 You have studied how light rays can be reflected and how they can be refracted. Think about **reflection** and **refraction**.
- **a** Make a list of ways in which they are similar.
- **b** Make another list of ways in which they differ.

Extension question

8 A disco mirror-ball sends patches of light across the walls as it turns. Explain how it works.

SAT-STYLE QUESTIONS

1 The diagram shows a ray of light shining onto a flat mirror.

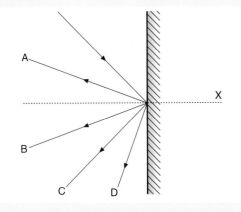

a Which of the rays (A, B, C or D) shows correctly the path of the ray after it has been reflected by the mirror? (1)
b Name the line marked X. (1)
c Copy the diagram, and label the incident and reflected rays. (2)
d Mark two angles which are equal. (1)

2 Benson is experimenting with a glass block. He shines a narrow ray of light at it. He tries different positions of the glass block.

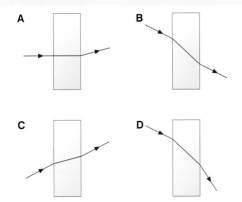

For each of the diagrams, say whether it shows correctly how the ray could have behaved. (4)

3 Reese shone a ray of white light at a prism, and saw a spectrum on a piece of white card.

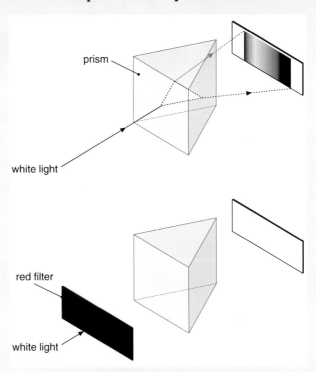

a She put a red filter in the path of the ray of light, as shown in the second diagram. Describe how the appearance of the spectrum would change. (1)
b She then put the filter between the prism and the white card. What would she see on the card? (1)
c Explain why Reese used a piece of *white* card in this experiment. (1)

Key words

Unscramble these:
flecter
crafter
quepoa
clanternuts
marttins

8L

Sound and hearing

COMING SOON

8L1 Changing sounds
8L2 Seeing sounds
8L3 How sounds travel
8L4 Hearing things
8L5 Noise pollution

Yes, sound definitely does travel through the ground!

What's it all about?

Hearing is a remarkable sense. When you hear someone speak, you can guess all sorts of things about them – young or old, male or female, are they indoors or outdoors, speaking in their native tongue, and so on.

Unfortunately, not everyone has perfect hearing. As we get older, our hearing deteriorates. Some people are born with poor hearing, or they may be totally deaf.

Scientists and engineers have developed many ways of detecting and measuring sound, and for improving hearing. They can only do this because they have a scientific way of thinking about sound.

 ## What do you remember?

You already know about:
- sources of sound.
- sound travelling through different materials.
- the difference between pitch and loudness.
- changing the pitch and loudness of some musical instruments.

1 Which of these will sound pass through?

air   **the ground**   water   wood

2 Which word means how high or how low a note is?

height   loudness   pitch   vibration

3 Describe how an object moves as it makes a sound.

4 How could you show that sounds can travel through wood?

The Scientificalifragilistics

Making music together can be fun. Each instrument has a part to play, and each player must know how to make different notes.

a) How does the sound change if you hit a drum harder?

b) How many ways can you think of to change the note made by a guitar?

c) How do other instruments make different notes?

Musicians have to show some consideration for the people around them. Loud music can be annoying.

d) Can listening to loud music be hazardous, as well as annoying?

Now, after three: one, two, three . . .

Changing sounds

8L1

LEARN ABOUT
- energy and loudness
- pitch and frequency

A guitarist can play notes that are high or low, loud or soft. They can play classical, rock, folk, jazz – all kinds of music.

Good vibrations

Sounds are made when things **vibrate**. You may be able to see the strings of a guitar as they vibrate, although they only move a small amount, and they move very fast. In wind instruments, it is the air inside which vibrates, and you can't see that.

A tuning fork is useful to a musician because it produces a single musical note. When the fork is struck, its two prongs vibrate. You may not be able to see these tiny vibrations, but the photograph shows what happens when a vibrating fork touches the surface of some water. The vibrations cause the water to fly everywhere.

Different notes

You should know how to make different notes on different musical instruments. To make a louder note, you have to put in more energy. You strum the strings harder, or blow harder. So the **loudness** of a sound tells you about its **energy**. A loud sound has more energy than a soft sound.

Don't get mixed up: a note can also be described as 'high' or 'low'. A high note has a higher **pitch** than a low note. Most musical instruments produce notes of different pitches.

Q1 How does a pianist make a louder note? At which end of the piano keyboard are the notes with high pitch?

Twang that ruler

- Press one end of a ruler onto the bench. Twang the other. Watch the ruler vibrate and listen to the sound it makes.

- How does the loudness of the sound change as the vibrations die away? Use the idea of energy to explain what you observe.

- You can change the pitch of the note by changing the length that vibrates. How can you show that a shorter ruler vibrates more frequently (more times each second)?

- Attach a heavy mass to the free end of the ruler and repeat your experiments. What changes do you observe?

Care: Keep your feet away from heavy masses.

Getting in tune

When a band or an orchestra is about to play, they tune up. A band sounds bad if the guitarists play slightly different notes. They need to be sure that they don't sound 'out of tune', so one guitarist plays a note. The others adjust their guitars to play exactly the same note. Then they make sure that the other five strings match the first one.

In the recording studio, the engineer has the job of making sure that all of the instruments are in tune with each other

Q2 How does a guitarist adjust the note produced by a string?

At an orchestral concert, the oboist plays the note A, and the other performers adjust their instruments to match. They are making sure that their instruments produce the same number of vibrations each second. Another way to say this is that the notes must have the same **frequency**. The frequency of a sound tells you how many vibrations there are every second. The more vibrations per second, the higher the pitch.

A low note has a low frequency; a high note has a high frequency.

Some musicians use tuning forks to be sure that they are tuned to the right note. Others use an 'electronic tuning fork', which is an electronic device that produces a sound of the desired frequency.

Q3 Look at the photo of the tuning fork on the opposite page. How many times does it vibrate each second?

LINK UP TO
MUSIC

You will learn about more aspects of musical sounds when you study Soundscapes.

SUMMARY QUESTIONS

1 ☆ Which words tell you about the pitch of a sound? Which words tell you about its loudness?

   high   loud   low   soft

2 ☆☆ Copy and complete these sentences:

   If two musical notes have the same frequency, their . . . will be the same.

   A sound with more energy will be . . .

3 ☆☆☆ Look at the photo of the Japanese women playing musical instruments. Say as much as you can about how these instruments work.

Key words

energy
frequency
loudness
pitch
vibrate

Seeing sounds

8L2

- amplitude and frequency
- displaying sounds with an oscilloscope

On the screen

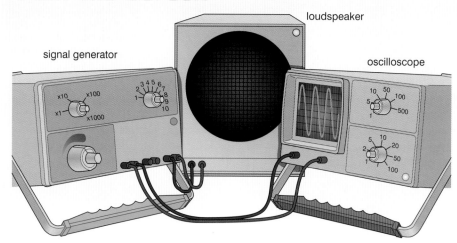

loudspeaker

signal generator

oscilloscope

We can't see sounds; we hear them. However, there is a way to make sounds visible, using some electronic equipment. Here's what you need:

- A **signal generator** makes sounds with different frequencies. You can also change the loudness.
- A **loudspeaker** lets you hear the sounds from the signal generator.
- An **oscilloscope** lets you see a trace of the sound on its screen.

The trace on the screen changes as the sound changes pitch and loudness.

Making sense of sounds

- Watch how the oscilloscope trace on the screen changes as the loudness and the pitch of the sound are changed.

- Your teacher will show you how the dot moves across the screen to make the trace. The sound makes the dot move up and down as it moves along. (You can think of the trace as a graph of the sound. The graph has time along its x-axis.)

- Listen to a square wave. Can you relate its sound to the trace you see?

How the trace changes

A   B   C

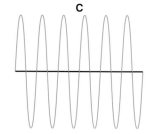

This is a soft sound; the trace doesn't go up and down very much.

Now the sound is louder. The trace goes up and down more.

Now the frequency is higher. More vibrations are squashed into the same interval of time.

Q1 Which two traces have the same loudness? How can you tell?

Q2 How can you tell that the first two traces have the same frequency?

● Amplitude and loudness

When there is no sound, the oscilloscope trace is a flat line across the middle of the screen. As the sound gets louder, the trace goes up and down more. We say that its **amplitude** has increased.

● The greater the amplitude, the louder the sound.

Take care! The amplitude is measured from the middle of the trace straight up to the highest point. The oscilloscope screen has a grid to make it easier to measure the amplitude of the trace.

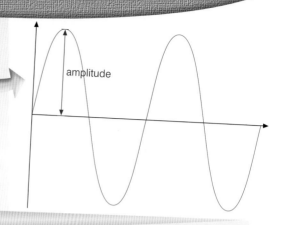

amplitude

Capturing sounds

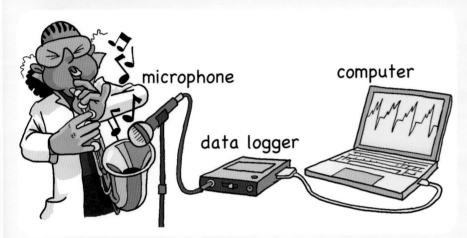

microphone

data logger

computer

● If you connect a **microphone** to a data logger, you can record sounds and then look at them on a computer screen, just like an oscilloscope.
● Try things like clapping your hands, whistling and singing (preferably not all at the same time).
● You may be able to look at the patterns produced by different musical instruments. Even when they are playing the same note, their traces are different – that's why one instrument sounds different from another.

SUMMARY QUESTIONS

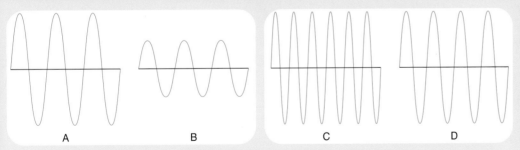

A   B   C   D

1   ☆ Look at the diagram. Which trace (A or B) has the greater amplitude? Which sound is louder?

2   ☆☆ Look at the diagram again. Which trace (C or D) has the greater frequency? What difference would you notice if you heard these sounds?

3   ☆☆ Sketch diagrams like the trace on an oscilloscope screen to show:
    a) a sound which gets louder and then softer
    b) a sound which gets more and more high-pitched.

Key words

amplitude
loudspeaker
microphone
oscilloscope
signal generator

How sounds travel

8L3

LEARN ABOUT

- how sound travels through materials
- the speed of sound
- the wave model of sound

● Solids, liquids, gases

Have you ever heard a recording of your own voice? It can sound odd – embarrassing, even. The reason is that when you hear your voice as you speak, the sound usually reaches your ears in two ways: through the air, and through the bones of your skull. When you hear a recording, the sound arrives only through the air, and it sounds different.

So sounds can travel through a gas (air), and through a solid (bone). It can also travel through liquids such as water.

Q1 How could you show that sound travels through water?

In space, no-one can hear the door bell

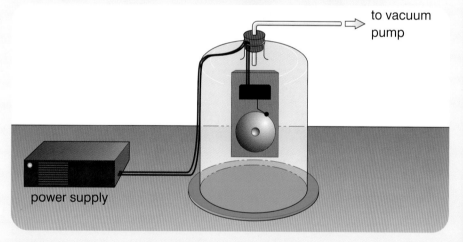

to vacuum pump

power supply

In this experiment, a door bell is ringing inside a bell jar. It sounds rather faint, because the sound has to travel through air and then glass.

As the air is pumped out of the bell jar, the sound fades away. You can still see the bell vibrating, but you can't hear it.

When the air is pumped out, there is a **vacuum** in the jar. This experiment shows that sound cannot travel through a vacuum – there must be a material for it to pass through.

Q2 Explain why we can see the Sun, but we can't hear it.

Dolphins and whales communicate underwater using squeaks, grunts and other sounds. Unfortunately, human noises made by ships etc. make it harder for them to keep in touch with each other.

● The speed of sound

If you are ever locked up in a prison (or a boarding school), remember that you can communicate with the other inmates by tapping on the pipes. This shows that sound can travel easily through solids.

In fact, sound travels much faster through solids and liquids than through the air.

Speed of sound:

in steel = 5100 m/s

in water = 1500 m/s

in air   =   330 m/s

To understand these differences, and why sound can't travel through a vacuum, you need to understand how sound travels.

● Sound waves

Put your ear to the table. Tap the table gently. The sound of your tapping reaches your ear.

Remember that the table is made up of many, many tiny particles. Because the table is a solid, they must be packed closely together.

When you tap the table, your finger causes the particles next to it to vibrate. These particles push on their neighbours, which push on their neighbours, and so on. So the **vibration** is passed on from one particle to the next, until it reaches your ear.

The particles of the table don't travel all the way from your finger to your ear. They have fixed positions, and they **oscillate** back and forth. It's the vibration that travels from your finger, through the table to your ear.

In a gas, such as air, the particles are farther apart. When the air is made to vibrate in one place, the sound is passed on when the particles collide with one another. However, because they are farther apart, they collide less often than in a solid or liquid, so the sound travels much more slowly.

Q3 Explain why sound can't travel through a vacuum (empty space).

● The wave model

Scientists say that sound travels as waves. Sound waves are not exactly the same as waves on the sea, but if you have ever been in a swimming pool with a wave machine, you will understand why we talk about **sound waves**.

The wave machine pushes the water next to it back and forth. That water pushes on the next lot of water, and so on. The result is a wave that travels from one end of the pool to the other.

Q4 Does water travel from one end of the pool to the other?

SUMMARY QUESTIONS

1 ✰✰ Look at the list of key words on this page. Which two have the same meaning? What is their meaning?

2 ✰✰ How could you show that sound can travel along a metal rod?

3 ✰✰ Put these in order, from slowest to fastest:

a snail   **sound waves in air**   **light**
an Olympic sprinter   **sound waves in steel**

4 ✰✰✰ A class of pupils is waiting in line. How could you use this to demonstrate the way in which a sound travels through a solid material?

Key words

oscillate
sound wave
vacuum
vibration

LEARN ABOUT
- range of hearing
- how ears work

What can you hear?

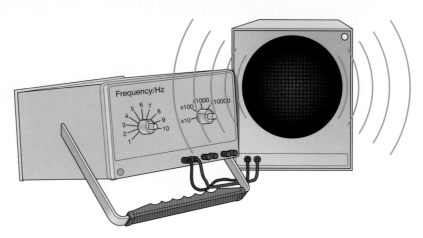

The **signal generator** will let you test your hearing. If you turn the **frequency** higher and higher, eventually you will not be able to hear the sound coming from the loudspeaker. Its frequency is too high.

Similarly, if you turn the frequency down, the sound will eventually become inaudible. This usually happens at about 20 Hz (**hertz**) – that is, 20 vibrations per second.

Hearing test

Devise a safe way of finding out which member of the class can hear the most high-pitched sound, and who can hear the faintest sound. Take care! Remember that people might try to cheat by claiming that they can hear a sound when they can't, so you need to build an anti-cheating method into your test.

High and low

Children usually have a **range of hearing** from about 20 Hz to about 20 000 Hz (20 kilohertz). As you get older, your range of hearing decreases. It also gets harder to hear faint sounds.

You probably know that many animals, including cats and dogs, can hear higher notes than humans can. You can buy dog-whistles which are inaudible to us but which a dog will respond to.

Q1 How could you show that such a dog-whistle really does produce a sound?

Elephants make sounds with very low frequencies, which travel over long distances through the ground. They can hear sounds of much lower pitch than humans.

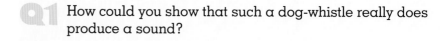

In your ear

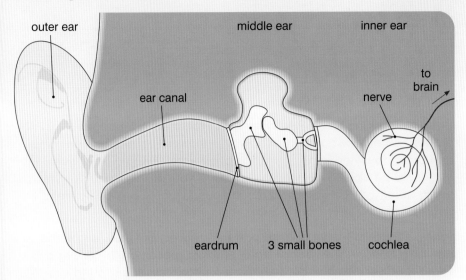

outer ear — middle ear — inner ear

ear canal

nerve

to brain

eardrum — 3 small bones — cochlea

When a sound enters your ear, it pushes on your eardrum. Eventually a signal travels up the nerve into your brain.

Remember that the sounds that enter your ears travel as vibrations in the air. How does that end up as something in your brain?

- The vibrating molecules of the air push back and forth on your **eardrum**.

- Your eardrum presses on the three small bones (the hammer, anvil and stirrup).

- The stirrup passes the vibrations on to the fluid of your inner ear. The cochlea detects this, and sends a message along the nerve to your brain.

You can see that the ear is a very complex organ. It allows you to detect very small differences in sounds, so that you can recognise hundreds of different voices and all kinds of musical instruments.

As you get older, the three small bones become stiffer and the sensitive cells in the cochlea start to die. This makes it harder to hear high pitched sounds and faint sounds.

A sense of direction

Did you say something?

We have two ears. If someone makes a noise to your right, the sound will reach your right ear first, a tiny fraction of a second before it reaches your left ear. Your brain uses this information to judge the direction the sound is coming from.

- Devise a safe investigation into this aspect of hearing. How much better are two ears than one for judging the direction of a sound?

SUMMARY QUESTIONS

1 ☆ Which of the following is *not* a bone in your ear?

   anvil   eardrum   hammer   stirrup

2 ☆☆ Explain what is meant by *range of hearing*.

3 ☆☆ Draw a block diagram or flow chart to summarise how we hear sounds.

4 ☆☆ Explain why it is dangerous to poke things into your ears.

Key words

eardrum
frequency
hertz
range of hearing
signal generator

8L5 Noise pollution

● Noise annoys

If you lived in the Stone Age, your ears would have been good at picking up all the sounds around you – the rustling of small animals and birds, the wind in the trees, distant voices. It would have been vital for you to be able to detect any threats to your own survival, as well as being able to detect your prey. Loud sounds would have been relatively unfamiliar.

Today, sounds still play a large part in our lives, but they tend to be artificial sounds – the roar of traffic, music, speech on the television. These loud sounds blot out the fainter, natural sounds around us.

These artificial sounds are not necessarily bad – loud music can be very enjoyable. However, the sound that one person is enjoying can be very annoying for another. Any unwanted sound is called **noise**. Noise in the environment is often described as **noise pollution**.

Q1 Give some examples of sounds which are a pleasure for one person but which other people regard as noises.

Could this be your idea of how to enjoy music?

● Noise harms

Noise isn't just annoying. It can be harmful.

- People who live in areas where there is a lot of noise – for example, from traffic or aircraft – may find it hard to sleep, and they can become stressed.
- People who work in noisy places need to wear ear protection. Better still, the noise level should be reduced.
- People who listen to music with the volume turned up high, especially through earphones or at concerts, can harm their ears.

The problem is that constant loud noise harms the ears. The small bones and the cochlea may be damaged, so that the person cannot hear soft or high-pitched sounds. You may not notice it happening at the time, but the effects last a lifetime.

This girl is having her hearing tested. The electronic box produces sounds – loud and soft, high and low – and the girl presses the button as she hears them.

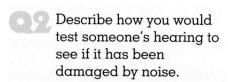

Gruesome science

Twenty per cent (20%) of people in the UK live in areas where traffic noise levels are above the accepted limit.

Q2 Describe how you would test someone's hearing to see if it has been damaged by noise.

Measuring noise

Sounds can be measured using a **sound-level meter**. This has a microphone, to detect the sounds, and a display which shows the sound level. The level of sound is usually measured in **decibels** (dB).

- 0 decibels – the faintest sound you can hear.
- 50 decibels – quiet conversation.
- 80 decibels – a door slamming.
- 110 decibels – a pneumatic drill.
- 130 decibels – the threshold of pain.

Q3 Guess how many decibels these score:
a) a watch ticking at a distance of 1 metre
b) loud conversation
c) a loud car horn.

Sound insulation

People who work in noisy places should protect their hearing by wearing ear defenders. These look like headphones, but they contain materials that are good at absorbing sound.

- Devise a safe way of studying sound **insulation**. How can you compare different materials, to discover how good they are at absorbing sound?

This technician is testing ear defenders. When he fires the gun, the microphones measure the sound level. Two other microphones inside the defenders measure the level of sound reaching his ears.

SUMMARY QUESTIONS

1 ☆ Give a two-word phrase which means 'noise'.

2 ☆☆ List some examples of noise pollution that might damage people's hearing at home and at work.

3 ☆☆ Describe how you could use a sound-level meter and a data logger to find out about noise levels near your school or home. What results would you expect to find?

4 ☆☆☆ People who live near a main road may have double-glazing fitted free of charge to reduce the noise. Find out other ways in which traffic noise can be reduced.

Key words
decibel
insulation
noise
noise pollution
sound-level meter

Read all about it!

IDEAS AND EVIDENCE

Using science today

Ultrasound at work

Ultrasound is any sound which is too high-pitched for us to hear. This usually means that its frequency is greater than 20 kilohertz (20 000 vibrations per second).

Ultrasound is now regularly used to scan expectant mothers, to show the developing baby in the womb. Ultrasound **waves** are passed into the mother's body, where they are reflected by the different materials of which she and her baby are made. The **reflected** waves are collected by a **detector**, and then analysed by a computer to produce an image of her baby.

Don't feel left out if you are a boy – you may still get scanned one day, if you have gallstones, for example.

Ultrasound scans have replaced X-rays, because X-rays were found to cause cancer in a small number of babies each year. As far as anyone can tell, ultrasound has no harmful side-effects.

There's another use of ultrasound in medicine. If you have kidney stones, they may be treated by directing a beam of ultrasound at them. This shatters them to a fine powder, which then comes out in the patient's urine.

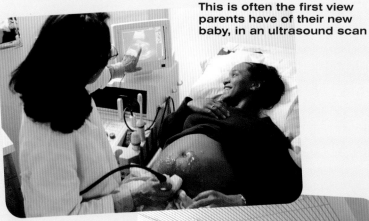

This is often the first view parents have of their new baby, in an ultrasound scan

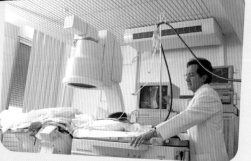

This doctor is using ultrasound to break up the patient's kidney stones. An X-ray image helps to make sure that the ultrasound goes to just the right place.

Bats and ultrasound

You probably know that bats use ultrasound to find their way around in the dark. They emit high-pitched squeaks, which we cannot hear. Then they listen for the reflected sounds, so that they can build up a picture of their surroundings. They can distinguish between rough and smooth surfaces, and they can detect tiny insects which are their prey.

The frog-eating bat from Panama can eat as many as 40 frogs in a night. It simply listens for their croaks. It also knows how to distinguish between edible and poisonous frogs.

Some species of insect emit ultrasound to confuse any bats that may be after them. It's a real ultrasound arms race out there!

In order to detect ultrasound, bats must have special ears. They have big earflaps to gather the reflected sound. So that they do not deafen themselves, the three small bones inside their ears move apart as they emit their squeaks. From the X-ray photograph, you can see that bats also have very large **cochleas**, for even greater sensitivity.

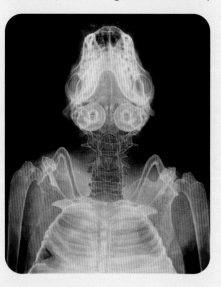

In this X-ray image, you can see the large, curled-up cochleas at the back of the bat's skull. These help it to detect very faint sounds.

THE HUSH CREW

Drum out of use

- A loud sound has a large amplitude.
- A high-pitched sound has a high frequency.
- Sound travels as vibrations of particles. This means that it can travel through solids, liquids and gases, but not through a vacuum.
- Noise is unwanted sound.
- Loud sounds can damage your hearing.

DANGER! AVOID THESE COMMON ERRORS

Don't get confused between 'high' sounds and 'loud' sounds. Sometimes we talk about turning the volume up high, but that makes the sound louder, not higher.

Remember that sound needs a material to travel through, because it is the vibrating particles that pass the sound on. The particles don't travel with the sound – they oscillate back and forth as the sound is passed from one particle to the next.

Key words

cochlea
detector
reflected
ultrasound
waves

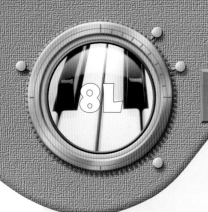

REVIEW QUESTIONS
Understanding and applying concepts

1   Look at the three diagrams showing the traces of three sounds (A, B and C), as shown by an oscilloscope.

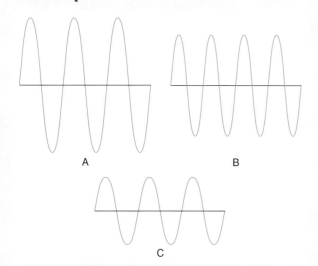

a   How does the pitch of the sounds change, from A to B to C? Explain how you can tell.
b   How does the loudness of the sounds change, from A to B to C? Explain how you can tell.

2   The photograph shows a stethoscope. At one end is a thin, flexible diaphragm which the doctor presses onto the patient's chest. The hollow tubes lead up to the doctor's ears. Explain in as much detail as you can how the stethoscope helps the doctor to hear what is going on inside the patient.

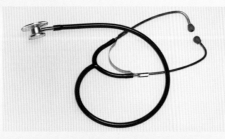

Ways with words

3   We talk about a sound having a 'high' pitch. The word 'high' usually describes how tall something is.
a   Explain what it means to say that a sound has a high pitch or a low pitch.
b   Suggest a way of remembering these meanings of the words 'high' and 'low'.
c   Give the meaning of the word 'frequency', and suggest a way of remembering it.

Making more of maths

4   You can work out the frequency of a sound from its trace on an oscilloscope.

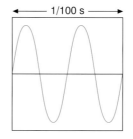 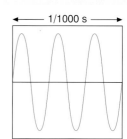

In the first diagram, you can see that there are two complete waves on the screen. The width of the screen represents one hundredth of a second (0.01 s).
a   Draw a sketch to show what is meant by 'one complete wave'.
b   If two waves fit in to one hundredth of a second, how many waves fit in to a whole second?
c   What is the frequency of this sound?

The second diagram shows the trace for a different sound. The oscilloscope controls have been changed, so that the width of the screen represents one thousandth of a second (0.001 s).
d   How many complete waves are there across the screen?
e   Does this wave have a higher or lower frequency than the first sound? Work out its frequency.

Thinking skills

5 Our senses help us to learn a lot about the world around us. Seeing and hearing are particularly important and these depend on light and sound.

In what ways are light and sound similar? In what ways are they different?

Extension question

6 Pip was blowing her own trumpet into a microphone. The drawing shows the trace which appeared on the oscilloscope.

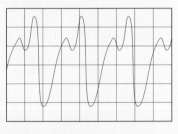

Describe how the particles of the air move when someone plays the trumpet. (You might find it easier to demonstrate this, rather than writing a description.)

How would the movement of the particles change if Pip played a higher note? Or a louder note?

SAT-STYLE QUESTIONS

1 Benson was investigating the different notes produced by his flute. He played it next to a microphone, which was connected to an oscilloscope. The diagrams show some of the traces he observed.

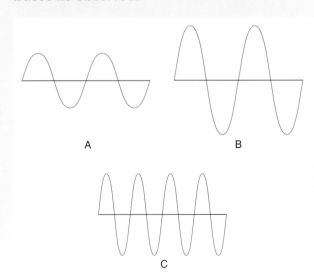

A

B

C

a Which diagram represents a loud, high-pitched note? (1)

b Which diagram represents a loud, low-pitched note? (1)

c Which diagram represents a soft, low-pitched note? (1)

2 Pip and Molly were investigating different materials, to see which was the best absorber of sound. Molly put squares of material over her ears, and Pip played her trumpet nearby. Molly judged which material let through the least sound.

a List *three* things which Molly and Pip should keep the same for this to be a fair test. (3)

b Why would it be better to use a signal generator and a loudspeaker to produce the sound, rather than using a trumpet? (1)

3 Small children have to learn that it is dangerous to poke things into their ears, as this can damage the eardrum.

a Describe how the eardrum moves when a sound enters the ear. (1)

b How does its motion change if the sound gets louder? (1)

c How does its motion change if the pitch of the sound gets lower? (1)

Key words

Unscramble these:

chipt
eosin
murdera
cholace
timaduple

Best practice in Sc1

Researching – using secondary sources

> Now I need to find the answer to the question: 'What's inside a ladybird?'

- Mike can use reference material to find out the structure of a ladybird's body.

DIFFERENT TYPES OF ENQUIRY

> Science is never boring... there are so many different ways to find the answers to scientific questions.

- Scientific enquiries (Sc1 activities) are all about finding the answers to questions.
- Here are some of the strategies you can use. The one you choose depends on the question you want to answer.

Observing and exploring

> Just how many ladybirds can live on this rose bush and what do they eat?

- This is an example of a question that we could start to answer by observing and counting ladybirds.

Fair testing – controlling variables

> Sometimes we need to carry out a fair test to answer a question like 'What affects the pitch of a note made by a stretched string?'

- In some enquiries we can carefully control all the variables that might have an effect, and just vary the one under investigation. This is a fair test.
- So Molly might investigate the effect of the length of the string on pitch. In this case she would systematically vary the length of the string, keeping all other variables that might affect the pitch the same.
- This will show us how one variable (the length of the string) affects another variable (the pitch of the note).

Pattern seeking – surveys and correlation

Do the weeds we find in a field differ in different parts of the field?

- Sometimes we want to know how one variable affects another, but there may be lots of factors that we can't control. In these enquiries we need to increase the size of the sample we look at before we can see any real patterns that come out of our data.

Using models and analogies

I find sound much easier to understand now I can visualise a sound wave.

So can we use this model to explain about the amplitude and frequency of a note?

- We can use models to help investigate our questions. For example, in Year 7 you used a water pump to help explain how a battery works in an electrical circuit. In Year 8 we use molecular model kits to represent atoms and molecules. This helps us answer questions such as 'Why do we get twice as much hydrogen as oxygen when we break down water using electricity?'
- The better a model, the more things it can help explain and the more correct predictions you can make using it.

Identifying and classifying

What type of rock is this?

Here, use this key.

- Sometimes we want to identify things, such as plants, animals, rocks, compounds or stars. We can use a variety of methods to help us, for example, keys, descriptions, chemical tests. At other times we might want to classify something to a particular group. For example, is an element a metal, non-metal or metalloid? Or which group is this animal in?

Using and evaluating a technique or design

Are you sure this circuit could work a set of traffic lights?

- In this type of enquiry you are solving a problem using a technique, which might involve a sequence of steps. Or you might be using your science to design a solution to a problem, such as making a burglar alarm.

Key words

analogies
classifying
enquiry
model
variables

Best practice in Sc1

PLANNING HOW TO GATHER YOUR DATA

1. Reese and Pete are studying a pendulum. Their teacher asks them 'What affects how quickly a pendulum swings?'

What affects how quickly a pendulum swings?

2. First of all, they list all the variables that might affect the swinging pendulum. This is the start of planning their fair test.

Length of string, mass of the bob at the end, height you release it from... Er that's it I think.

What about the colour of the string...? Only joking!

3. Reese and Pete have now identified all the key variables in their investigation.

4.

What shall we investigate then?

The length of the string? Let's see how that affects how many swings it does in, say, 20 seconds.

5.

Right, let's sort out all the variables...

Planning a fair test.

We will change:
The independent variable.

We will measure its effect on:
The dependent variable.

We will keep these things the same:
The control variables.

The length of the string

The number of swings in 20 seconds

The mass of the bob

The height of release

You can use these questions below to help you plan and carry out fair tests.

Investigation planner

Have you thought about these?:

1. What are you trying to find out?
2. a) What do you think (predict) will happen?
   b) Why do you think this will happen?
3. What are you going to change each time? This is your **independent variable**.
4. How can you judge the effect of changing your independent variable? What are you going to observe or measure each time? This is your **dependent variable**.
5. What will you keep the same each time to make it a fair test? These are your **control variables**.
6. How will you carry out your tests? How many values for your independent variable will you choose to test?
7. Is your plan safe? Could anything go wrong and somebody get hurt? (Check with your teacher.)
8. What equipment will you need?
9. How many readings will you need to take? Do you need to repeat tests?
10. What is the best way to show your results? A table? . . . and a bar chart? . . . or a line graph?

Questions

A group were investigating friction.

They wanted to see how the mass in a shoe affected the force needed to move the shoe.

- The title of their investigation was phrased as a question. What is the title of the investigation?
- What type of enquiry would answer their question?
- What was the independent variable in their investigation?
- What was the dependent variable?
- Which variables did they have to control?

RECORDING YOUR DATA

The story continues . . .

We'd better plan a table to put our results in.

Yes, let's do it properly... Remember that the independent variable goes in the first column and the dependent variable goes in the second.

Length of the string (cm)	Number of swings in 20 seconds			
	1st test	2nd test	3rd test	Mean

Key words

control variables
dependent variable
fair test
independendent variable

Best practice in Sc1

1.

How many different lengths shall we investigate?

We need at least 5 different lengths to draw a graph from.

2.

Here we go then...

Length of the string (cm)	Number of swings in 20 seconds			
	1st test	2nd test	3rd test	Mean
10.0	32	33	31	32
20.1	23	22	21	22
30.0	17	19	18	18
39.8	16	17	15	16
50.0	14	14	14	14
60.2	14	14	13	13
80.1	12	11	11	11
100.0	10	10	10	10

3.

Now that we've done our testing, what shall we do with our data?

This can go on a line graph.

4.

So our dependent variable... the number of swings in 20 seconds... goes on the y (vertical) axis.

Exactly, Pete. Then we can draw a line of best fit through our mean results... no 'dot-to-dot' now!

5.

Number of swings in 20 seconds

(graph: x-axis "Length of the string (cm)" from 10 to 100, y-axis from 10 to 40, showing a decreasing curve)

ANALYSING YOUR EVIDENCE

THE END IS NIGH!

- Having carried out your enquiry, you should try to answer your original question.
- You should also judge whether or not any predictions you made are supported by the evidence collected.
- Any patterns in your data should be explained using your scientific knowledge and understanding.

EVALUATING YOUR EVIDENCE

As you carry out your enquiries, and certainly at the end of your activity, you should always consider the strength of your evidence:

- Can you draw a **valid** conclusion using the data collected? For example, you might choose a poor range for the 'Length of the string'. A narrow range of 10.0. 10.2, 10.4, 10.6, 10.8 and 11.0 cm might yield data that points to no pattern or only a slight **correlation** (link) between the length of string and the rate of swing. You need a wider set of values for the length of the string to get the data from which to draw a valid conclusion.

- Is your evidence **reliable**? If you, or somebody else, were to do the same investigation, would they come up with the same data? If they do, you have collected strong evidence for any conclusions you come to. This is why we carry out repeat readings in some investigations – to generate reliable data. Therefore, if you have large differences within sets of repeat readings, your data could be unreliable and you can't place much trust in your conclusions.

- How could you improve your enquiry? Suggest any improvements you could make to the quality of the evidence collected. Think about the points above.

- You could also consider any patterns you spot – ask yourself 'Are they likely to extend beyond the range of values you chose to investigate?' How could you check this out?

- If you are doing a 'pattern seeking' enquiry think about the size of the sample you chose. Was it large enough to be confident in your conclusions?

Ah-ha, the pattern is clear now.

Are you quite sure about that?

Questions

How would you tackle these questions? Choose from the types of enquiry described on pages 210 and 211:

- How does temperature affect how quickly copper sulphate dissolves?
- What is the temperature on the surface of Jupiter?
- How can you make your own thermometer?
- What type of insect is this?
- Do men have a faster pulse rate than women?
- Why do metals expand when we heat them up?
- What happens when calcium metal is added to water?

Key words

analysing
conclusion
correlation
evaluating
reliable
valid

8A Food and digestion

8A1 & 8A3 Find out what this is: BMI – Body Mass Index. Why are doctors worried about the nation's BMI?

8A3 Visit the World Health Organisation's web site to find out about where in the world people are well fed, and where they are malnourished.

8A5 People are encouraged to eat a low-fat diet for their health, but there are problems for children who do not get enough essential fatty acids in their diet. Find out about essential fatty acids and why we need them.

8A5 Dr William Beaumont was a pioneer doctor in the USA. He had a patient with an injury to his stomach. Dr Beaumont was able to use this patient to find out what the stomach does. Find out more about Dr Beaumont and his work.

8A6 Washing powder enzymes digest food spilt on your clothes. Devise an experiment to find out how good they are at removing food stains.
You will need to decide:
- what foods to use – such as ketchup or blackcurrant juice,
- how to make each stain the same,
- your washing technique,
- the temperature of your wash,
- how you are going to measure stain removal.

rmance

8B Respiration

8B1 Some animals and bacteria, such as glow worms, some tropical fish and angler fish, use light energy. Find out about how one of these organisms uses light.

8B2 William Withering made one of the earliest scientific investigations of a natural remedy. Find out about his work developing digitalin made from foxgloves for heartbeat problems.

8B3 There is much less oxygen at high altitudes, yet people live and work there. Find out about differences in the blood of people who live in high mountains compared to dwellers at sea-level. How do mountaineers who tackle high mountains such as Everest, or fighter pilots cope with a shortage of oxygen?

8B5 Find out about how animals, such as insects or reptiles, obtain oxygen and release carbon dioxide.

Key words

Research these new words:
emphysema
food additive
haemoglobin
heartbeat
metabolism

8C Microbes and disease

8C3 Try making yoghurt at home with an adult to help you. Some commercial yoghurts contain live bacteria so you will need one of this sort as your source of bacteria. Remember to keep things clean when you do it.

8C4 Look out for reports of outbreaks of infections such as food-poisoning, 'flu, BSE, cholera. Monitor the spread of the infection and what health authorities are doing to limit the spread.

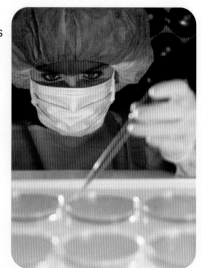

8C5 During the spring and summer the air is full of flower pollen. We breathe it in and it gets into our lungs. Some people are sensitive to pollen antigens and develop hay fever. Find out what happens in hay fever.

8C6 'Flu is a severe infection. Each year it claims lives. Vulnerable people are encouraged to have a vaccination that will protect them from infection. Find out who is offered the vaccination and why.

8D Ecological relationships

8D4 Research a mutualistic relationship in which each partner provides something the other needs. You could look at lichens, or hermit crabs and sea anemones.

8D4 Find out what happened when sand eels in the North Sea were extensively fished for fish meal.

8D4 Investigate the introduction of any alien species you find in your survey.

8D5 Plan making a model rock pool in your laboratory. You should think about how to keep the water cool if you want to keep British species, as well as oxygenating the water.

a) How will you provide rock pool habitats such as crevices and sand to dig in?

b) Which species of animals and plants and how many would it be reasonable and humane to keep in your rock pool?

c) Will you need to feed your inhabitants or can your food web sustain itself?

Key words

Research these new words:
allergy
antibiotic resistant
limestone pavement
measles
parasites

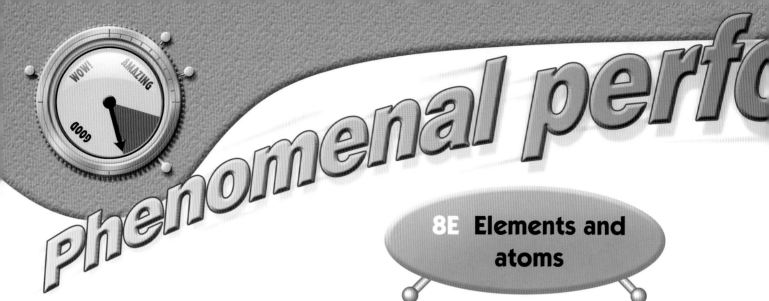

8E Elements and atoms

8E1 Do some research to find out the Ancient Greeks' theory about elements.
Give an example of how they could explain things using their theory.

8E2 The mass of the smallest atom, hydrogen, is about 1.7×10^{-27} kg.
a) The mass of a carbon atom is roughly 12 times greater than that of a hydrogen atom. What is the approximate mass of a carbon atom?
b) If you have 1 g of hydrogen atoms, how many hydrogen atoms would there be?

8E3 a) Find out how Ytterby, a village in Sweden, has played an important part in the naming of chemical elements.
b) Make a list of other chemical elements that have been named after places.
c) Make a list of chemical elements that have been named after people.

8E4 Caffeine is a compound found in tea, coffee and chocolate. Look at this model of one of its molecules.
a) What is the chemical formula of caffeine?
b) Explain why caffeine is called a compound, and not an element.
c) Compare the caffeine molecule with the molecule of theobromine shown on page 90. What is the difference between the two molecules?

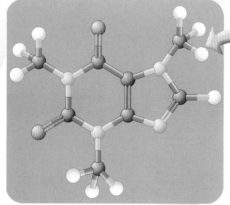

A molecule of caffeine

8E5 There is a group in the Periodic Table whose elements are very unreactive. For a long time people thought that they would not react with other elements at all. However, in the 1960s their first reaction was discovered.
a) Write a paragraph about this group of elements.
b) Give an example of a compound that can be formed from one of these elements. Write down its chemical formula and the word equation for its formation.

8F Compounds and mixtures

8F1 Find out how we get the element sulphur from underground. Include a diagram to explain the process.
Give another source of sulphur that has become increasingly important.

8F2 The 'combining power' of phosphorus (P) can be 3 or 5.
a) Give the formula of the two chlorides that phosphorus can form.
b) Draw a molecule of carbon dioxide, showing its chemical bonds.
c) Draw a possible structure for a molecule of ozone, O_3.

8F3 a) Draw a flow diagram that shows how we separate gases from air.
b) Look at the uses of the gases we extract from liquid air on page 99. Choose one use of a gas. Then draw a poster giving details of this use and why the gas is used in this way.

8F4 a) Explain how you would test a sample of a colourless liquid that you suspected was pure water.
b) Why wouldn't anhydrous copper sulphate or blue cobalt chloride paper help you prove the sample was *pure* water?
c) Using particle theory, think up an explanation of why salt water has a higher boiling point than pure water.

This sulphur is being stored following its extraction

Key words

Research these new words:
atomic clocks
graphite
LCDs
UPAC
uranium

8G Rocks and weathering

8G1 Crude oil is found trapped underground.
Do some research to find out how we find out where to drill for oil.
Describe what a 'cap rock' is and how porosity of rock is important in explaining the location of the crude oil underground.

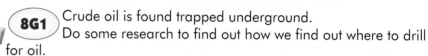

8G2 Find out about the formation of underground caverns in limestone regions in more detail.
Include a word equation that describes how stalactites and stalagmites are formed.

Drilling for oil near Mexican Hat in Utah, USA

8G3 **a)** Describe how physical and chemical weathering could combine in the weathering of a granite rock face.
b) Why can biological weathering be described as another form of physical weathering?

8G4 Explain how erosion can explain why a river meanders.
Find out how this leads to the formation of an oxbow lake.
Illustrate your answers with diagrams.

8G5 **a)** What do sharp boundaries between bedding planes tell us?
b) Explain how the boundaries between some beds of rock merge into each other.
c) A bed contains mixed sizes of rock fragments. Think of a set of conditions that could explain how these fragments were deposited together.

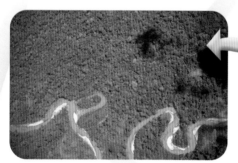

This river in Ecuador is forming an oxbow lake

8G6 Draw a poster that explains the different ways that fossils can be formed.

8H The rock cycle

8H1 Explain why some sandstones are soft and crumbly, whereas other are very hard.

8H2 An exposed cliff face shows thick sedimentary layers of a soft brown sandstone and thinner layers of chalk.
How could the changing face of the Earth over time explain how these might have been formed?

8H3 Find out more about the 'earth movements' responsible for the formation of metamorphic rock. You can research one of these questions:
- How can we see where the boundaries between tectonic plates lie?
- What is 'subduction'? (Include a diagram to illustrate your answer.)
- Why is San Francisco at risk from earthquakes?
- What is 'seafloor spreading'?

8H4 Plan a safe investigation you could do to find out how one factor affects the viscosity (runniness) of lava. You can use syrup to model the behaviour of the lava.

8H5 In 1995 the volcano on Montserrat, a tiny island in the Caribbean, erupted after lying dormant for centuries. Find out how the volcano on Montserrat affected the lives of people on the island.

A new delta of land has formed on the island of Montserrat

Key words

Research these new words:
Giant's Causeway
magnetic reversal
metaquartzite
Richter scale
salt domes

81 Heating, cooling

811 We have nerve-endings in our skin to detect temperature. The skin of our lips is particularly sensitive. Try touching some different clean objects on your lip. Can you tell if they are at different temperatures? Explain what the word 'sensitive' means here. Can you suggest a reason why our lips need to be sensitive to temperature? Take care! Don't touch anything too hot or cold with your lips, or surfaces that might be contaminated with bacteria or hazardous chemicals.

812 Draw a picture or a diagram of a room. Include some things which are hotter than the room – radiators, people, etc. – and things which are colder – the windows, perhaps. Add arrows to show how heat energy moves about in the room.

813 People and other animals live in the frozen Arctic. Find out how insulating materials make this possible.

814 The diagram shows a bimetal strip. It is made from two different metals, welded tightly together. When it is cold, it is straight, but when it is heated, it bends. Which metal has expanded more? Try to explain why this happens. Find out some uses of bimetal strips.

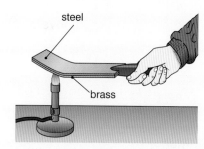

steel

brass

816 The Gulf Stream is a convection current. It brings warm water from the tropics to western Europe. Find out how this affects our climate. What would happen if climate change meant that it stopped flowing?

8J Magnets and electromagnets

8J3 The Earth's magnetic poles keep moving. Very gradually, they wander around in the Arctic and Antarctic regions. This means that, from one year to the next, a compass needle points in a slightly different direction.

An Ordnance Survey map shows how to take account of this. Find an OS map, and look at the part where the symbols are explained. How fast does magnetic north move?

Do some research. Find a map which shows how the positions of the Earth's magnetic poles have varied over the centuries.

8J4 Audio and video tapes are covered in tiny particles of magnetic material. Find out how electromagnets are used to magnetise these when music or a TV programme is recorded. How do magnetic materials help computers store information?

8J5 Many ammeters and voltmeters have a needle which moves across a scale to show the current or voltage. Inside, they have a small coil of wire, and a permanent magnet.

Examine a meter like this, and try to see the coil of wire. Use a plotting compass to detect the permanent magnet.

When a current flows through the coil, it moves round. Try to explain how this works.

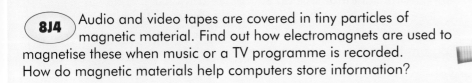

Magnetic recording makes use of electromagnets

Key words

Research these new words:
magnetic declination
magnetic reversal
thermochromic paint

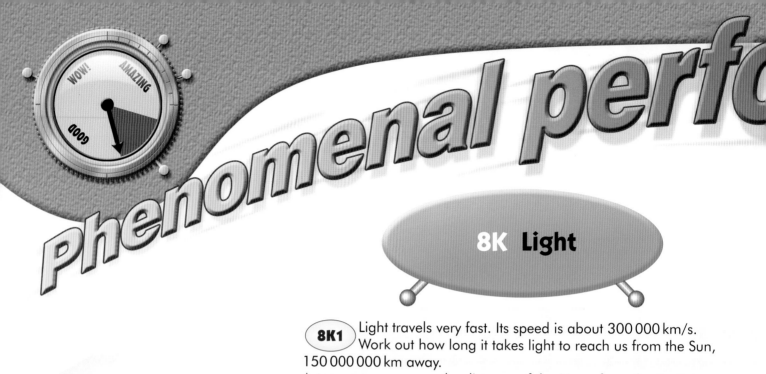

8K Light

8K1 Light travels very fast. Its speed is about 300 000 km/s. Work out how long it takes light to reach us from the Sun, 150 000 000 km away.
Astronomers measure the distance of the Moon from the Earth by finding how long it takes for a ray of light to travel to the Moon and back. If it takes light 2.7 s for this round-trip, how far away is the Moon?

8K2 A mirror reflects all of the light that falls on it. So does white paper. What's the difference? Can you draw a diagram to help your explanation?
(Hint: Think about how rough or smooth their surfaces are.)

This giant mirror reflects the Sun's rays. It's part of a solar power station in France.

8K4 Explain why mirrors can be useful to these people: dentists, drivers, shopkeepers, astronomers.

8K5 Windows are made of flat sheets of glass. Some rooms, such as bathrooms, have windows with a different kind of glass. The thickness of this glass varies, so you can't see clearly through it. Use the idea of refraction to explain this.

8K6 What colours are not part of the spectrum? Can you explain why they do not belong to the spectrum?

rmance

8L Sound and hearing

8L1 Draw a design for a musical toy for a child. Explain how they can use it to make sounds of different pitches and loudness.

8L2 Find out about the frequencies of notes on the musical scale. Can you find out about the mathematical relationships between them?

8L3 Heat travels quickly through steel, and so does sound. Heat and sound both travel more slowly through air. What's the connection?

8L4 As we get older, our range of hearing tends to decrease. In particular, it is harder to hear high-pitched sounds and softer sounds.
Devise a way of representing in a diagram the range of someone's hearing. How would the diagram change as someone got older?

8L5 Imagine that you lived under the flight path at an airport. How could you try to cut out the noise of low-flying aircraft?
How would you react if the airport proposed to increase the number of aircraft landing and taking off at night?

GLOSSARY

absorption　when something (e.g. light or sound) is absorbed, so that it no longer exists. When nutrients or gases, such as oxygen pass into the body. **pp. 181, 188**

aerobic respiration　a process that uses oxygen to release energy from glucose. **p. 22**

alveolus　an air sac in the lungs. **p. 30**

amino acid　made when proteins are digested. **p. 12**

amplitude　a measure of the size of a sound vibration. **p. 199**

amylase　a digestive enzyme that breaks down starch. **pp. 12, 15**

anaerobic respiration　a process which releases energy from glucose without using oxygen. **p. 27**

angle of incidence　the angle between a ray of light and the normal at the point where the ray hits a surface. **p. 184**

angle of reflection　the angle between a reflected ray of light and the normal at the point where the ray reflects off a surface. **p. 184**

angle of refraction　the angle between a refracted ray of light and the normal at the point where the ray refracts at a surface. **p. 184**

antibiotic　a substance that kills bacteria. **pp. 44, 52**

antibody　a substance made by white blood cells that stops infections. **p. 49**

antigen　a marker substance on the outside of cells. **p. 49**

antiseptic　a substance that kills micro-organisms in wounds. **p. 52**

artery　a muscular blood vessel that carries blood away from the heart. **p. 25**

arthropods　a group of animals with hard external skeleton and jointed legs. **p. 60**

atom　the smallest particle that can still be identified as an element. **p. 80**

attract　pull towards you with a force. **p. 163**

basalt　a fine-grained (made up of small crystals) igneous rock made when molten rock cools quickly and crystallises at or near the surface. **p. 133**

beam　a wide ray of light. **p. 178**

boiling point　the temperature at which a liquid becomes a gas. **pp. 100, 155**

bronchus　the airway that leads from the trachea into a lung. **p. 29**

calcium　a grey metallic element. It is found in minerals we need for strong bones. **p. 6**

capillary   a tiny blood vessel specialised for supplying cells with oxygen and nutrients and removing wastes. pp. 25, 26

carbohydrate   a type of nutrient that provides us with energy. Starch and sugar are carbohydrates. p. 5

Celsius scale   the scientific scale of temperature. p. 143

cementation   the process in which dissolved solids come out of solution to 'stick' rock fragments together. This helps to form sedimentary rock. p. 126

change of state   a change from one state of matter (solid, liquid or gas) to another. p. 154

circulatory system   the system that sends blood round your body. pp. 24, 34

classification   a way of organising animals and plants into groups with similar features. p. 60

colony   a group of bacteria growing on nutrient agar jelly. p. 42

compaction   the process in which pressure builds up on sediment as layers are deposited on top, resulting in the particles fusing together. This helps the formation of sedimentary rock. p. 126

compete   organisms compete for the resources they need, such as light or food. p. 66

composition   details of the substances found in a material. p. 97

compound   a substance made up of two or more different types of atom. The different elements in the compound are always present in the same ratio. pp. 84, 95, 97

conduction   when heat energy travels through a solid material. p. 152

conserve   save; don't waste; stop animals and plants dying out. p. 152

consumer   an animal that eats plants or other animals. p. 66

contract   get smaller; muscle action that moves body parts. pp. 28, 148

convection   energy transfer by a hot liquid or gas as it flows. pp. 151, 152

convection current   the circulation of a liquid or gas when hot material rises and cold material replaces it. p. 150

core   a piece of iron or steel inside an electromagnet; makes it stronger. pp. 168, 171

decibel (dB)   the unit of loudness of a sound. p. 205

decomposer   an organism that breaks down dead plant and animal remains. pp. 60, 66

deficiency disease   an illness caused by not having enough of a nutrient. p. 6

degrees C (°C)   the unit of temperature measurement. p. 142

denatured   a denatured enzyme has changed shape, so that it cannot work. p. 14

density   calculated using density = mass/volume. p. 151

Key words

on key people
Alexander Fleming
antibiotics
Robert Koch
growing bacteria
William Gilbert
magnetism

GLOSSARY

deposit
verb – to lay down or settle an object in a place.
noun – the object that settles down.
pp. 114, 117

diaphragm
muscles used in breathing that separate your chest and your abdomen. **p. 28**

diet
all the different foods we eat. **p. 8**

diffusion
the tendency for particles to move about randomly and to spread out and mix with each other. **p. 3**

digestion
breaking down large insoluble molecules in food into smaller soluble molecules that can be absorbed. **pp. 12, 15**

disinfectant
a powerful substance, such as bleach, that kills micro-organisms. **p. 52**

eardrum
the first part of the ear to vibrate when a sound enters. **p. 203**

electromagnet
a magnet made from a coil of wire, operated by an electric current. **p. 168**

element
a substance made up of only one type of atom. Elements cannot be broken down chemically into simpler substances. **p. 79**

energy
the ability to make things happen. **p. 196**

enzyme
speeds up chemical reactions in the body. **pp. 12, 14, 16, 44**

erosion
the wearing away of rocks as they rub against each other. **p. 115**

evaluate
consider how good an experimental method is. **p. 165**

excretion
removing harmful materials made by the body. **p. 31**

exhale
to breathe out. **p. 28**

expand
get bigger. **p. 148**

faeces
undigested food and bacteria that pass out of your digestive system. **p. 11**

fatty acid
made when fats are digested. **p. 12**

fermentation
the process in which micro-organisms such as yeast feed and produce wastes such as alcohol. **p. 44**

fibre
indigestible material in plant foods. Fibre is mainly cellulose from plant cell walls. **pp. 4, 11**

filter
a coloured material through which light can pass. **p. 188**

food web
a set of linked food chains in a habitat. **p. 66**

formula
the abbreviation that tells us the number of each type of atom in a molecule, e.g. H_2, CH_4, H_2O. **p. 85**

freezing point
the temperature at which a liquid becomes a solid. **p. 155**

frequency
the number of vibrations in a second. **pp. 197, 202**

gabbro
a coarse-grained (made up of large crystals) igneous rock that is rich in iron-bearing minerals. **p. 135**

gas exchange absorbing oxygen and releasing carbon dioxide in the lungs. **p. 30**

glucose the main energy source for respiration. It is made by digesting carbohydrates **pp. 12, 22**

glycogen glucose is stored in muscle and liver cells as glycogen. **p. 13**

gneiss a metamorphic rock formed in the intense pressure and heat during mountain-building episodes. It is recognised by its light and dark bands. **p. 130**

granite a coarse-grained (made up of large crystals) igneous rock that is rich in minerals bearing silicon and oxygen. **pp. 108, 111, 133, 135**

haemoglobin a protein found in red blood cells. It carries oxygen round the body as oxyhaemoglobin. **p. 26**

heart an organ that pumps blood to the body and to the lungs. **p. 25**

heat energy energy moving from a hotter place to a colder place. **p. 144**

hertz (Hz) the unit of frequency; 1 hertz = 1 vibration per second. **p. 202**

hydrochloric acid an acid you make in your stomach. It kills bacteria in your food and helps to digest protein. **pp. 10, 15**

igneous rock types formed by solidifying molten rock. **p. 132**

image a picture of something, formed by light. **p. 182**

immune system defends us against infectious micro-organisms. **p. 48**

immunisation giving someone a vaccine to protect them from an infection. **p. 50**

immunity our body's ability to resist an infection. **pp. 48, 50**

incident ray a ray of light which strikes a surface. **p. 184**

incubator keeps things at a warm temperature. **p. 43**

infectious disease a disease caused by a micro-organism that can spread from one person to another. **p. 46**

infra-red radiation invisible radiation similar to light, spreading out from a hot object. **pp. 150, 178**

inhale to breathe in. **p. 28**

inoculate to spread bacteria on nutrient agar jelly to give someone a vaccination. **p. 42**

insulation a material which prevents heat or sound energy from travelling. **pp. 153, 205**

invertebrate an animal that does not have an internal backbone. **p. 60**

inverted upside down, or left-right reversed. **p. 184**

iron a metallic element we need to make red blood cells. **p. 6**

lactic acid an acid made in cells by anaerobic respiration. **p. 27**

large intestine a section of your digestive system that extracts water from undigested food remains. **p. 11**

Key words

on key people
Stephen Sparks
volcanoes
James Dewar
low temperatures
Marie Curie
radium

GLOSSARY

laser a source of a narrow beam of light. p. 178

lipase an enzyme that digests fats. p. 12

loudness how loud or soft a sound is. p. 196

loudspeaker a scientific device used for making sounds. p. 198

luminous describes something that gives out light. p. 182

magnetic field the area around a magnet where it can affect magnetic materials. p. 166

magnetic material any material which is attracted by a magnet. p. 162

magnetised turned into a magnet. p. 170

malnutrition not having the correct balance of nutrients for health. p. 8

melting point the temperature at which a solid turns into a liquid. p. 100

metamorphic rocks whose structure and/or mineral content has been changed by the action of heat and/or pressure. p. 130

micro-organism a living thing that is usually too small to be seen with an unaided eye. p. 40

microphone a scientific instrument used for collecting sounds. p. 199

mineral compounds of an element that plants and animals need to make their cells. Also means a solid element or compound found naturally. pp. 4, 6, 108

mixture two or more different substances mixed, but not chemically combined, together. A mixture does not have a fixed composition, i.e. the ratio of the different substances present can vary. pp. 94, 97, 98

model a 'picture' constructed by scientists to help explain the way things work. p. 184

molecule groups of two or more atoms bonded together. p. 84

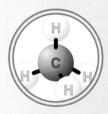

nickel a magnetic metallic element. p. 162

noise unwanted sound. p. 204

noise pollution unwanted sounds in the environment. p. 204

non-luminous describes something that doesn't give out light; it is seen by reflected light. p. 182

normal the line at right angles to a surface, where a ray of light strikes the surface. p. 184

north-seeking pole the pole of a magnet which points north. p. 166

nutrient a food component that is essential for health. p. 4

nutrient agar jelly a food for growing bacteria. p. 42

obese being so overweight that your health suffers. p. 9

obsidian igneous rock with a shiny black appearance and glassy texture. It forms from small eruptions of magma that cool down so quickly that no crystals have time to form. p. 133

opaque   describes a material that will not transmit light. **p. 181**

oscillate   move back and forth in a regular way. **p. 201**

oscilloscope   a scientific instrument used for displaying sounds. **p. 198**

pancreas   an organ that makes digestive enzymes. **p. 10**

particle model   a way of thinking about matter as made up of many tiny particles. **p. 149**

pasteurisation   treating milk to kill harmful microbes. **p. 54**

penicillin   a type of antibiotic. **p. 52**

percentage cover   a way of measuring plants that grow in clumps. **p. 64**

Periodic Table   a table of the chemical elements arranged so that similar elements line up in vertical columns (called groups). **p. 83**

peristalsis   the way that muscles in the digestive system contract and relax to push food along. **p. 10**

permanent magnet   a magnet which doesn't require a current to make it work. **p. 168**

petri dish   a dish for growing bacteria. **p. 42**

pH   a measure of how acidic or alkaline a solution is. A pH of less than 7 is acidic, a pH of more than 7 is alkaline. **p. 15**

pitch   how high or low a note sounds. **p. 196**

pole   where the magnetic force of a magnet is most concentrated. **p. 163**

pooter   a suction device for catching tiny animals. **p. 63**

population boom   the result of animals having plenty of food and few predators so that they live and breed successfully. **p. 68**

predator–prey relationship   this is concerned with the changes in the population size of a predator and the prey it eats. **p. 69**

primary colours   the three colours from which all other colours of light can be made. **p. 188**

producer   a plant. It converts light energy into food energy. **p. 66**

proportion   the relative amount of a part present in the whole, usually expressed as a fraction or percentage. **p. 97**

proportional   when one quantity increases in step with another. **p. 171**

protease   an enzyme that digests protein. **pp. 12, 15**

protein   a nutrient that we need to grow. **p. 4**

pumice   an igneous rock formed from 'volcanic froth' that solidifies rapidly. **p. 133**

pure   made of a single substance. **p. 101**

pyramid of numbers   a pyramid that shows how many organisms there are at each step of a food chain. **p. 70**

Key words

on key people
William Beaumont
digestive enzymes
Amadeo Avagadro
atoms
Isaac Newton
the spectrum

GLOSSARY

quadrat — a device for measuring the number of plants in an area. p. 64

radiation — when heat travels outwards from a hot object in the form of infra-red radiation. pp. 150, 152

random sampling — a method of gathering unbiased data about the plants and animals in an area. p. 64

range of hearing — the range of frequencies which someone can hear, from lowest to highest. p. 202

ratio — the relative numbers of constituents in a whole, e.g. each type of element in a compound. p. 103

ray — a very thin beam of light. p. 182

ray diagram — a diagram to show where light travels. p. 183

red blood cell — a cell that is specialised for transporting oxygen round the body. p. 26

reflect — bounce off a surface. pp. 180, 189

reflected ray — a ray of light after it has been reflected by a surface. p. 184

reflection — when something (e.g. light or sound) bounces off a surface. p. 181

refraction — when light bends as it travels from one material into another. p. 186

repel — push away from you with a force. p. 163

respiration — the release of energy from glucose. pp. 22, 27, 44, 70

ribcage — the bony cage made by your ribs and breastbone that protects your heart and lungs. p. 28

saliva — a digestive juice that is made in your mouth. It breaks down starch. pp. 10, 15

sampling — selecting small samples of something to measure, then applying the findings to the rest. p. 64

schist — a metamorphic rock formed from mudstones and shale that are subjected to high pressure and moderately high temperatures during mountain-building episodes. p. 130

sediment — rock fragments that are deposited. p. 115

sedimentary — rock types formed from the compaction and cementation of sediment. p. 127

sensitive — able to sense small differences or changes. pp. 142, 165

signal generator — a scientific instrument used for making sounds of known frequencies, through a loudspeaker. pp. 198, 202

slate — a metamorphic rock formed when mudstone or shale is subjected to high pressure. Its minerals line up in parallel layers, enabling it to be cleaved along the plane of the minerals. p. 130

solenoid — another name for the coil of an electromagnet. p. 168

sound wave	how sound travels, passed along by vibrating particles. **p. 201**
source	where something (e.g. light) comes from. **p. 178**
south-seeking pole	the pole of a magnet which points south. **p. 166**
spectrum	when light has been split up into all the colours it is made from. **p. 187**
starch	a carbohydrate. A nutrient we need for energy. **p. 4**
steel	a metal, made mostly of iron. **p. 162**
sterile	having no living micro-organisms. **p. 42**
stomach	an organ in which food is churned up and protein is digested. **p. 10**
symbol	the abbreviation of the name of each chemical element, e.g. hydrogen = H, lead = Pb **pp. 80, 85**
temperature	a measure of how hot or cold something is. **p. 142**
thermal conductor	a material that is good at conducting heat. **p. 146**
thermal insulator	a material that is bad at conducting heat. **p. 146**
thermometer	an instrument for measuring temperature. **p. 143**
trachea	the airway leading from the back of the throat to the lungs. **p. 29**
transect	in ecology, samples taken along a line to see how the plants and animals in an area change. **p. 64**
translucent	describes a material that lets light through but through which you can't see clearly. **p. 180**
transmission	when something (e.g. light or sound) is allowed to pass through a material; the method by which micro-organisms spread from one person to another. **pp. 46, 181**
transmit	allow light or sound to pass through. **pp. 180, 188**
transparent	describes a material that lets light pass through. **p. 180**
transport	the moving of rock fragments (by the action of gravity, wind, rivers, sea or glaciers). **p. 114**
upthrust	the upward force on an object in a liquid or gas. **p. 151**
vaccination	giving someone a vaccine to protect them from a disease. **p. 50**
vaccine	a solution that contains fragments of micro-organisms. It provokes the immune system into protecting the body. **p. 50**
vacuum	empty space. **p. 200**
vein	a large blood vessel that conveys blood to the heart. **p. 25**
ventilation	the movement made by your diaphragm and ribcage to move air in and out of your chest. **p. 28**
vibrate	move back and forth at a regular rate. **pp. 196, 201**
villi	minute projections on the surface of the small intestine that provide a large surface area for absorbing nutrients. **p. 10**
vitamin	a type of nutrient required in small amounts. **pp. 4, 6**
weathering	the breakdown of rocks in nature. **p. 110**
white blood cell	a cell in the immune system specialised for protecting against invading micro-organisms. **p. 48**
yeast	a type of fungus. It is used to make bread. **pp. 44, 54**

Key words

on key people
Robert Boyle
gases
Georg von Békésy
the inner ear

ACKNOWLEDGEMENTS

Alamy Images: 14b, 33r, 113, 128t, 146t, 205t; **Brownie Harris/Corbis:** 132l; **Corel 7 (NT)** 106b, **Corel 18 (NT)** 67, **Corel 39 (NT)** 110, 111, **Corel 124 (NT)** 40t, **Corel 183 (NT)** 129m, **Corel 205 (NT)** 27, **Corel 244 (NT)** 66, **Corel 253 (NT)** 30, **Corel 301/Royal Sovereign by William Velde (NT)** 6, **Corel 406 (NT)** 124t, **Corel 416 (NT)** 8t, **Corel 417 (NT)** 151b, **Corel 434 (NT)** 118, **Corel 452 (NT)** 217l, **Corel 465 (NT)** 38b, **Corel 515 (NT):** 92t, **Corel 516 (NT)** 106t, **Corel 517 (NT)** 60b, **Corel 527 (NT)** 194, 227r (all 4), **Corel 541 (NT)** 45, 54l, **Corel 559 (NT)** 217br, **Corel 604 (NT)** 227l, **Corel 620 (NT)** 219, **Corel 669 (NT)** 14l, **Corel 759 (NT)** 50t, 171, **Corel 763 (NT)** 72m, 92b, **Corel 768 (NT)** 217tr, **Corel 776 (NT)** 22; **Digital Stock 7 (NT)** 42br, **Digital Stock 12 (NT)** 26; **Digital Vision PB (NT)** 76b, **Digital Vision 1 (NT)** 168, **Digital Vision 2 (NT)** 4b, **Digital Vision 5 (NT)** 46b, 58b, 182t, **Digital Vision 6 (NT)** 140, **Digital Vision 11 (NT)** 20b, 20t, **Digital Vision 13 (NT)** 200, **Digital Vision 14 (NT)** 132r, 124b, **Digital Vision 15 (NT)** 226, **Digital Vision 17 (NT)** 4t, **Digital Vision 18 (NT)** 151t; **Gerry Ellis and Michael Durham/Digital Vision LC (NT)** 58t, 218b; **Dr B Booth/GSF Picture Library:** 116t, 116bl, 129b, **GSF Picture Library:** 127tr, 128b, 130b, 134l, 134r, **GSF/Rida/GSF Picture Library:** 127l; **Holt Studios:** 60t, **Holt Studios/Wayne Hutchinson:** 68; **i100GC (NT)** 188; **Illustazione Italiana/Mary Evans Picture Library:** 136; **Illustrated London News V2 (NT)** 54r; **Ingram ILV2CD5 (NT)** 16r; **Jeremy Woodhouse/Digital Vision WT (NT)** 202, 224; **Karl Ammann/Digital Vision AA (NT)** 150; **Lawrie Ryan:** 82; **Mark Boulton/CEC:** 16l, 62, 143, 162t; **Milepost 92½:** 148; **Photodisc 4 (NT)** 225br, **Photodisc 6 (NT)** 64, 140, **Photodisc 18 (NT)** 182b, 184l, 208, **Photodisc 24 (NT)** 9, 119b, 196t, 197b, **Photodisc 37 (NT)** 176, 189, 193, **Photodisc 40 (NT)** 206tl, **Photodisc 45 (NT)** 197t, **Photodisc 46 (NT)** 98b, **Photodisc 54 (NT)** 156b, 166, 225tr, **Photodisc 67 (NT):** 2; **Photodisc 72 (NT)** 38t, 47tl, 76t, 160, 167, 218t, 225l;

Science Enhancement Programme: 146b; **Shout/ Rex Features:** 142; **Spectrum Colour Library:** 130t; **Science Photo Library:** 44, 47r, 88b, 88tr, 88tl, 120tr, 172l, /**CMS:** 33m, /**Eye Of Science:** 10, 33l, /**Alfred Pasieka:** 12, /**Adam Hart-Davis:** 222t, /**Bernhard Edmaier:** 223, /**Biophoto Associates:** 7, /**Dee Breger:** 129t, /**Dr Arthur Tucker:** 145, /**Jim Amos:** 156t, /**Kaj R Svensson:** 108r, 127br, /**Martin Dohrn:** 120br, /**St Bartholomew's Hospital:** 34, /**AJ Photo/Hop Americain:** 206bl, /**Andrew Lambert Photography:** 86, /**Andrew McClenaghan:** 42t, 52, /**Annabella Bluesky:** 204, /**BSIP Boucharlat:** 102r, /**BSIP Chassenet:** 98t, /**BSIP, Laurent:** 43, /**Charles D Winters:** 100l, 108ml, /**Cordelia Molloy:** 102l, /**Crown Copyright/Health & Safety Laboratory:** 205b, /**Dave Roberts:** 206br, /**David Hardy:** 133br, /**David Nunuk:** 221, /**David Parker:** 109, 187, /**David Scharf:** 48tr, /**David Taylor:** 169, /**Dirk Wiersma:** 133m, /**Dr Morley Read:** 222b, /**Dr Gary Gaugler:** 40b, /**Dr Linda Stannard, UCT:** 41, /**Dr P Marazzi:** 46t, /**E R Degginger:** 108tl, /**Eric Grave:** 40m, /**ESA:** 172r, /**George Bernard:** 133l , /**Gusto:** 72l, /**Los Alamos National Laboratory:** 178, /**Martin Bond:** 32, /**Martin Land:** 119t, /**Maximilian Stock Ltd:** 42bl, 100r, /**Merlin Tuttle:** 206tr, /**Pascal Goetgheluck:** 72br, /**Peter Menzel:** 48b, /**Richard Megna:** 162b, /**S Nagendra:** 50l, /**Science Pictures Ltd:** 47l, /**Sheila Terry:** 120tl, 133tr, /**Simon Fraser:** 116r, /**Sinclair Stammers:** 120bl, /**Stanley B Burns, MD & The Burns Archive NY:** 50r, /**Steve Allen:** 196b, /**Tony McConnell:** 152r, 158, /**Will & Deni McIntyre:** 50bm; **Still Pictures/Tom Koene:** 8b, /**Martin Bond:** 152l; **Stone/Getty Images:** 190.

Picture research by Liz Savery and Stuart Sweatmore

Every effort has been made to trace all the copyright holders, but if any have been overlooked the publisher will be pleased to make the necessary arrangements at the first opportunity.